The DOG OWNER'S ENCYCLOPEDIA

of HELPFUL HINTS and TRADE SECRETS

This comprehensive book contains over 2,000 helpful hints and trade secrets for owners of all dogs and other pets. These solutions and trade secrets were researched, gathered and submitted by dog owners (professionals and non-professionals) and from other pet owners over a 36-year span.

In order to help the reader find a particular helpful hint, tip, important fact or a just plain great idea (quickly and easily), some may have been cross-referenced under more than one of the 199 topics. Also to assist the reader, these amazing secrets and valuable solutions have been alphabetized within each category or topic.

The reader may note that, sometimes, when an obvious warning was contained within a hint, that warning was italicized so the reader would be alerted and then could take extra caution. The words "he," "him" and "his" are to be viewed usually as gender neutral.

This handy book will become an integral part of your library—whether you have a kennel, many pets or a single loving family pet. This one-of-a-kind reference book will assist you in providing your pet with a quality life along with the special care he or she deserves.

Read and enjoy!

Published by Nancy Lee Cathcart
9428 Blue Mound Drive
Fort Wayne, IN 46804
www.sheltie.com
s.pacesetter@sheltie.com

When using any commercial product, always read and follow the directions carefully. When
reference is made to any trade or brand name, no endorsement by Nancy Lee Cathcart is
implied nor is any discrimination intended.

Even though every effort was made to confirm that product names, addresses, phone
numbers, e-mail addresses and website addresses were correct at the time of creating this
book, it cannot be guaranteed that they will remain current after printing.

Always check with your veterinarian and/or with other appropriate qualified professionals
to make sure these suggestions are safe for your pet before attempting to use them as the
information contained in this book is not intended to be a substitute for professional
guidance.

ISBN: 978-0-9912298-0-2

Table of Contents

Bitches

(Also see "WHELPING"—"'In Whelp' Bitches")

Bitches With Puppies

A product called Probiocin (live culture lactobacillus) is excellent for enteritis in newborns and to fight E. coli. Definitely use this if any antibiotic is given. Also, give it to their dam. «»Editor's note: based upon reading and research in nutritional biochemistry, Natren Acidophilus and Life Start are excellent (1/2 teaspoon of each in 1 ounce of lukewarm water for adults and especially for the new mother).«»

From the time my puppies are about a week old until they are about three weeks of age (while Mom is still cleaning up after them), I do the following while cleaning out the whelping area. I hold the pup for Mom, placing her pup upside down on my lap and let Mom clean this puppy. Of course, I am seated on the floor. Mom seems to appreciate this and does a thorough job (since she has no squirming puppy to contend with). It is also a good way to get puppies familiar with being handled at an early age (which we should be doing anyway). Puppies don't mind it a bit as Mom is tending to them. It seems to form a bond between all of us. This is, also, how I begin cutting each puppy's toenails.

Have you ever had a bitch who, for any reason, has been unable to nurse her babies? Unfortunately some of us have. I have a solution for allowing the mother to clean up her babies without allowing the babies to nurse. Use a baby's sleeper (30-pound size) for a medium-size dog. Place the bitch's front legs through the sleeper's arms, snap the snaps down her back, cut the feet out and hem with an elastic piece inside each leg. Sew or move the snaps in the crotch area so that the pups cannot sneak inside. The sleepers are cotton and, therefore, are cool. The mother cleans her puppies and you feed them. This way is much easier for both of you.

Here's a super stew recipe for bitches who have whelped a litter: combine one pound stew beef, one large beef kidney and one pound of beef liver. Simmer along with two sliced onions and two or three carrots. Flavor with 1/3 package dried onion soup. This will take about three hours of cooking time. Feed this to bitches for three to four days after they have whelped. It seems to help clean them out and bring in your bitch's milk. Feed it several times a day and begin to add kibble by the morning of the third day.

If, unfortunately, a bitch "in whelp" picks up fleas or you find yourself with small infested puppies, use Johnson's Baby Oil on the inside of legs, tummy, on the head and under the tail and throat. The fleas will vacate immediately and the bitch will not object. The same treatment may be used on the mother without side effects. Although they look greasy the first day or so, the oil will be totally absorbed. For chasing down a lone flea, put the baby oil in an old nose spray bottle or an eyedropper, release a drop of oil on the flea and he will immediately expire.

If you have a first-time mama who is less than enthusiastic with diaper duty, try spreading a little peanut butter on the new puppies' tummies and bottoms. Mom should get the idea in one or two applications of the peanut butter.

If your dog has just had a litter and doesn't have enough milk for the new arrivals, give her a few swallows of beer and this will bring on milk in abundant quantities. The small amount of alcohol will not affect her puppies.

One of my young bitches refused to eat after whelping her first litter. Normally she's a glutton, however I couldn't tempt her to eat anything...even her favorite cheese. I offered her many food goodies—with no success. Then I stumbled upon beaten raw egg mixed with a little milk. She loved it. Soon she was accepting her dry food with the egg mixed in and later she ate the dry food only. «»Editor's note: based on nutritional biochemistry, a diet which contains an excess of raw egg whites quickly and almost invariably leads to a biotin deficiency. In raw eggs, biotin is typically bound to a sugar-protein molecule (the glycoprotein called avidin) and cannot be absorbed into the body unless the egg is cooked, allowing the biotin to separate from the avidin protein.«»

To get a C-sectioned bitch to accept her pups, use your fingers and gather the discharge from her vulva and smear it on her pups. One sniff will tell mom that these puppies are hers.

To help pick up loose stools of females after whelping, use potting soil. Leave some over the spot after pickup as it absorbs and helps keep the flies away.

When it came to weaning my puppies, I had trouble drying up the milk in a couple of my bitches. One bitch just kept producing milk despite my cutting her food, water, etc. I found a good way, without any drugs, to dry her milk up. I took a bath towel, soaked it in water, folded it and froze it in a plastic bag. Then I placed the bitch in her crate and placed the frozen towel under her. I didn't do this at night, but only for short periods during the day. I made sure the bitch was in a fairly warm room and didn't become chilled. It took only one to three hours of treatment for three or four days to begin this drying-up process. The towel, after being used, may be replaced in the freezer to be ready for the next treatment.

Dams Needing Help

(See "WHELPING"—"Dams Needing Help")

"In Season" Bitches

Bothered by unwanted dogs around your property when a bitch is in season? Try vinegar. When the bitch puddles, pour white vinegar on the spot immediately. I have done this for years and I have never been bothered by unwanted male visitors.

Everyone knows about the panties that are available in a pet store. They make them for bitches who are in season. These panties offer the light day pads with pants that have Velcro on the sides to keep them on. Instead of using those, I just use my son's old underwear. I cut a hole in the back and you have a very inexpensive way of keeping things clean while your bitch is in heat.

Give your "in season" bitches Nullo tablets. It cuts the odor of heat and doesn't get your male or your neighbor's males upset.

If you are traveling with a bitch in season, put a drop or two of Oil of Citronella in her crate and the males will not know she is in season. *Keep citronella candles, oil products and insect coils out of your dog's reach. The citronella plant (also called the mosquito plant) is actually a member of the geranium family. Grown as a mosquito repellent plant, this plant poses a risk to dogs. The American Society for the Prevention of Cruelty to Animals cautions that all members of the geranium family (Pelargonium) are toxic to dogs...as they contain the active toxins geraniol and linalool.*

My standby for years for bitches who are in heat and to avoid those red-splattered messes (or worse, total confinement of a beloved pet to the kennel) is this: I put little boys' underpants (for medium-sized dogs,) on the bitch, hole side up. (The bitch's tail goes through the hole.) Then I take half of a stick-on panty shield or a mini-sanitary napkin, line it up with her vulva and stick it to the underpants. After the first five minutes, the dogs don't usually notice, especially if you distract them and play with them.

Since our girls are in the house a lot, I have found that a pair of boy's underpants work beautifully on a dripping bitch and after she has been spayed. Turn the pants so that her tail may be pulled through the fly. This keeps them on much better than those contraptions you may buy. A mini pad may be used inside also. A boy's size 6 to 8 fits most medium-size girls. Mine never seem to mind wearing them, in fact, they seem to enjoy the laughs and extra attention they get. I used this idea when one of my older girls was spayed, using pants a size larger. It kept her from chewing out her stitches, but still let the air in.

To remember which bitch is in season, cut a long piece of red polar fleece and tie into a bow. It is easily slipped on and off of any bitch who is in season and reminds you who to be careful about (especially early in the morning when you are not quite awake).

We feed Shaklee's Vitamin B-Complex to our show dogs. We find that some of our bitches become edgy when they are "in-season" and being shown at the same time. Vitamin B-Complex is a natural relaxant. From what we understand, you can't overdose your dog as the unneeded excess is passed through the urine. We begin giving these vitamins two days before the show (once the night before and once more in the morning of the show). We feed 3 to 5 tablets (250 mg.) each time (depending on the individual dog).

When you have a bitch in for breeding, do your boys go out of their minds even when separated by as much distance as space will allow? Try burning scented candles in the room with the bitch. *Make sure each lit candle is beyond the reach of your pet.*

"In Whelp" Bitches
(Also see "FEEDING"—" 'In Whelp' Bitches")

Before breeding your bitch, measure around her belly (use a measuring tape or even a piece of string which you may mark with a felt tip pen). Two weeks after the breeding, take the measurement again. If it's increased, she's probably in whelp.

I use a Fisher-Price nursery monitor in my back bedroom where I keep mothers with their very young babies or my "in-whelp" bitches. I can go about my daily household chores and hear constant feedback as to what's happening in there. The monitor is so sensitive that you may even hear the mother's breathing. It's no substitute for constant supervision but it helps relieve my anxiety as to what's going on in there at all times. It has been very helpful and its cost is moderate.

There was a discussion on the internet as to whether it was okay to bathe a bitch who is in whelp and due in about a week-and-a-half. When my bitches are pregnant and too big to pop in the tub, I spray Self Rinse Plus where the bitches are dirty and then wipe clean. It's very easy and less stressful on the mother-to-be.

When my bitch is in whelp and her whelping day is very close, I have been taking her temperature (rectally) twice a day. The only drawback is when I have to wash the thermometer and disinfect it. Since I wash it by hand, I find it very unsanitary. But one

weekend while looking at all the goodies in the drugstore next to the temperature strips, I found a great product called Oral/Rectal Thermometer Covers. These are oral and rectal sheaths for thermometers. Rectal sheaths are pre-lubricated so they'll will be no more hassles with Vaseline. The thermometer is left clean and this process is so simple and sanitary.

When you have a bitch who has been bred, it helps to condition her nipples. This helps to prevent the possibility of them becoming sore or cracked. (The procedure is similar to that used for mothers who plan to breast-feed.) You take a soft toothbrush and lanolin and brush the breasts and nipples with the oil on a daily basis. This also helps to heal nipples that may become injured due to the bitch scratching herself, etc.

Oxytocin
(See "WHELPING"—"Oxytocin")

Spaying Bitches

Since our girls are in the house a lot, I have found that a pair of little boy's underpants work beautifully on a dripping bitch. Turn the pants so that her tail may be pulled through the fly. This keeps them on much better than those contraptions you can buy. A mini-pad may also be used. A boy's size 6 or 8 fits most medium-size bitches. My girls never seem to mind wearing them, in fact, they seem to enjoy the laughs and extra attention they get. I also used this idea when one of my older girls was spayed...using pants a size larger. It kept her from chewing out her stitches and still let the air in.

Taking An "In Whelp" Bitch's Temperature
(See "WHELPING"—"Taking A Dog's Temperature")

Whelping Bitches
(Also see "FEEDING"—"Whelping and Feeding")

During whelping when my bitch goes into a rest period, I wait no longer than one hour. Then I fill a dish with ice cold milk and torn-up white bread. Then I offer this to the bitch. More often than not, she will drink the cold milk which seems to prompt labor once again. Those bitches who don't eat the bread will usually go back and gobble that up, too (once they have finished whelping). I have used this method from my first litter and ever since that litter. Several other breeders (who have called me desperately in the middle of the night) tried my somewhat old-fashioned method have told me that this method worked for them. The vet, of course, is the last resort if labor does not start up shortly.

Instead of bathing or cutting off the skirts of bitches after whelping (in order to remove the blood), wipe the blood off by using straight hydrogen peroxide and then dry with a towel or paper towels. Pour or sponge the hydrogen peroxide through her skirts and then squeeze out with a dry towel. Her skirts will become beautifully clean. *Be sure to completely dry everything before returning mom to her pups.*

The new type of surface thermometer (such as Digitemp which may be found in the medical section of any store) would be a very valuable item for a pet owner to keep handy. The surface thermometers measure the surface temperature and not the internal temperature (as rectal thermometers do). The directions for them state that the surface temperature of humans (measured on the forehead) is five degrees below internal temperature. So when used on humans, normal would be approximately 94 degrees. Since a dog's internal temperature is normally 101 degrees, this thermometer should read about 96 degrees for his surface temperature. I have checked this temperature reading on my own dogs and found it to be accurate (at a normal 96 degrees surface temperature). I measure by holding the strip against the least hairy place on the inner thigh or belly of my dog and the whole procedure takes less than 30 seconds. Used as a quick check on a bitch close to whelping, you should be able to spot the temperature drop which would produce a reading of 94 degrees or below. Although it will not measure fractional changes, it is an easy-to-use tool to check for high or low temperatures when you are watching for a large deviation from normal.

Breedings

Actual Breeding

I like to use Astroturf (artificial grass carpet) in my breeding pen as it provides excellent footing. This non-slip surface is rubber-backed and is easily hosed off and sterilized.

K-Y Lubricant Jelly, often used for breeding those too-tight bitches, is now spermicidal (kills sperm). If your tube states, *"Not Sterile,"* it is the new variety which kills sperm. H-R Lubricating Jelly is sterile and non-spermicidal. It is available through your vet and is manufactured by Holland-Rantos Co., Inc. or HR Pharmaceuticals, Inc. (http://www.hrpharma.com/products/). It is distributed by Youngs Drug Products Corp., 865 Centennial Avenue, Piscataway, NJ 08854 (732-885-5777).

One of the best purchases we've ever made was an adjustable mechanic's seat which is a small padded stool that is adjustable in height and mounted on swivel casters (allowing it to roll easily from one spot to another). This rolling stool has been invaluable in saving my knees and back while grooming and when assisting in natural breedings or collecting semen from stud dogs for artificial insemination (AI). The swivel casters allow me to move around with the dogs, so they are always within my reach. We bought ours from Northern Tool and Equipment, 800-533-5545, 800-221-0516 or www.northerntool.com.

Sometimes when breeding dogs, either the stud or the bitch is just a little taller than the other and a little help is needed. We use roofing shingles. Either add or subtract, whatever is needed to get the job done.

When breeding dogs, I find it very worthwhile to have both the stud dog and the bitch lie on their sides after the tie has been established. To accomplish this, it is best to have someone assist you in turning them. This is done by taking hold of their hind legs which are opposite you and pulling both dogs towards you. This prevents the two dogs from collapsing and hurting themselves during a prolonged tie. The length of the tie does not appear to be affected. Also, both dogs seem to enjoy the tummy rubs given.

Artificial Insemination (AI)

When collecting semen for artificial insemination, I use disposable baby bottle liners. They're sterile.

Housing "In Season" Bitches

Bothered by unwanted dogs around your property when a bitch is "in season"? Try vinegar. When the bitch puddles, pour white vinegar on the spot immediately. I have done this for years and I have never been bothered by unwanted male visitors.

Give visiting "in season" bitches Nullo tablets. It cuts the odor of heat and doesn't get your male or your neighbor's males upset.

If you are housing a bitch who is "in season," put a drop or two of Oil of Citronella in her enclosure. The males will not know she is in season. *Keep citronella candles, oil products and insect coils out of your dog's reach. The citronella plant (also called the mosquito plant) is actually a member of the geranium family. Grown as a mosquito repellent plant, this plant poses a risk to dogs. The American Society for the Prevention of Cruelty to Animals cautions that all members of the geranium family (Pelargonium) are toxic to dogs...as they contain the active toxins geraniol and linalool.*

To remember which bitch is "in season," cut a long piece of red polar fleece and tie into a bow. It is easily slipped on and off of any bitch who is "in season" and reminds you who to be careful about (especially early in the morning when you are not quite awake).

When you have a bitch in for breeding, do your boys go out of their minds even when separated by as much distance as space will allow? Try burning scented candles in the room with the bitch. *Make sure each lit candle is beyond the reach of your pet.*

Long Ties

Overly long ties can be very frustrating. I've found that elevating the bitch's rear helps to break the tie. Straddle the bitch and hold her up gently by the stifles, pushing back a little toward the male. It sometimes requires repeating this motion a few times in succession, but it works for us in probably 90 percent of the cases and has been a real blessing numerous times.

Stud Dogs

When sending out pedigrees of stud dogs, photocopy the dog's OFA and CERF certificates right on the back of each pedigree. If sending out pedigrees of puppies, you could include the dam's certifications or sire and dam if you reduce the certificate's size. By doing that, no one has to research the accuracy of the statement "normal eyes and hips."

Misc.

Before breeding your bitch, measure around her belly (use a measuring tape or even a piece of string which you may mark with a felt tip pen). Two weeks after the breeding, take the measurement again. If it's increased, she's probably in whelp.

I use a puppy calendar for all my dog notices and health activities (such as wormings, vaccinations, breeding, due dates, trips, etc.). At the end of each year, pertinent information is transferred to individual dog records. All calendars are kept in a file cabinet for easy access.

Ears

Bracing and Weighting Ears
Which Should Tip Forward

An outstanding article is available which discusses (in detail) how to brace your puppy's ears. A photocopy of this four-page article is still available for purchase for $5.25. Contact Nancy Lee Cathcart at s.pacesetter@sheltie.com.

A fine product that I have found to provide weight to the tip of the ear (add more to the ear tips...if you wish) and also works nicely for softening the ear leather, is the overnight cream put out by Mary Kay cosmetics. It works on rough, dry elbows, too.

An easy way to brace puppies' ears so they start carrying their ears high is to use nylon fiber tape. After the ears are glued with Speed Sew (ear tops to inside bottom of ear), fold a 4 1/2-inch-long piece of fiber tape until it is 1 1/4" wide and 4 1/2" long. Slip this tape through and in front of the ears so they are correctly set or a little more tightly set than needed. Attach the two ends of tape with another small piece of fiber tape. The ear brace may easily be removed by taking off the connecting piece of tape. Removal of the ear brace while puppies are playing together will keep the tape from pulling the glued fur out. Nightly use of the ear brace produces showy high-set ears.

A very good friend of mine informed me of a glue that works wonderfully on ears called Fabric-Leather Cement (by the Vala Company, 700 West Root Street, Chicago, Illinois 50609). We found ours at a farm-supply store. The appearance and fragrance resemble that of the popular, more expensive brand used by many Sheltie and Collie owners.

Being thoroughly disgusted with the quality of the caps on Speed Sew tubes, I decided that I would have to solve the problem of cracked caps myself. I searched through my medicine cabinet and found that the cap on Fougera antifungal cream (athlete's foot medicine) fits the Speed Sew tube perfectly. I'm sure there are other products on the market which have interchangeable caps or, maybe, the seller could provide extra caps.

Having trouble finding Antiphlogistine? It may be ordered from Omaha Vaccine Co. Send for their catalog: P.O. Box 7228, 3030 'L' Street, Omaha, NE 68107-0228. It comes in a tube and the consistency is perfect.

Hooflex Hoof Softener (a horse product available at feed stores or call 800-889-8967) makes an excellent lubricant for those hard-to-tip ears. Don't be afraid to comb those ears in order to get rid of dead hair and to also stimulate new hair growth.

I found the most marvelous device for weighting ears—plastic bandages. They hold very well and yet are easily removed without taking out too much hair. Be sure to peel them off by pulling in the same direction as the hair grows or, in other words, with the lay of the hair. They are wonderful to use during showing when the more permanent types of tippers are a hassle to keep putting on and removing. I find the 3/4-inch size the best general weight but have used several size (including the spot bandages when just a little weight is needed).

If, on a cold day, you are showing a dog whose ears tend to fly up in cold weather, try wringing out cotton or a cloth that's been dipped in hot water (it may be carried in a wide thermos) and holding it to the ears before going into the ring. *Be sure it's not too hot because you wouldn't want to burn your dog's ears.* Or...you may cup the ears in your hands and blow your warm breath on them.

If you are having trouble with a puppy's ears wanting to stand up, but the ears are too small to begin bracing, try this: take a piece of carpet tape (Sears has the best), cut it to the size of the ear and tape the ears to the side of the puppy's head. This works like a charm for me and when the tape loosens, the ears are over nicely and they stay that way.

If you have a dog with flying ears who is allergic or sensitive to most preparations, try the antibiotic ointment called Furacin. This is an antibiotic which is found in feed stores and is used as a wide spectrum antibiotic ointment for horses, dogs, etc. I had a two-year-old dog who had semi-soft ears, but when *I used pine tar I was horrified to find his hair fell out in clumps until his ears were almost bald.* I first got the rest of the dried pine tar out by using Goop and slapped a helpful amount of the Furacin ointment on both sides of his ear. It seems to soak in and soften while soothing at the same time. His ears are tipping now and except for making the hair yellow and greasy, it seems to work for tipping ears. It is very easy to wash out. (The yellow comes out with washing, also.)

If you like a mud-type weight (if an ear flies just before a show or when tape weights need to be off) and you can't find Denver Mud or Antiphlogistine, you may make your own. The recipe is half water and half glycerin, mixed with dry potter's clay to the consistency you prefer. It comes off easily and completely with a damp washcloth.

If you want to correct a temporary high ear with weight on the inside tips of the ears, try mixing equal parts of water and glycerine (not much) with dry potter's clay to give a consistency of heavy cream. It comes off with a damp washcloth or wears off in a week or two. It is very much like the old antiphlogistine.

I have found a new glue for fixing ears. It's available at Farm & Fleet stores or at discount stores in the camping and boating departments. It is Tehr-Greeze—a white fabric-leather cement. It dries almost instantly and is easily removed with a small amount of solvent. Just put a small amount on the hairs located on the outer edges of the ear—no need to put any on the skin itself. «»Editor's note: based upon a vet's recommendation, here is a method to prevent causing harm to the ear when bracing or gluing your dog's ears: temporarily place a pencil on the inner part of the ear (at the place where you want the ear to fold over), and gently fold the ear over the pencil. You will then be able to safely glue or brace the tip of the ear in place without creasing the ear itself. Hold for a few minutes so the glue may adhere to the ear hair. Gently slide the pencil out from the ear. *By placing a pencil at the fold (before bending the ear over) you will not cut off the circulation since the ear will not be creased when folded.*«»

I have had great success with giving advice on ear training to new puppy owners. Instead of complicated instructions regarding the use of moleskin, double-edged tape, etc., I give them a photocopy of Marilyn Dooley's excellent article, "As The Twig Is Bent." «»Editor's note: a photocopy of this four-page article is still available for purchase for $5.25. Contact Nancy Lee Cathcart at s.pacesetter@sheltie.com.«»

I keep a lunch pail available for what I call "Ear Gear." This kit contains: masking tape, moleskin, white bandage tape, skin adhesive and remover ("Skin Bond"). Anytime I have a puppy with ears which are standing straight up (when they should be tipped), I know immediately where all my supplies are located. Because all of these items are in one place (the lunch pail), I don't put off bracing my puppy's ears.

In addition to using starting fluid on moleskin to help the moleskin adhere longer to the ears, try cleaning the ear first with nail polish remover instead of alcohol *(check with vet for safety)*. This makes the moleskin stick much longer.

I never liked the thought of using engine starter fluid on the moleskin for bracing my dogs' ears. I prefer to use Show Adhesive. It comes in an aerosol can. It's what I use to hold problem hair and hard-to-hold hair together when I showed registered Shorthorns at cattle shows. It may be purchased at farming-goods stores, through wholesale catalogs or directly through Farnam Companies, Omaha, Nebraska 68112. It really works.

Instead of antiphlogistine or gum for weighting ears, I use a dab of toothpaste. It works perfectly and washes off easily. Besides, it's always available.

Instead of gluing ears up, try using the small groomers' rubber bands or dental bands. Take small tufts of hair from each side of the ear as you would when you are gluing, but instead intertwine the tufts and then wrap them in a rubber band to make a pony tail. No mess. Carefully cut the rubber band when you're ready to release the ears. «»Editor's note: according to vets' recommendations and for your dog's protection and safety, *don't put any part of your dog's ear in rubber bands or dental bands because putting bands on any part of the ear itself may cut off blood circulation and that part of a dog's ear may then become damaged or actually die).*«»

I've rediscovered using antiphlogistine (also known as Denver Mud) to tip a dog's ears. It's best features are that it does not cause hair loss, that it does not irritate the skin and it comes out with just water. I use mine straight from the tube—at room temperature. It quickly dries hard (like gum…in a matter of minutes). To speed up the drying process even more, use powdered grooming chalk on the antiphlogistine. I was surprised when I tried this product again since years ago it was a very runny and messy product to use on a dog's ears. Now I like the consistency of either putty or caulking.

Moleskin will stick to the inside of a dog's ear much better if you spray the moleskin with engine starting fluid just before applying the brace to the ear. You may buy this product quite cheaply at any auto parts store and it does not irritate the dog's skin the way heated moleskin sometimes can. When you want to remove the brace, simply spray the starting fluid onto a cotton ball and work the brace off making sure no fluid touches the ear itself.

Most of us, at one time or another, find the need to brace a puppy's ears. I am no longer using engine starter fluid as I had in the past. I found the odor offensive and I always worried about using such a product on tender skin. Instead, I now clean the ears with alcohol, then allow them a few minutes to dry. Then, to soften the adhesive on the back of the moleskin I heat the adhesive with a cigarette lighter. Cut the piece of moleskin to the size you need. Then remove the plastic or paper backing. Holding the moleskin in one hand by a corner and the lighter in the other hand, I allow the flame to pass over the entire surface of the adhesive carefully turning the piece of moleskin as needed so it is entirely heated. Be careful not to ruin your manicure or burn yourself. Set the piece on the edge of the table while you continue with the second piece of moleskin. *Test each piece for warmth and adhesive quality before applying to the inside of the animal's ear because you certainly don't want to burn your puppy's ear.* This same technique may be used on adhesive tape, which some of us roll up and use to bring down the tip of the ear to the moleskin, which is at the base of the ear. I find the ears stay braced far longer. I have no problem getting them to stay in place three weeks at a time—if need be.

My six-month-old male was able to lick off Hooflex, tear off tape and tear loose Speed Sew along with everything else I used on one of my dog's stubborn ears. While in the midst of refinishing floors, I noticed that coarse sandpaper really was quite heavy. I glued a piece of it to each ear tip (sand-side out) with Speed Sew. The sandpaper weights lasted almost indefinitely, were almost unnoticeable and the pup left them alone. I used 50-D-weight paper on this particular dog's rather large ears. Size of the sandpaper piece and weight of the paper can control the amount of weight added to the ear tip. Paper may be cut to any shape and placed on the portion of the ear tip where weight is necessary. This dog's sandpaper was glued to the inside half of the tip since his ears tended to break to the outside. It worked extremely well.

Save those yellow plastic squeeze-type containers. They are great for dispensing pumice for weighting ears (just squeeze onto the ears).

There is a new fabric glue on the market called No More Pins. It is made by Loving Touch, Elizabeth, New Jersey 07207. It takes a little longer to dry than Speed Sew, but it is water-soluble and comes right out with just a few drops.

To create ear braces which don't cause hair loss: first, clean the inside of the ear so that it is dry and free of all oil or wax. Second, trim the long hairs and apply a piece of moleskin from the break to the top of the ear canal. Then, gently apply a glob of antiphlogistine to the inside of the ear tip and fold it over, pressing it against the moleskin. This will hold for many days—even weeks, depending upon the activity of the dog and how many "friends" he has to pull on his ears. As the antiphlogistine dissolves in water, remove the braces by washing off the antiphlogistine. No hair loss, no strain, no pain. If you can't find antiphlogistine, ask a pharmacist to order it for you—most grocery store or drugstore pharmacists will order it for you.

We buy moleskin in 4-yard bulk packages. The backing is plastic (not paper) and is very hard to start peeling off. Use the tip of an ice pick to break through the plastic backing to make an area where you can start peeling. To make moleskin stickier, heat the back with a cigarette lighter to melt the glue. *Allow the glue to cool before placing the moleskin in the dog's ear since you wouldn't want to burn your dog's ear.*

When bracing my puppy's ears, I had been gluing his ears and despite all the glue-removers, he was becoming a little head-shy when I worked on his ears. Moleskin was recommended. He didn't mind the moleskin after a while, but his ears were still not up enough toward the top of his head. I let the moleskin set well (about 1/2 hour). Then I peeled back the upper 1/2" just 1/8" or so from the edge of the inside of his ear. I very carefully took a needle with strong tapestry thread and sewed one edge of the moleskin to the edge of the moleskin on the other ear going back and forth a few times (for added strength). It worked well and stayed braced for two weeks and held the ears up on top of his head. It came off either by itself or easily (without the trauma of glue and gook).

When I need to weight one of my dog's ears, I use Vogue Stickum. It is made for silk flowers. It sticks really easily and isn't as messy as gum. You may purchase it at any craft store.

When taping your dog's ears, try spraying engine starter fluid onto the sticky side of the moleskin before sticking it to the ear leather. The ether in the starting fluid really helps the moleskin adhere to the ear leather. When you want to remove the brace, simply spray the starting fluid onto a cotton ball and work the moleskin brace off making sure no fluid touches the ear itself.

When weighting a dog's ears with antiphlogistine, you can get it off relative easily by using a half-and-half mixture of glycerine and water. Mix with enough powdered potter's clay to create the consistency of heavy cream. Remember any weighting preparation is for short-term use only (e.g., to weight a flying ear during teething). This should wear off in a few days, or it may be removed with a washcloth and warm water.

Cleaning Dog's Ears and Your Hands

(Also see "GROOMING"—"Cleaning" and "Cleaning Your Hands")

A good way to get pine tar, Ear Tip, etc., off your hands is washing them with kerosene. It works fast and is not quite as smelly as gas.

Johnson's Baby Oil is good for cleaning inside the ears. It may also be applied to small puppies who may have picked up fleas. It will be totally absorbed by the coat in a day or so and may be used on the head and face.

Waterless hand cleaner (usually available in auto parts stores) makes for an excellent cleaner at ringside or when grooming before going to the ring. It will clean off those hard-to-rid traces of pine tar or lubricants which might still be on your dog's ear leather.

We use Baby Wipes for a multitude of reasons (for example: cleaning up a mess in the car, cleaning a "just-used" thermometer, cleaning any area that's been stitched or sutured, a quick ear cleaning before a show, on a messy puppy's face and on babies just learning to eat from a pan). The least expensive ones contain more moisture, and you'll be surprised how many uses you'll find for them.

You may use hydrogen peroxide to remove a foreign object from deep in your dog's ear providing you *first check with you vet to make sure the hydrogen peroxide is appropriate. Also, check with your vet for the correct percentage of hydrogen peroxide for this purpose.* Even foxtails may be bubbled out. You may use an ear syringe or just gently pour the peroxide right from the bottle into the ear. Hold the dog's head, fill the ear with peroxide and then hold the base of the ear between your fingers and gently move it about. The peroxide will begin to bubble to the surface bringing the object with it. You may need to repeat the process several times to get results.

Your dog's ears may be washed out with a drop of vinegar in water. Mix in a small bottle. This is the same thing many vets use except it doesn't have any coloring.

Ear Care and Ear Health

(See "HEALTH"—"Ear Care and Ear Health")

Ear Grooming

Baby powder behind your dog's ears and in their petticoats will provide a nice light fragrance and will also keep the hair from matting. If you are traveling to the southern part of the United States, purchase some Brown Sugar Baby Powder. It is light brown in color which is perfect for sable-colored dogs.

Fuller's Earth Powder is an easy and dry way to get rid of that "stringy" or "raggedy" look behind the dog's ears. Fuller's Earth is a very fine-grained astringent powder that is beige in color. It is perfect for sables. Since it may be completely brushed out, it is also usable on other colors. Sprinkle in behind the ears. I use a soft plastic salt shaker. Rub the powder in with your fingertips and use a flea comb to get most of it out. Then brush with a pin brush or a clean chalking brush.

Encouraging The Use Of Ears

Encourage your puppies to use their ears without constant human contact. An inexpensive child's pinwheel toy (with the wooden handle shortened, taped and tied to the fencing of their outdoor play area) attracts their attention as the wind spins it. Be sure to fix it securely (above their reach when they're standing on their hind legs) and reposition it as they grow. Wind chimes also attract their attention. In addition to using their ears, when cocking their heads from side to side while trying to figure it all out, they assume adorable poses for candid shots for camera buffs.

Removing Ear Braces and Weights

A hint that helps in removing Speed Sew from your dog's ear is Spray 'N Wash. If you put your finger through the loop of the ear, spray the glued area, then massage the ear and the ear will come apart very easily. Then spray the stubborn areas and massage. Comb out with a fine comb. It sure helps to keep most of the hair on the ear, and it's hard to tell that the ear has ever been glued.

For removing glue in puppy ears at matches (or if a puppy is allergic to other removal agents), I use Uni-Solve pads. They are made for human ostomy patients for glue removal, are extremely gentle on sensitive skin and are sold through most pharmacies. The individually wrapped pads make this product convenient for the tack box, too.

For removing Speed Sew, use lighter fluid *(keep fumes away from fire and check with your vet for safety)*. Grease the fold with Hooflex paste daily (which will soften the ear muscle). Hooflex is a dressing for a horse's hooves and is available in tack shops.

I discovered a way to remove Speed Sew quickly and easily. I applied a little Vaseline to the dry Speed Sew and let it set for a while. Then I went back to it and was surprised to see how easily it came off. The best part is that it is very effective.

If you are a believer in pine tar for erratic ears, you probably know how difficult it is to remove before a show. Forgetting about a puppy match the next week, I quickly slapped some pine tar on my teething puppy. I just as quickly removed it with Goop hand cleaner—even after 12 hours of drying time in the sun. Just rub in and wipe off with a wet cloth.

If you have a dog with flying ears who is allergic or sensitive to most preparations, try the antibiotic ointment called Furacin. This is an antibiotic which is found in feed stores and is used as a wide spectrum antibiotic ointment for horses, dogs, etc. I had a two-year-old dog who had semi-soft ears, but when *I used pine tar I was horrified to find his hair fell out in clumps until his ears were almost bald.* I first got the rest of the dried pine tar out by using Goop and slapped a helpful amount of the Furacin ointment on both sides of his ear. It seems to soak in and soften while soothing at the same time. His ears are tipping now and except for making the hair yellow and greasy, it seems to work for tipping ears. It is very easy to wash out. (The yellow comes out with washing, also.)

I'm sharing some information on a product which I bought from Cherrybrook Company. It has turned out to be super. The product is, ADHEEZ-OFF and is available from the Cherrybrook Company, Rt. 57, Box 15, Broadway, NJ 08808, 800-524-0820. I bought it to see if it would help take off the gooey, sticky residue left on puppies' ears after the moleskin brace is put on or comes off and it does. One squirt and the stickiness dissolves, and the sticky residue comes cleanly off your fingers, too. It also takes labels off products you buy at the stores (the ones that labels stick on forever). I've found another use for it as it also removes pine resin from my dog's paws—even between my dog's pads. It worked like a miracle product. If you can no longer find ADHEEZ-OFF, you might want to try STR Adhesive Remover or other adhesive remover products (which are safe for your dog's ears).

To remove glue or Goop from puppies' ears, try De-Solv-It. It is available in the laundry soap section of stores. It whisks away glue, gum, etc., without irritating skin (the way some solvents will).

To remove that glue or moleskin adhesive that we use in training ears (without irritating the ear leather or causing excessive hair loss), I have found a product called Detachol. It is available through pharmacies or directly from the manufacturer (Ferndale Laboratories, 780 W 8 Mile Road, Ferndale, MI 48220, http://www.ferndalelabs.com, 248-542-4701). It's also available through other sources. It comes in a 4-ounce plastic bottle with an applicator tip and is available in either cases of 12 or 36 bottles per case. This product has no caustic fumes and is not harmful to the skin. It is a pure petroleum distillate product used as surgical adhesive remover. I use it straight from the bottle or on a cotton ball. It dissolves the glue or moleskin adhesive as you massage it in with your fingers. I use a cotton ball to apply it when removing a moleskin brace (working under the bottom of the brace in an upward motion toward the top of the ear). *Do not pull the brace off.* Let the Detachol melt the glue and the moleskin will lift off easily. In the case of a large glue gob mixed into the long hairs on the sides of the ears, apply directly from the bottle and massage it in with your fingers (working from the top downward). As the glue softens, use a fine-toothed comb to separate the hair at the top and proceed downward as the glue melts. *Do not try to comb through from the skin upward as this is how you really lose hair.* When the glue is removed, the hair will look very oily, depending on how much of the Detachol you have used. You may towel off some of the oil, then either powder and brush out the balance or leave it to dissipate overnight on its own. I have had great success with minimal hair loss even in the messiest of situations. I have even used it to dissolve tar from the belly coat of a dog who got involved with a newly seal-coated driveway. Then I used terry-cloth towels to absorb the melted tar matter. Try splitting a case between club members. It makes a lovely hostess gift along with a tube of adhesive when kennel-hopping or traveling.

When I glued pups' ears, I would end up cutting the glue out of the hair—sometimes leaving ugly "chopped" areas. I came across an easier way to remove the glue with less hair loss. I now use Goop hand cleaner. Put a small amount on your finger and rub it thoroughly over the glue and the hair close to the glued area. Sometimes, depending on the amount of glue used, the glued area will start breaking loose. If it doesn't begin to break loose after about a minute of rubbing the Goop in, let it set for about five minutes. The hair and glue should be easier to remove and comb out. After getting out the glue, the Goop that remains may be "dried" by applying a bit of Fuller's Earth.

When weighting a dog's ears with antiphlogistine, you may get it off relatively easily by using a half-and-half mixture of glycerine and water. Mix with enough powdered potter's clay to create the consistency of heavy cream. Remember any weighting preparation is for short-term use only (e.g., to weight a flying ear during teething). This should wear off in a few days, or it may be removed with a washcloth and warm water.

Softening Ear Leather

A product which I have found works for softening ear leather, plus providing weight (add more if you wish), is the overnight cream put out by Mary Kay cosmetics. It works on rough, dry elbows, too.

A puppy of mine had an ear which broke high. The only moisturizing thing I had on hand was Vaseline Vitamin E cream. On this pup, it sunk right into the ear leather and the next day the ear was in its proper place. It worked for me and it can't hurt to try it.

As an ear softener, I have found that Corn Huskers lotion works quite well. It's jellylike, has a pleasing fragrance and very easy to remove. It may be removed by brushing it out or by rubbing a little baby powder into it. It's also great for holding the weight on the ear tip. Furthermore, it's really inexpensive.

If you have a dog with flying ears who is allergic or sensitive to most preparations, try the antibiotic ointment called Furacin. This is an antibiotic which is found in feed stores and is used as a wide spectrum antibiotic ointment for horses, dogs, etc. I had a two-year-old dog who had semi-soft ears, but when *I used pine tar I was horrified to find his hair fell out in clumps until his ears were almost bald.* I first got the rest of the dried pine tar out by using Goop and slapped a helpful amount of the Furacin ointment on both sides of his ear. It seems to soak in and soften while soothing at the same time. His ears are tipping now and except for making the hair yellow and greasy, it seems to work for tipping ears. It is very easy to wash out. (The yellow comes out with washing, also.)

The very best thing I have ever found to keep ear leather supple when puppies and adults are going through an "ear-flying stage" is CHAP-ANS. Unfortunately, it is no longer being made (so I am told). So I have spent the last two years trying every product under the sun. Aside from the fact that nothing really worked to my satisfaction since everything had a drawback (such as having an unpleasant odor, stickiness, it was too hard to put on, too hard to take off, etc. Finally, after getting the worst sunburn of my life, I dug out my jar of Deep Magic moisturizing cream. Why I never thought of it before and why I remembered it when I was sunburned is another story. Anyway, I tried it on my puppy's flying ears. Not only does it have a light fresh smell, but it is absorbed completely into the ear leather. Best of all, it works. It is currently available in drugstores as a cream or in a squeeze bottle as a lotion.

Stopping the Chewing of Ears, Braces and Weights

A very good product, which I have used for years, is Thum. It's a human baby product for thumb sucking, nail biting, etc. This works better than Bitter Apple for stopping any type of chewing problem. It will not stain fabrics or furnishings. For coat chewing or ear chewing, dab on with applicator or put a few drops on a toothbrush and comb through the coat or the ears. It will not stain coats and it stops puppies from pulling on their props or weights. It will not make pups sick to their stomach if they should get some of it into their mouths. It is inexpensive and it works.

If your puppies lick the weight-adding mixture you have put on their ears, try spraying Bitter Apple on their ears.

I would like to pass on a helpful hint to those who have dogs who are attracted to ears which have been taped or glued, etc. I have a dog at my house who wouldn't let ears alone for a second (would actually chew the moleskin out of ear of another dog before I finished working on the second ear). You can get "oil of cloves" at the drugstore (which is bitter and burns the tongue). I use a Q-Tip (dipped into the bottle) and rub it in a few places inside and outside the ears which have been fixed. I also make sure each dog who is tempted to fake a lick gets one from me first (I take the same Q-Tip and rub it on the tongue of the offending ear chewer). Putting it in their mouth creates an immediate dislike for the smell (as well as the taste), and I have never had a repeat offender. It is a good idea to repeat the application on the ear every three or four days.

Keeping adhesive ear braces on a pup is a real job when you have to put the pup back in with his littermates who think tearing off ear braces is great fun. I have a great solution. I "chalk over" the white-colored adhesive. Use brown chalk for sables, black for tris and gray for blues. It works.

Eliminating Bad Behaviors

Barking and Too Noisy

Barking can be a hard behavior to modify because it's a self-rewarding activity for your dog. When he barks, he almost always makes something happen. When your dog barks at the mailman, for example, the mailman leaves (because your dog doesn't know that dropping off the mail and walking away is the mailman's job). Your dog, instead, thinks his barking has scared the intruder away.

Do you have an early and noisy riser in your kennel? I do. He wakes everyone up. So I put a sheet over his enclosure (just as is done with a bird). Now he stays quiet until I remove the sheet and it's time to get up.

Do your dogs bark? I use those plastic lemons with lemon juice in them. When your dog barks, squirt him in the back of the throat. The dog cannot bark and will hate the taste. It does not take long to figure out not to bark. It is not harmful and provides him with Vitamin C.

I have a problem in that I live in the country. My neighbor puts his cows out in the pasture next to my property, which aggravates my dog...so they bark, bark and bark. I finally went back to the "old can full of rocks" solution (or, in my case—pennies), and it seems to work much better than the water super-soaker. I also have used a "barker breaker" (that emits a high-pitched sound) which doesn't seem to work much at all. Shaking the can and finally throwing that can toward the dog or pup (without hitting any dog, of course) seems to work best of all. Even my 13-week-old seems to respond. This action is, of course, accompanied with a command of "Quiet" or using the "No bark" command.

There are a lot of handy uses for your spray bottle besides misting when line-brushing. With the bottle always full of water and water only, set the nozzle on "stream." It will squirt across a room. My aim is not that good but I can generally get a barking dog's face and/or mouth very wet from across the room. Even if you just hit the body or dampen an ear, you do get their attention. If you don't think it shuts them up, try it. Also, my dogs are not afraid of the spray bottle, they merely respect it because they drink from it at shows. At hot outdoor shows, you may not have a bowl of water handy but you probably have a spray bottle within reach. My dogs love to have this water sprayed into their mouths, however you need to *make sure the nozzle is reset to "spray" (so it's not too strong) and that they do not receive too much, too rapidly because they might then vomit.* If you have sloppy drinkers and you are ready to go into the ring, but "Superdog" looks like he could use a drink, a squirt in the mouth is a lot neater than water slurped all over his ruff. I also use the spray bottle to rinse chalk off my hands when I'm in a hurry or off my shoes, clothes, etc. Believe it or not, I have been known to squirt the thing in my own mouth or at my nervous husband.

To get your dog's attention, put a few pennies in an empty soda can and shake. The noise will make him stop what he is doing...such as barking and can be a good training tool.

To train your dog not to bark, first, train your dog to "Speak!" for a yummy treat. Praise him when he barks. After a few barks, tell him, "Enough!" or "Stop" using a deep and firm, no-nonsense voice. Immediately give him a doggy treat.

It's difficult for him to bark when his mouth is stuffed with a doggy treat...so he has no choice except to obey your command to stop barking. Now tell him what a good dog he is for being quiet. To stop unnecessary barking, this training is going to take a few weeks to sink in. Be persistent and consistent in doing the same steps and don't give up. Some breeds (like Shelties) are naturally noisy and will take more work to train than others. Even when your dog understands what's expected of him, he may still bark more often than you'd like. Now, you have a way of getting his attention and letting him know what you want. Even if you have to say "Stop!" or "Enough!" each time he barks when he's not supposed to, you'll be doing much better than when you didn't have a way to communicate with him at all. When you're sure that your barking dog totally understands the meaning of the word "Enough" or "Stop," you may start correcting him when he ignores it. If he doesn't obey your command to stop barking, give him a sharp tug on his collar and scold him by strongly stating, "NO! Enough!" Before long, you'll be able to use the word "Stop" or "Enough" to stop him before he even begins his barking.

Too much barking? I attended a handling workshop about a year ago and was told the way to handle this problem was to "spritz" the dogs with water. Since the "barkies" occurred when they were out in their pens, the spray from a normal spray bottle wasn't able to reach my dogs. Because of this, I bought one of those super-soaker squirt guns for kids and it reached a long distance.

When having dinner at a friend's home, we often laugh at the antics of her male canary. When we wish to "turn him off," we place the cover over his cage. One day a noisy dog was, as usual, exercising his lungs as I was putting the others away. I placed a towel over the front of his airline crate and he became silent.

When the doorbell rings, your dog barks to let you know that something is out there and sure enough, you come to check on your visitor. If he barks for his dinner, you usually bring him food. Yelling, scolding or throwing things are rarely effective as corrections for this inappropriate barking because he's still making something happen with his barking...even if that something isn't very nice. A better way to quiet your noisy dog is to teach him to start and stop barking on command.

With a barking dog, you may use all his barking episodes as training opportunities. When the doorbell rings, praise him for barking to alert you, then tell him "Enough!" or "Stop!" and then reward him with a treat when he stops. He's going to learn that you want a few barks and then silence. Make sure you praise him for barking when he's supposed to and then stopping ("Enough!" or "Stop!") on command.

Biting

To train your puppies to bait (but not to puncture your fingers), feed them through the crate or fence wires. At a later date, put them with older, stable dogs and train them to bait in a group and to only take the tidbit when called by name. You want the whole group's attention even when someone else gets the treat. Be sure that each dog receives a reward when the correct baiting occurs.

Chewing

A good substitute for chew sticks are unpeeled carrots. Cut each carrot into 4-inch to 6-inch lengths. My pups love them and usually end up eating the raw carrots.

All puppies will love this—take a small rag or old washcloth, soak it in water and wring most of the water out. Then freeze it. They will love the coldness on their sore gums and will choose chewing on the rag or washcloth instead of furniture, etc.

A piece of rope tied to a table leg or a doorknob makes a great teething aid for puppies, and your pups are not as likely to chew on furniture, etc.

Are you tired of pups chewing on everything but the rawhide chews that you provide? Soak them in some bouillon or broth for a few minutes (the rawhide chews, not the pups) and watch the renewed interest.

If you are having problems with puppies chewing everything in sight, take a shoelace and tie it around the leg of a chair. I guarantee it will keep their attention to the point that they will ignore all the other goodies including your shoes, feet, toes, etc. If you want to go first class, use a leather shoelace.

If you have a coat chewer in your kennel, try black pepper as a cure. Kennel your chewer with one of the "victims" after you have sprinkled lots and lots of pepper in the victim's coat (only in the areas normally chewed). This method worked like a charm for me.

I keep a stock of chew sticks by my telephone because that's when my puppies (and some juvenile delinquents) decide to chew on everything they know they shouldn't be chewing. If I can't leave the phone, I can divert their attention with a bribe they love.

Secure electrical cords to baseboards or make them inaccessible to your dogs. *If your dog chews on them, he may suffer electric shocks, burns and could possibly die.* To hide those cords (which can't be made inaccessible), you may place empty paper towel rolls or toilet tissue cardboard rolls over the cords. Place construction-type cardboard on the walls to cover over cords which can't be put into cardboard tubes.

There is a toy I have found very good for puppies. Take about four rawhide bones and then tie each one together with strips of rawhide strings. The strings may be bought at any local saddle shop or in the section of your store where they sell shoestrings. These toys will keep your puppies from playing tug-of-war with your drapes and will keep them occupied for hours.

To get your puppy's attention, put a few pennies in an empty soda can or on any empty can and shake the can. Having the lid on the can keeps the pennies or pebbles inside the can. The noise will make him stop what he is doing and may be a good training tool.

To help keep your puppy from chewing on the furniture, carpet, etc., be sure he has his own rubber toys. On furniture (table, chair legs, etc.) on which he is chewing, try putting a little oil of cloves on the wood. The odor should keep him away and if not, the bitter taste will.

We moved to West Germany. We were here less than two months when our six-month-old puppy decided that grabbing on to our older dog's tail and yanking on it for long periods of time would be great fun. Since I didn't know how to say "Bitter Apple" in German, I was at a loss as to what to do. Finally an idea came to me. The juice from a jar of jalapeno peppers applied liberally to our older dog's tail put a stop to the problem in short order.

When dogs lick or chew their feet, the white hair often turns pink or rusty-looking. To stop the chewing and allow the feet to get white again, apply Dr. Scholl's Athlete's Foot Spray Powder liberally once a day.

When pups start teething around our place, we did practically everything possible to keep furniture, carpet, etc., from being destroyed. I tried commercial products, vinegar, etc. They didn't work. In desperation I was going to try quinine but it was pretty expensive. So I tried the next best thing which was tonic water. It cost me less than a dollar and there was no more chewing. I would suggest that before trying this, test the tonic water on an inconspicuous spot first as some fabric might discolor.

Cleaning and Staying Clean

I keep a towel on a hook right outside my back door. I have taught my dog to sit and wait (when he comes inside) until I wipe all four feet. As dogs are creatures of habit, I must wipe his feet and even on the driest of days, he will wait and "paw the air" (until I wipe him). It really cuts down on the amount of water and mud that he tracks into the house. He stays cleaner between bathings and my carpet stays cleaner between vacuumings.

Digging

Ever own a determined digger? Ever wonder what to do with your daily collection of doggy dung? Simple—just deposit problem "number 2" into problem "number 1" and pack over with 2" to 4" of dirt.

If you have a dog who is a persistent digger, try filling the hole with doggy waste. Then fill the hole with rock and/or dirt. Most fastidious dogs will refuse to dig in their own waste.

I had a puppy with a habit of digging into my chicken cage and stealing the chickens. As this could become hazardous to his health, I devised something that keeps dogs from either digging out of or into another kennel. I had tried burying large cement blocks under the edge, but they always just dug under the blocks so I cut chicken wire into 12-inch-wide strips and carefully secured it to the bottom pole of the kennel with baling wire all the way around. Then I buried it in about 10" of dirt. When the dogs dug and hit the chicken wire, they can go no farther and usually give up after a few tries. Be sure to lay a strip inside and outside of the kennel to prevent digging in or out.

The secret to avoid digging is simple: no toenails means no digging. If a dog's toenails are trimmed every week or filed very gently every few days with a roto tool, they will remain so short the dog cannot grab with them. Trimming must be constant to maintain a short toenail.

Eliminating Other Bad Behaviors

There are a lot of handy uses for your spray bottle besides misting when line-brushing. With the bottle always full of water and water only, set the nozzle on "stream." It will squirt across a room. My aim is not that good but I can generally get a barking dog's face and/or mouth very wet from across the room. Even if you just hit the body or dampen an ear, you do get their attention. If you don't think it shuts them up, try it. Also, my dogs are not afraid of the spray bottle, they merely respect it because they drink from it at shows. At hot outdoor shows, you may not have a bowl of water handy but you probably have a spray bottle within reach. My dogs love to have this water sprayed into their mouths, however you need to *make sure the nozzle is reset to "spray" (so it's not too strong) and that they do not receive too much, too rapidly because they might then vomit.* If you have sloppy drinkers and you are ready to go into the ring, but "Superdog" looks like he could use a drink, a squirt in the mouth is a lot neater than water slurped all over his ruff. I also use the spray bottle to rinse chalk off my hands when I'm in a hurry or off my shoes, clothes, etc. Believe it or not, I have been known to squirt the thing in my own mouth or at my nervous husband.

To get your puppy's attention, put a few pennies or pebbles in an empty soda can and shake (keeping your finger over the opening). This unpleasant noise will make him stop what he is doing and may be a good training tool.

Escaping and Jumping

As a breeder of dogs, at one time or another you have probably rushed to the aid of a yelping puppy *to find a pup who has managed to get his head wedged between the bars of the exercise pen.* In a panic you work to remove the puppy's head from between the bars (while he fights with all his might to resist your help). Newspaper and cardboard modifications to the exercise pen's bars are fine but these fixes make it impossible to fold up the exercise pen. I found that if you take a roll of weaving strips (used to repair lawn chairs) and weave those strips in and out of the bars of the exercise pen, it then becomes safe, escape proof and easy to fold up and to transport. This weaving material is usually the same height as the exercise pen's bars.

I have a couple of large pens where several dogs run together. When they're excited, they all jump against the gate making it almost impossible to open without an "escape." One day when coming home to the excited group, I noticed a throw-can of pennies that I'd left by the pen when silencing a barking episode a few days earlier. A simple shake sent the dogs scurrying. I now keep such a can by each gate and may easily enter even when the dogs are excited.

To discourage dogs from jumping out of an exercise pen, I attach about a 4-inch piece of fine chain to his web collar. At the end of the chain a tennis ball is attached *(make sure the chain is no longer than 4" because you don't want your dog to be able to chew the tennis ball).* When my dog jumps, the ball bounces against him and he is quickly discouraged from this practice.

To protect the outside of our wooden storm doors from our happy and bouncy dogs, my husband covered the panel below the window with a sheet of plexiglass. It allows the wood to be seen, and yet it protects it from scratches and is easily cleaned of muddy paw prints. Now the dogs who like to bounce against the door can't cause any damage to our wooden door.

Housebreaking
(See "TRAINING"—"Housebreaking Your Dog")

Stool Eating

If your dog is eating stools, try feeding your dog pancreatic digestive enzymes (because this disgusting habit is probably due to the dog's lacking in those enzymes). Give your dog one Nutri-Dyn Pan-5-Plus tablet (available for purchase in many health food stores) before feeding. This tablet is a powerful pancreatic enzyme which may be crushed and mixed with your dog's food. You may prefer to feed your dog twice daily and use half a tablet with each separate feeding.

I think I've found a solution for that awful habit of stool eating: one tablespoon of crushed pineapple or pureed pumpkin given daily has stopped my medium-sized dog from his eating stool.

To put a stop to that canine "poop-scooper" in the back yard, try sprinkling Accent on his food. This seems to discourage him from eating any of his stools.

Temperament Problems and Encouraging Good Behavior

Do you have a new dog who is standoffish? Have you tried everything to win him over and nothing seems to work? Try doing this for a while—do nothing. In other words...basically ignore the dog while playing with the other dogs. Try isolation for a while. After a few days or a week, the dog will be dying for attention. It really works.

Ever have a dog who has to be dragged and pushed into a crate? I avoid this by teaching my puppies to happily pile into their crates on command by bribing them. As soon as they are in their individual crates, I reward each puppy by giving him a Milk Bone (or other doggy treat) as soon as he is inside the crate. I also make them get into their crates for their meals. Now it's a race for the crates as soon as I say "Cookies" or "Suppertime." Thank heavens, there is no chasing all over at bedtime or when company arrives. It's great at the shows, too, because they enter their crates willingly.

If you have a dog who is a little apprehensive when a judge comes up to go over him, just take hold of a few hairs along the side of his head and below his ears. Hold him gently, but firmly, with your right hand and take a short hold on the lead with your left hand. You will find this will steady your dog and he will not pull away from the judge.

If you need to contain your puppy in a crate, remember to put a favorite toy inside the crate.

I have discovered a great way to help those young puppy hopefuls adjust to the noise and echo sounds of indoor shows. I bring the puppy into the house (where he feels secure and comfortable) and play my home videos which I've taken at various shows. It has worked great for me. You can start off with the volume low and slowly increase it as your dog begins to become more and more secure.

I have found an easy solution to instilling self-confidence when show-training young dogs. I work the young dog on a brace with an older, seasoned show dog. It helps the youngster to relax and soon he will start to imitate and compete with the older dog. Then he will begin to enjoy ever minute of it.

I purchased an adult dog who was lead-trained but needed a little more individual attention and socialization. Having given seminars on time management and being short on time myself, I decided to combine the two. I put an Obedience lead on him and tied it to my left-side belt loop. I then proceeded to do some of my daily chores around the house and yard. A very good example which worked well with him was when I cooked or cleaned up after our dinner, he was by my side. The smell of food kept his attention, familiarized him with me and I got the kitchen cleaned— all at the same time. This can also prove to be an excellent time to practice baiting since your dog is ready and the bait is handy.

Is your tremendous show prospect a clinging vine? Dogs who become very attached to their person also tend to rely on that person for their self-confidence. For a week or so, place him in a strange household (preferably with someone who knows and loves dogs). It'll do wonders when he is forced to be self-reliant.

Many breeders complain about their litters going through a screaming stage at about three weeks of age and I have witnessed this many times in other people's homes, however I have never had a screaming stage with any of my puppies at any age. I attribute this to the habit (which my whole family indulges in): they pick up the pups and cuddle them often (starting when they are two or three days old). Newborn pups can't see or hear, but they can feel and smell. We hold them on our laps and stroke them and let them snuggle right up under our chins while they sleep. In this way, each pup is used to the smell and the feel of humans long before their eyes and ears open. My pups are eager to see people and develop good temperaments.

The fastest and safest way to warm a puppy (if he is small, weak or cold) is to carry that pup in the front of your blouse or shirt (making very sure that he can't slip out while your carrying him). I had to prove it to myself with two small premature puppies weighing only 3 1/2 ounces. They wouldn't nurse so I carried them around all afternoon in the front of my blouse and, presto ,they are now three weeks old, fine and healthy. «»Editor's note: based upon reading and research, handling puppies in this manner will also help their temperaments when it comes to bonding with humans and wanting to be cuddled.«»

To get puppies accustomed to the large amount of noise at shows, take a tape recorder with you to the next show and record some of those many noises. Try to get a lot of announcing, especially when the announcer is playing with the microphone (flicking his thumbnail on it, blowing on it, etc.) which always happens when you have a puppy in the ring for the first time. Play this for the puppies, starting when they're about two to three weeks of age, often (be sure it is loud enough to be heard, but not so loud as to frightened the puppy) to get them accustomed to it. Mealtime is a good time to play it so they associate the noise with something good.

To help your puppy become well-socialized, try introducing him to the following new and safe encounters or experiences: meet a bird, a small animal, a large animal, a man with a beard, a lady with a hat, a baby, someone who looks different than you, a different home, balloons, a store, a vehicle and various outdoor locations; ride an elevator, an escalator, a boat and anything which moves; crawl over objects, through a tunnel, under coverings and overhangs, into enclosed areas (like boxes); listen to children playing, music, different sounds and noises; watch unusual lighting effects, an umbrella opening and closing; walk near anything which is tall and moves, various-sized fans blowing air; walk

over safe surfaces (like pebbles, water, slippery places, flat gratings, etc.), a wobbly bridge, up and down a staircase, something that rocks or moves, near running sprinklers, etc. Slowly introduce your puppy to as many safe and yet new adventures as possible (making sure that he's not ever overwhelmed or frightened). Each time an encounter might be unknown to your puppy and may possibly frighten him, be sure he is prepared and immediately give him a treat. Always be looking for new ways to expose your puppy to unknown ventures so he will become well-socialized.

Train your dogs to accept strange noises and objects which flap in the wind because they may encounter them in the show ring (whether inside or outside). Around your kennel area, hang up some wind chimes, an American flag and some of the pretty wind socks.

We all know not to call dogs to us for punishment (otherwise they'll never come), but sometimes we don't realize what, to a dog, is considered as punishment. I noticed my usually friendly and obedient dogs were refusing to come when I called them. I then realized that every time I called them to me it was because I intended to kennel them and they knew it. Now when I call them to me, I pet them and let them go their way before kenneling them (usually with food waiting for them...inside their crates).

When show-training young dogs, I have found an easy solution to instill self-confidence. I work the young dog on a brace with an older, seasoned show dog. It helps the youngster to relax, and soon he starts to imitate and compete with the older dog and begins to enjoy every minute.

You can let your young puppies crate train themselves by placing a small crate (#100 Vari Kennel crate) in their play yard. Since they are able to come-and-go as they please, they seem to accept being crated much more readily.

Enclosures— Crates, Cages, Pens and Whelping Boxes

Bedding, Mats, Footing, Etc.

A good way to keep puppies clean and free of newspaper print is to fill their pen with shredded computer paper. I first line the pen with newspaper and then put a large mound of shredded paper over this. I've found that it keeps puppies drier and free of newsprint, too. My husband brings this home in large plastic bags from his office.

A terrific bedding for dog crates is a product called a Trail and Action Pad by Pacific Crest Designs. This is a polyethylene cushion sold for camping, etc. It is sealed to make it moisture resistant. The cushion is difficult for pups to grab or to chew. It's easily cut to fit a crate. It cushions and insulates and may be hosed down if it becomes soiled. You might try searching the internet for foam sleeping pads if you can't locate these Trail and Action Pads.

At garage sales I buy pillow cases, crib sheets and receiving blankets for our crates. The pillow cases fit perfectly over the crate pillows, the crib sheets get wrapped around the pillows (and may be washed after every show). I put the receiving blankets in at night for the dogs to wad up and use for sleeping. I always take extra crib sheets in case one gets dirty. You may also clothespin the receiving blankets on wire crates in the car to keep the sun from shining on the crates.

Ever wonder what to do with your old pillowcases? I buy one-inch thick foam rubber and have it cut to fit the size of my crates. Just slip the foam piece into the pillowcase and you have an instant crate pad. The fabric is extremely durable. You may machine wash and dry them and pillowcases are the perfect size for medium-sized dog crates. When traveling, if you have a dog who drools or who gets carsick, place the piece of foam in a 13-gallon-size trash can liner to protect it from moisture and then slip it into the pillowcase. For larger crates or whelping boxes, use the sheets. Just stitch up the sides to, make a giant envelope.

For better smelling crates, take nylon netting and cut into 8" x 10" pieces. Take two pieces and seam up all the sides, leaving a 3-inch or 4-inch opening. Turn inside out and fill with cedar chips. Stitch opening shut. Toss underneath the grill floor.

For those of us who travel with wire cages which have metal pans, I put shower mats in the bottom. I buy the ones with the holes in them and suction cups on their undersides. This keeps the mat in place, allows for liquids to go into the holes and away from my dogs and provides a non-slip surface for the dog. They are also very easy to clean.

Here's a twist for the outdoor or indoor dog bed. I filled a durable cloth pillow case with one-half cedar shavings and one-half of those white packing pellets *(make sure dogs don't eat the pellets)*. The cedar shavings give the bed a nice fragrance, and the white packing pellets absorb the dog's body heat (providing him with a nice winter bed in his doghouse). I stitched in a zipper but a piece of Velcro with a flap would serve nicely, also. I have heard that cedar shavings repels fleas.

Hospital supply stores sell washable, moisture-proof pads for use in hospital beds. They are soft, absorbent (they stay dry on top...wicking moisture to the absorbent filling in the center) and provide firm footing for nursing puppies. They are also the perfect size (30" by 34")—which will fit most medium-sized whelping boxes. Ours have been machine-washed, bleached and dried repeatedly and have held up well through many litters over a number of years.

I buy Softex Bath Mats at Walmart. They are 17" x 36" and have tiny suction cups on the bottom of each mat. In the winter I keep my puppies in a dog room where the floor may get cold because the flooring is vinyl (on top of concrete). I put two of these mats together and the puppies may then lie on top of them which keeps the pups off the cold floor. Water will drain through these mats and best of all, they are machine washable. Also, because of the tiny suction cups on the bottom, the mats don't scoot around. This eliminates the need for newspapers in the area of my home where the mats are positioned. The mats also work well as a floor in the #200 Vari Kennel. There is also a smaller mat (16" x 23") which fits perfectly in the crate. I found the smaller mats at Target.

I found that when I was raising puppies who were still nursing, the ruts around the bottom of a very large crate (which I used as a whelping box) could be eliminated by rolling newspapers, taping them together and then putting them inside the crate. *This keeps the puppies from getting sat upon by their mother* (especially when she has seven puppies and she's having a difficult time getting them situated so everyone may nurse).

If you are tired of papers covering the entire puppy area, try this: after my puppies get the idea what the papers are for, I take my metal tray from a puppy crate and line it with papers. Placing this in the puppy play area, I remove the rest of the papers and they quickly get the idea that this is their spot. The tray is a nice size, providing your puppies room for walking and still find their favorite spot but is small enough to provide the puppies room to play. Your puppies soon learn where to go, the tray is easily cleaned and the puppies can't slide into messes as they spend the rest of their time playing. The tray is also nice when you have carpeting (since papers leak but metal does not).

I have always felt sorry for dogs who have to lie on the bumps found at the bottom of a Vari-Kennel. I had a set of old TV trays and discovered that they perfectly fit the bottom of a size #200 kennel. Now if the dog rearranges its bedding, he is still lying on a flat surface. Also, when shipping a dog, the paperwork, etc., is protected under this new floor.

I keep my puppies in a mesh-sided playpen (which may be a reasonably priced item through a second-hand shop or at a garage sale) while being housebroken. I place towels (which are easy to change when an accident occurs) on the bottom of the playpen. By keeping the puppies in the playpen, they may be kept anywhere the family is gathering (without the worry of soiled carpets), and they may be quickly shuttled outside when necessary. I also teach them to bark when they need to go out.

Instead of using sawdust shavings for puppies, I use the cedar shavings which you may purchase at Walmart (contained in a very large bag). It's inexpensive and your puppies will smell so good.

Interested in inexpensive crate mats? Visit yard sales for comforters. A twin-size comforter will make four crate mats (each approximately 18" x 26"). Simply cut the comforter into four equal pieces. Fold each in half (right sides together) and sew around the edge of 2 1/2 sides. Turn through the open 1/2 side and stitch. To further secure, stitch a line approximately 2" to 3" in from the edge around all four sides.

I use old bath towels (instead of newsprint) on the bottom of my puppy pen. This gives newborns plenty of traction for finding "mum," is easy to change, simple to wash and my puppies are always clean.

I went to a plastic supply company and bought scraps of high-impact styrene (which were .060" thick). The store cut them for me (at no cost) into 16" by 22" sheets (four each) and I took the remaining pieces home. The 16" by 22" pieces fit into a #200 crate without having to round the edges. They fit on top of the grates. Now there are no slots for toes or tiny paws to slip through and any wetness runs off under the grate. They're washable and bleachable and odor doesn't cling. They may even be used without a grate although the .080" might be a bit better for that use (which is more expensive, of course). I was able to purchase "liners" for four #200 crates, one #500 crate (my whelping box) and enough left over for another #200 crate, if I ever needed it. If people are afraid of puppies chewing the edges, the sheets may be cut a tad larger and then just round the edges for a closer fit.

Need shredded paper to line puppy pens or when shipping dogs? Shredded newspaper (without any print) or IBM computer paper makes excellent absorbent material and, as an extra bonus, there is no dirty newsprint ink all over the dogs.

Never use wood chips as bedding for young pups because of the possibility that the chips harbor the bacteria Klebsiella. *This organism may cause death in puppies and may make their dam very ill.*

Our Vari Kennel crates come with a removable board (placed at the bottom of the crate—which covers those horrible plastic bumps molded into the bottom of the crate). Some people let their dogs sleep directly on those bumps...which is uncomfortable. If you take the measurement of the old board to a lumber yard or a hardware store, they will cut another board or boards the same size for you (but without the holes as seen in the original board).

People's baby playpens make great puppy playpens. Those with the mesh sides keep even the smallest babies in and yet they may see out. Most of the playpens have a plastic rim around the bottom which holds in the shavings. We cut a scrap piece of linoleum to fit the bottom. It covers the handle holes in the floor and makes it waterproof. I get mine at garage sales and save money.

Putting indoor-outdoor carpeting in the bottom of the whelping box may be deadly to your puppies if their urine or their mother's urine saturates the carpet and the pups then lie in it. The chemicals with which the carpet is treated may combine with the strong urine to produce a chemical similar to sulfuric acid. Well-washed carpeting has probably had all the dangerous chemicals removed. Old throw rugs which have been washed and re-washed are probably the safest and provide the pups secure footing. Be sure to wash these rugs at least once a day to avoid odor and problems with bacteria.

Rather than spend a lot on commercial vinyl tiles for cages and pens, I suggest you go to a good carpet or linoleum store. I picked up an end of linoleum which was also coated with plastic on its reverse side. It made great pads for my outdoor dog houses as they are sturdy and easily washable.

Recycle all those dog food bags by cutting off their ends and then splitting the bag lengthwise. Put the bag under the news-papers in the exercise pen or puppy playpen. Doing this makes cleaning up easier. Just roll it up so it's a contained bundle and toss. I buy Purina Pro Plan and the inside has kind of a plastic coating for moisture control.

Reuse old crib bumpers as liners for dog beds, crates or for whelping areas. They are especially useful for geriatric dogs to lean against.

Rubbermaid Sure Grip (for drawer lining) is great for lining crates, puppy pens, tubs, tops of counters and any surface which you may use for measuring, grooming, etc. It's inexpensive, comes in great colors and you just throw it in the washer when it needs cleaning.

Standard-sized zippered plastic pillowcase covers are excellent for protecting the inner foam cushions for the #200 crate pads. The size is just right and they are wonderful to have when those "accidents" happen.

The waterproof lap and crib pads made for babies are handy to use for puppy whelping boxes. They are waterproof, washable and provide good traction for the pups. They also last a long time, and the puppies do not get their toenails caught in the fibers (as they sometimes do with carpeting).

Those washable and reusable air-conditioning filters make nice beds. When my crate's dog floors finally gave out, I used these filters. They may be put into the washing machine (gentle cycle only) and washed. You may also sprinkle flea repellent (such as Sevin dust) underneath each filter.

To give newborns something for good footing (which will stay in place and is easily cleanable), cut up and edge flat mattress pads. A Sears king-size makes four pads which exactly fit a Kennel

Aire whelping crate.

To keep your puppies as clean as possible, put shredded newspaper (preferably paper without the print) in their pens when they become old enough to be messy.

Unable to find rubber matting or other suitable flooring for your dog's crate? Try a non-skid bath mat as a substitute. With this rubber matting, cleaning is simplified just by removing and hosing it off. If you have a solid crate, this type of matting is also excellent to place on the top of the crate because it will provide firm footing for grooming.

We use grill floors in the bottom of our airline crates. In my search for something to pad the floor for my chewer/spinner, I remembered an old Girl Scout idea of making newspaper mats. Open a double page of newspaper, fold the long side up about 2 1/2 inches. Then flip that part over and press. Keep flipping until finished (about seven times). Make 12 and then start weaving. Leave ends long enough to tuck under. These mats last my spinner about a week. It's a great way for the kids to keep busy, too.

We went to a metal fabricator in our area and had pans made for all our exercise pens, which we keep in the house. These pans are flat with a one-inch lip at their edges (which keeps the liquids in and helps to stabilize the pens as well). Not only are they easy to clean, they stop puppies from digging up the linoleum. You may also use them to protect carpeting under an exercise pen.

When a puppy begins spending the night in a crate but isn't old enough to last the night without wetting, I hook two wire crates together. If a puppy is small or the crate's large, I put bedding in one half of the crate and newspaper in the other half. (I put computer paper over the newspaper to keep the puppy from getting newsprint on himself.) When the puppy's old enough to last the night without having to wet, I take away the crate along with the newspaper.

When grooming puppies or unsure adults, I place a bath mat (the kind with carpeting on one side) on top of my grooming table. You may find them in any department store in various colors. The bottom of the mat secures nicely to the grooming table and your dogs will feel more comfortable because they are on more secure footing. After each grooming session, I shake this bath mat outside and it's usually as clean as it was when it was new. You may also put it in the washer and dryer. They are great mats for inside your dogs' crates.

When puppies are two weeks old, I put a 12" by 16" cardboard bed (along with a baby receiving blanket and a heating pad) in their whelping box. Then, I put disposable diapers over the newspaper in the rest of the box. (Use diapers without elastic legs so they'll lie flat.) The diapers are more absorbent than newspaper and also provide good footing. The puppies leave their bed to eliminate on the diapers. I also put computer paper over the newspaper to keep the puppies cleaner.

When shipping a dog, there are drawbacks in using a hard board as the crate's bottom *because it may flip over and injure the dog. Shredded paper may also cause a problem during ship-ping since it may block air circulation.* Try using a thick stack of newspaper (either pinned or sewn into a pillowcase). This pillow-case may be emptied and laundered easily and provides a safe and absorbent crate mat.

When the trays of your metal dog crates start rusting, buy some peel-and-stick floor tiles (random patterning like marbling in pale colors work the best). Cut and fit them tightly into the metal tray. Seal the edges with silicone caulking so that these trays are then waterproof. The light-colored tiles make any soiled patches plainly visible.

When traveling, we place Kitty Litter in the bottoms of our crates. The litter quickly absorbs those seemingly inevitable tummy upsets, leaves no odor, keeps coats clean and provides a more comfortable journey. We also use Kitty Litter in the base pans of our Puppy-Aire crates.

When whelping, I use newspaper during and after delivery of each pup and I always have to scramble to open up new newspaper after each pup. I work in housecleaning for a medical center and noticed that staff members have these blue pads that they use for babies, etc. These pads have plastic on the bottom and then the absorbent material is on top. What an easy way to keep things dry and clean.

Cleaning

A tire scrub brush is a great solution for scrubbing down dirty Vari Kennels or other plastic crates. The brush easily reaches into corners and is stiff enough to clean thoroughly (without leaving scratches).

Detachol removes ear braces. Now...I am also suggesting that you try using Detachol for removing the glue residue left on your shipping crates after you tear off the shipping documents or the airline's labels. I tried every other type of cleaning product and nothing else has removed this black gunk as effectively as Detachol. It will also remove the price tags which stores love to put right in the middle of the lenses on those new sunglasses you just purchased (without scratching the lens). Best of all, it removes tar or blacktop chips from your carpeting, kitchen flooring and your dogs' coats. Just apply it liberally (in the case of tar) and sop up with a towel (as it dissolves the tar into a runny mess). Then wash thoroughly to remove the Detachol residue.

For those of us who travel with wire cages which have metal pans, I put shower mats in the bottom of each crate. I buy the shower mats with the holes in them and suction cups on the underside (this keeps the mat in place, allows for liquids to go into the holes and away from my dogs and provides a non-slip surface for the dog). They are also very easy to clean.

How do you clean fiberglass shipping crates which have greasy coat oil and dirt on them? Separate the crate and rinse each part (with hot water, if possible). Spray the inside with Grease Relief. Let it stand for at least 20 minutes with about 1/2" water in the bottom of each section. Use a scrub brush to clean the crate. If you have ever tried regular soap and water or Comet Cleanser, you will sigh with relief at how much easier this is. Make sure there is no residue of Grease Relief remaining.

I found, quite by accident, that Clorox Toilet Wands are an excellent tool for cleaning airline crates. The long handles make it very easy to reach into the corners of even a #300 crate. They do a remarkable job of cleaning and disinfecting at the same time. Remember to rinse well...so no residue remains.

If you really want to get those fiberglass crates clean, just hose them down first, then spray them with Dow Bathroom Cleaner with scrubbing bubbles. Let this set, then rinse well. It will leave them clean (with little work required by you), and it disinfects and deodorizes. *Remember to rinse well.* It leaves my crates looking new.

I use flea shampoo when washing kennel blankets and puppy towels and when cleaning crates. This helps to control fleas in the crates and keeps the fleas off young puppies and their dam while in the puppy pen.

My puppies' playpen is in our dining room and having a no-wax floor sure helps. I encountered a problem when the newspaper print (both color and black-and-white) stained the floor. To remove those stains, I found that WD-40 worked well. First, make sure all puppies are out of the area to be sprayed. Spray the WD-40 directly on the stains. Use a clean, dry paper towel to rub the spots out. Then clean those areas thoroughly with soap and water. It works like magic and is safe for no-wax floors.

Nilodor is a wonderful product to use on pet odors. I keep a mist spray bottle filled with it at all times. Not only is it an easy way to freshen up the inside of crates, but it is also an easy way to freshen up the carpets.

One cleansing agent which works great for me when cleaning my Kennel Aire crates is Dow Bathroom Cleaner. There are other brands on the market, also. Just wet the crate first, then spray this bathroom cleaner all over the crate. The cleanser eats the gum-like substances without a lot of scrubbing required by you. Be sure to wash (with soap and lots of water) afterwards so no cleanser remains.

Rather than crawling in airline crates to clean them, use a (new and clean) toilet bowl brush. They are great for cleaning those out-of-reach corners.

To clean greasy crates, take them apart and moisten the soiled areas. Spray with the oven cleaner I use (Mr. Muscle). Mr. Muscle is a non-aerosol product. Let the foam set a few minutes and use a scrubby to loosen the grime. Wash thoroughly with soap and water so that no Mr. Muscle residue remains.

To clean out plastic Sky Kennels, first empty everything that you have inside them. Spray with Spray 'N Wash cleaner and then take them to a self-serve car wash and rinse them thoroughly. That sterilizes them and completely cleans them (both inside and out) without much work. Rinse off all Spray 'N Wash cleaner.

We have found a wonderful, convenient way to wash airline crates—all at the same time. If you have six or seven crates which need a good, basic cleaning and you are short on time, load them into the show vehicle or truck of your choice and drive them to the nearest do-it-yourself car wash. Make sure that all bowls and any of the "coop cups" are removed, as under the high pressure they may become dangerous projectiles. Line the crates up against the wall starting from the corner. Be sure to thoroughly rinse the crates and, whatever you do, make sure that you don't accidentally use the wax while going through the car wash. As a courtesy to other patrons, rinse any debris into the floor grate. This method may garner some strange looks but it is quite effective.

Crates and Cages

After the horrible theft of a dog at a show, we started locking our crates at shows. We bought a dozen or so very small locks from Sears. We lucked out in that they were all identical and the same key fits all the locks we purchased. Every crate in our house has a lock hanging on the door and no matter which crate gets taken to a show, there is a lock just waiting to be used. They are not heavy-duty locks but they do the job. It is doubtful that someone thinking about stealing a dog will bother one who is locked up. Even if the lock could be picked or broken, they will look for an easier target. I keep a key pinned to the inside of my bait pouch for quick access in case of an emergency.

Could you use an extra Sky Kennel for very little money? Then you should start taking advantage of yard sales, your local swap meets and flea markets. You would be surprised how many people have a crate in their garage which they needed years ago and no longer need. They are more than willing to unload it for a very reasonable price. Little do they know, that treasure is quite valuable to us.

Do you have an early and noisy riser in your kennel? I do. He wakes everyone up. So I put a sheet over his enclosure (just as is done with a bird). Now he stays quiet until I remove the sheet and it's time to get up.

For better smelling crates, take nylon netting and cut into 8" x 10" pieces. Take two pieces and seam up all the sides, leaving a 3" or 4" opening. Turn it inside out and fill with cedar chips. Stitch the opening shut. Then just toss it underneath the grill floor.

For those who have wire handles on crates or exercise pens, make it easier on your hands by covering those wire handles. Get an old piece of hose (a garden hose works well) and measure the amount of hose you'll need for the handle. Slice the hose on one side from one end to the other. Slip it over the wire handle and tape the hose shut. (I find friction tape works well.) Wrap the tape around the length of the hose several times. It makes crates and pens so much easier to carry.

In the house, I put carpet remnants between the crates and walls to protect the walls.

I want to issue a warning to anyone who uses or recommends using the dividers that come with the wire crates. I sent a pup to his new home and received a call that no breeder ever wants to get. It was from a sobbing, hysterical puppy buyer who got up to let her puppy out to potty only *to find the puppy dead (with his head hung between the divider and the crate). She said the divider fit in very tight and was hard to insert. The pup had somehow loosened one of the hooks which secures the divider and got his head caught. Not hearing a sound from him, she assumed that her puppy was unable to make a noise by having his airway cut off.* Later, she did call the company that makes the crates and also asked me to warn everyone I knew about this danger. I'm just sick over this and want to warn as many people as possible.

Crate Training
(See "TRAINING"—"Crate Training")

Feeding and Drinking Containers
(See "FEEDING"—"Containers")

Indoor Enclosures
Children's plastic pools are great for new puppies since the pool may be rinsed out to rid it of odors and/or messes.

For a new litter of puppies or kittens, confine them in a mesh playpen. Tape screen around a wooden playpen so pups or kittens can't get out.

For the people who need to leave their dogs in a kennel or in the house alone when they are at work during the day, I have found that it's a good idea to always turn on a radio whenever I am away. By turning on music, my dogs always have something consistent and soothing to listen to rather than hearing outside noises which may then cause them to bark. It works very well in an apartment, too.

For those of you who do not have a large uncarpeted indoor area which is suitable for young puppies (once they have outgrown the whelping pen or crate), here is what I do: I have a large carpeted family room which becomes a puppy play area. I purchase

a large remnant of Solarium or Congoleum vinyl flooring and put this down over the carpeting. Get a remnant at least six-feet-wide by twelve-feet-long. You can leave one end rolled up depending on how large a litter you have. Then connect a wire crate to an exercise pen or two using clip fasteners to hold them together. Now the babies have a crate to sleep in and a nice size area to play and eat in until they are old enough to go outside and then eventually to their new homes.

I found the most marvelous thing in the baby department of Walmart. It is called a "soft gate" by Gerry. It's a collapsible gate that's approximately 26" high and expands from 27" to 42". The whole thing fits into a carry case that's about 3" in diameter. It's great when traveling.

If you find stepping over your puppy gates getting more difficult as you grow older, try using a pair of shutters in the doorway. Also, while picking up the shutters at your local home improvement center, ask what they do with their wall panel samples once they are discontinued. At just one store we picked up 12 samples which would have been thrown away. With just minor trimming with a sabre saw, they make beautiful floors for your crates. Just be sure, if trimming for airline crates, to allow for the difference in size of the old and newer crates. They're easy to clean (even the grooves run the right way) and they are free.

I've loaned crates to puppy buyers to help them during the first few weeks with their new puppy. I found a marvelous pamphlet to send along with our usual six-page instruction and care sheets for the puppy. It is "A Pet Owner's Guide to the Dog Crate" and I cannot recommend it highly enough. These pamphlets may be ordered from Nicki Meyer Educational Effort, Inc., 31 Davis Hill Road, Weston, CT 06883. «»Editor's note: you may also be interested in reading an article by Nicki Meyer entitled "Dog Crates as Aids to Pet Owners" in the September/October 1981 issue of the *Sheltie Pacesetter* magazine on page 140. A photocopy of this ten-page article may be purchased for $7.90. Contact Nancy Lee Cathcart at s.pacesetter@sheltie.com for details.«»

Most people use exercise pens to keep dogs confined in a place. I do, too, but I also use my exercise pens to keep dogs out of certain places.

Simple and inexpensive pen tops for the 4' x 4' pens may easily be made from one single section of the type of pens which are built using individual sections. Our pen tops overlapped the 4' x 4's by about a foot, and I finally discovered that it was easy to bend that one foot over by standing on the pen section and pulling up. Then simply strap the top on with those elastic straps (bungee cords) that we all use to tie down pens, etc., to our station wagon racks.

The soft insulators which go around pipes are great for the tops of exercise pens. Just pop them on and the metal ex-pen will not mark or scratch your walls or anything they touch.

Thinking of redoing your kitchen or utility room floor and don't know which kind of linoleum will hold up best? With your next litter, ask a local flooring place for some tile samples (usually given free) and use them as a base underneath the newspapers in your puppy exercise pen. You will soon know which styles and brands will hold up best. If it can take the constant cleanup of puppy droppings, it can withstand anything. (I found that the deeper grooved designs, while being stylish, are far harder to clean.)

We went to a metal fabricator in our area and had pans made for all our exercise pens (which we keep inside the house). These pans are flat with a one-inch lip at their edges (which keeps the liquids inside and helps to stabilize the pens, as well). Not only are they easy to clean, they also stop puppies from digging up the linoleum. You may use them to protect carpeting under an exercise pen.

Newborns

An ideal cozy den for just weaned puppies (who are in a large whelping box) is a baby diaper box. Put a towel in it and watch them pile inside and sleep. Once it has turned into a chew toy, just replace it. They love it.

Children's plastic pools are great for new puppies as the pool may be rinsed out to rid it of odors and/or messes.

For a new litter of puppies or kittens, confine them in a mesh playpen. Tape screen around a wooden playpen with wooden slats so pups or kittens won't get out.

I found that when I was raising puppies who were still nursing, the ruts around the bottom of a very large crate (which I used as a whelping box) could be eliminated by rolling newspapers, taping them together and then putting them inside the crate. *This keeps the puppies from getting sat upon by their mother* (especially when she has seven puppies and she's having a difficult time getting them situated so everyone may nurse).

My husband's worn out T-shirts make excellent crate door cover-ups for newborns. I line up the shirt (XXL for a #400 crate) with the door. Then cut small slits under the shoulder seams to accommodate the width of the door hinges. When I put "Mom" out for exercise, I hang the T-shirt over the door to stop drafts and to remind me that she's still outside.

Use a 12-panel Extra-Aire by Kennel Aire exercise pen (or kennel panels) when keeping newborns or a litter of puppies in the house. Place a large plastic drop cloth *(after it's been aired out)* over the carpet or over whatever kind of flooring you may have. Then spread newspapers down and place shredded newspaper on top of the flat newspapers. If you can get newspaper without print, the print won't get onto the puppies. After the pups are whelped these may be changed easily. Surround the papers with a portable exercise pen which is 24" high. You may step over this and this pen will keep the puppies and their dam confined until the pups are weaned. If we have two or more litters at the same time, we put a partition in the middle. Each of our litters has it's own heating pad. A heating pad is needed, even in the summertime, especially if you're running your air-conditioning (as newborn puppies need about 85 degrees temperature for approximately their first seven days). By using this method we have never lost a pup past three days of age.

Outdoor Enclosures

(See "KENNEL MAINTENANCE"—"Dog Runs and Enclosures")

Puppies

An ideal cozy den for just weaned puppies (who are in a large whelping box) is a baby diaper box. Put a towel in it and watch them pile inside and sleep. Once it has turned into a chew toy, just replace it. They love it.

As a breeder of dogs, at one time or another you have probably rushed to the aid of a yelping puppy *to find a pup who has managed to get his head wedged between the bars of the exercise pen.* In a panic you work to remove the puppy's head from

between the bars (while he fights with all his might to resist your help). Newspaper and cardboard modifications to the exercise pen's bars are fine but these fixes make it impossible to fold up the exercise pen. I found that if you take a roll of weaving strips (used to repair lawn chairs) and weave those strips in and out of the bars of the exercise pen, it then becomes safe, escape proof and easy to fold up and to transport. This weaving material is usually the same height as the exercise pen's bars.

A way to keep puppies warm and busy outside in the late fall is to put the leaves you rake up into a 10' x 10' pen (size may vary) and put the puppies inside that pen. They'll have a ball because they love romping through the leaves. If there are some small twigs with the leaves, the pups may chew on them and play "keep-away." Once the pups tire out, the leaves will keep them warm.

A wise precaution to take (if you have small puppies exercising in a dog run which has the chain-link cyclone fence fabric) is to put 12" to 24" of 1-inch mesh or hardware wire all around the bottom and on its outside. *I had a seven-week-old puppy who put his head through the 2 1/2-inch diameter opening and got stuck.* While I held the puppy so he wouldn't struggle, a neighbor (who had heard the commotion) used pliers to unweave the fence (at its base) in order to free this puppy's head. If I had used the wire mesh, this could have been avoided. I was lucky because I hadn't left those pups unsupervised and I saw this dangerous incident as it was actually occurring.

During the summer months, I always purchase two of the kiddie wading pools. One day, while in a pinch, I found that the combination of a kiddie pool and an eight-panel playpen makes a great corral for toddling puppies and even for older puppies. It's waterproof and may be lined with paper. The extra kiddie pool may quickly replace the other pool when you're cleaning it.

Even though our puppies and visiting bitches are kept in air-conditioned areas, we often direct a fan toward them for extra cooling during those hot summer months. Since they are kept on newspapers, it used to be a big problem to keep the papers from blowing all over the place. I learned that by overlapping the newspapers (similar to shingles on a roof) and by starting at the farthest point away from the fan and putting each new section about halfway over the last, each paper holds the other in place. The last section (which is closest to the fan) is weighted with nice, fat complete sections of newspaper (for the extra weight needed to hold down the paper completely).

For a litter of puppies or kittens, confine them in a mesh playpen. Tape screen around a wooden playpen with wooden slats so pups or kittens won't get out.

For winter or inside puppies, I buy storage boxes for "litter box" training my puppies. I buy a big, deep storage box (and store stuff in the box) and use the lid for litter training young puppies. As the puppies get older, I use an "under the bed storage box" as a "litter box." By then, the pups have learned to use the "lid litter box," but as they get older the "under the bed storage box" works better since it is a little deeper and shavings stay inside better. The pups also have fun hopping in and out of the box.

Having trouble keeping those little puppies inside that wading pool? Try putting chicken wire around the pool. It's very flexible, comes in different heights and it's very easy to remove (so you may store it away for your next litter).

If you are tired of papers covering the entire puppy area, try this: after my puppies get the idea what the papers are for, I take my metal tray from a puppy crate and line it with papers. Placing this in the puppy play area, I remove the rest of the papers and they quickly get the idea that this is their spot. The tray is a nice size providing your puppies room for walking and still find their favorite spot but is small enough to provide the puppies room to play. Your puppies soon learn where to go, the tray is easily cleaned and the puppies can't slide into messes as they spend the rest of their time playing. The tray is also nice when you have carpeting (since papers leak but metal does not).

If you love "treasure hunting" at garage sales and flea markets like I do, keep your eyes open for those wooden (with plastic mesh) baby gates. I've collected them for years to lend to families with new baby puppies and I made a neat puppy pen from some of them. Simply take the two sides apart and saw off the wooden slide bars leaving two wooden framed mesh rectangles with those little rubber tips that usually fit against the door frame. Lay the rectangles on their sides so that the rubber tips are on the floor and then hinge the sides together. I use a pair (one gate) of these like a "fire screen" at our hallway, too. It's tall enough that the dogs get the hint to stay off the carpet and yet short enough so that we are not constantly tripping over it.

I have started a lot of people using chicken or rabbit cages for their new puppies (be sure wire does not allow pups' feet to fall through openings which might hurt their tender paws). These wire cages have pullout trays so unmentionables will fall through and keep the puppy high and dry. Also, be sure to clean out whatever does not fall through the wire. What's more, these cages are half the price or less than the same type of cage designed and sold specifically for dogs. I buy mine at a nearby animal feed store. They may be cleaned even while the puppy sleeps. After lining the trays with newspaper or brown sacks, I pour a little cat litter on the tray which absorbs all odors.

I keep my puppies in a mesh-sided playpen (which may be a reasonably priced item through a second-hand shop) while they're being housebroken. I place towels (which are easy to change when an accident occurs) on the bottom. By keeping them in the playpen, they can be kept upstairs with the family (without the worry of soiled carpets) and they can be quickly shuttled outside whenever necessary. I also teach them to bark when they need to go out.

I partition my kitchen off from the rest of the house when housebreaking a youngster by using indoor shutters and decorative wood trim. The trim pieces are cut, spaced and nailed along the outer edge of the doorway in such a way that one or more shutters may slide into the doorway (depending on the size of the puppy). They are easy for adults to step over but too high for a puppy to jump. The trim pieces and shutters may be stained or painted to match your decor.

Make a temporary puppy crate by joining two rectangular laundry baskets. Use wire to hinge these baskets together.

My puppies are self-fed and I found that the adults were getting too "porky" with their constant access to the puppies' food. I solved this problem without having to separate them. I made a creep-feeder (a pen so constructed as to exclude larger animals while permitting young animals to enter and obtain feed) out of a Kennel Aire crate. I used a rubber bungee strap or a piece of heavy wire to tie the crate door open and block off most of the crate entrance with an extra door that I had from a plastic crate. This was fastened, too, with rubber straps. The entrance is vertical and just wide enough for the pups to enter and "pig out" on the

bowl of food placed inside to the back of the crate. (You could use this same procedure with an exercise pen with a door.) The adults can't fit through the entrance and have to wait until feeding time for their measured portions.

Need a cheap exercise pen for puppies? Try a compost rack which may be purchased in the garden section of Walmart. It is a lightweight 4' x 4' x 3' plastic-coated metal cage.

People's baby playpens make great puppy playpens, too. Those with the mesh sides keep even the smallest babies in and yet the puppies may see out of this playpen. Most of the playpens have a plastic rim around the bottom which holds in the shavings. We cut a scrap piece of linoleum to fit the bottom which covers the "handle" holes in the floor and makes it waterproof. I get mine at garage and yard sales and save money.

Use a 12-panel Extra-Aire by Kennel Aire exercise pen (or kennel panels) when keeping newborns or a litter of puppies in the house. Place a large plastic drop cloth (after it's been aired out) over the carpet or over whatever kind of flooring you may have. Then spread newspapers down and place shredded newspaper on top of the flat newspapers. If you can get newspaper without print, the print won't get onto the puppies. After the pups are whelped these may be changed easily. Surround the papers with a portable exercise pen which is 24" high. You may step over this and this pen will keep the puppies and their dam confined until the pups are weaned. If we have two or more litters at the same time, we put a partition in the middle.

When a puppy begins spending the night in a crate but isn't old enough to last the night without wetting, I hook two wire crates together. If a puppy is small or the crate's large, I put bedding in one half of the crate and newspaper in the other half. (I put computer paper over the newspaper to keep the puppy from getting newsprint on himself.) When the puppy's old enough to last the night without having to wet, I take away the crate along with the newspaper.

You can let your young puppies crate train themselves by placing a small crate (#100 Vari Kennel crate) in their play yard. Since they are able to come-and-go as they please, they seem to accept being crated much more readily.

Traveling and Shipping

As safe as air shipping is, there was an unfortunate situation where a dog in a Sky Kennel was injured. The crate was accidentally tipped and the dog's leg was trapped. Tape down your pegboard floors before shipping.

For anyone who has a problem with drooling puppies and young adults (it's hoped they will outgrow it when mature), and if you want to show the puppies at matches or point shows, you don't want to give them any tranquilizers, Dramamine or other remedies because then they won't want to show. I have tried everything to prevent them from drooling...to no avail. In order to keep them from getting themselves and other puppies in the crate with them wet (because saliva takes forever to dry), I take old terry T-shirts and cut the arms out. The arm fits over the head and acts like a barber's bib. It catches and absorbs the saliva and keeps the puppy dry. Cut the length to reach to the pastern so the puppy may move around without stepping on the bib. Keep the bib on for a while when you get to the match (it takes them a few minutes to realize they aren't moving anymore), then remove the bib and you have a dry puppy.

I have always felt sorry for dogs who have to lie on the bumps found at the bottom of a Vari Kennel. I had a set of old TV trays and discovered that they are a perfect fit for the bottom of a #200 kennel. Now if the dog rearranges his bedding, he is still lying on a flat surface. Also, when shipping a dog, the paperwork, etc., is protected under this new floor.

In the past when returning a shipping crate, we have gone to UPS and paid a pretty hefty price. The crate had to be taken apart, UPS wouldn't insure and sometimes crates arrived broken. We learned that you may mail empty airline crates through the U.S. Postal Service. Leave the crate assembled, put a mailing label on top. The post office will affix stamps and off it goes.

Something we do all the time when shipping is to put the ever-present letters, photos and other papers under the false floor—all securely sealed in Baggies. This is much better than trusting our heavy-handed air personnel not to accidentally scrape off taped envelopes from the outside. Naturally, the health papers do go on the outside of the crate.

When shipping a dog there are drawbacks to using a hard board on the bottom inside of the crate *because that board may flip over and injure the dog. Including a lot of shredded paper inside the crate may block air circulation.* Try using a thick stack of newspaper (either pinned or sewn into a pillowcase). This can be emptied and laundered easily and provides a safe and absorbent crate mat.

Whelping Boxes

(See "WHELPING"—

"Bedding and Linings For Whelping Boxes")

After a period (years ago) when our bitches were having low-grade uterine infections, we threw away our whelping boxes and now use only cardboard cartons. These are easily obtained from a grocery store. We find Pampers and Bounty Towel cartons just the right size to fit in our Kennel Aire whelping crates. If the bitch soils it or rips up the cardboard carton, just put in a new one and then throw it away when you are finished with it. They're very sanitary with no chance of anything carrying over from a previous whelping.

An excellent whelping box is not a box at all but a 5' or larger plastic wading pool. There are no corners for puppies to get stuck in and the plastic is easily cleaned with bleach and water. *Just be very sure all the bleach has been totally removed before using it again.*

An ideal cozy den for just weaned puppies (who are in a large whelping box) is a baby diaper box. Put a towel in this box and watch them pile inside and sleep. Once it has turned into a chew toy, just replace it. Puppies love it.

A proper whelping box is made of an enclosed structure (including the top and bottom) to make a sort of den. Novice that I was years ago, I constructed such a box. This was a sturdy cardboard box cut out in front for the entrance of the dam. An approximately 4-inch lower part of the opening kept the puppies from crawling out at an early age. I never worried about guard rails, etc. When times were particularly cold, the box or den may be covered with a blanket to provide extra warmth. As time passed, I improved my whelping box or den by spraying the cardboard with lacquer for easier cleaning.

Children's plastic pools are great for new puppies. The pool may be rinsed out to rid odors or messes.

For a cheap exercise pen, I buy compost bins (used for storing leaves after raking, etc.). I quite often find them on sale at hardware stores. They are approximately 4' by 4' square and two or three bins may be attached together to make a larger pen. They make a great pen for the mom and her puppies and also make excellent whelping boxes. You may put them around a cardboard box and deliver the puppies inside and still keep the bitch enclosed.

For a new litter of puppies or kittens, confine them in a mesh playpen. Tape screen around a wooden playpen which has wooden slats so pups or kittens won't get out.

I have found a terrific place to whelp puppies in the house and that place is inside a closet. My box is made to fit two-thirds of the way and I use the last third for towels, etc. It is out of the way. There is a clothes rod in my closet on which to hang a light or a heat lamp. This whelping box is enclosed on three sides (which the bitch likes) and the fourth side may be blocked off using a short gate. Closet doors may be left open, taken off or closed part way to make a quiet, den-like area. I use a spare bedroom and can still hear the puppies easily. Give your next overnight guest a real surprise.

My husband's worn out T-shirts make excellent crate door cover-ups. I line up the shirt (XXL for a #400 crate) with the door, and I cut small slits under the shoulder seams to accommodate the width of the door hinges. When I put mom out for exercise, I hang the T-shirt over the door to stop drafts and to remind me that she's still outside.

Since I do not usually have more than one litter at a time, I only own one wooden whelping box. This year when I needed additional whelping boxes, I found a simple, good substitute. I have a large shipping crate (the fiberglass type). It may be easily divided into its two sections and becomes two makeshift whelping boxes. The only problem is that the bottom is not completely flat but by padding with papers and covering with carpet squares, they worked very nicely. Good idea? When it is not in use for whelping boxes, you have a nice large shipping crate instead of boxes stored and in the way, getting dusty.

Use a 12-panel Extra-Aire by Kennel Aire exercise pen (or kennel panels) when keeping newborns or a litter of puppies in the house. Place a large plastic drop cloth *(after it's been aired out)* over the carpet or over whatever kind of flooring you may have. Then spread newspapers down and place shredded newspaper on top of the flat newspapers. If you can get newspaper without print, the print won't get onto the puppies. After the pups are whelped these may be changed easily. Surround the papers with a portable exercise pen which is 24" high. You may step over this and this pen will keep the puppies and their dam confined until the pups are weaned. If we have two or more litters at the same time, we put a partition in the middle. Each of our litters has it's own heating pad. A heating pad is needed, even in the summertime, especially if you're running your air-conditioning (as newborn puppies need about 85 degrees temperature for approximately their first seven days). By using this method we have never lost a pup past three days of age.

We have used metal whelping pens for years and really like them, however when removing the metal rod to open the pen's front section, a tremendous screeching sound is produced when metal rubs on metal. This grating noise jars dogs, puppies and sleeping households. My husband replaced the metal rod with a wooden dowel rod with a similar 1/2-inch diameter. Now there is only quiet when the pen must be opened.

When I had to whelp my first large-breed litter, I discovered an excellent whelping box which was both practical and economical. I purchased a child's heavy plastic wading pool. Its plastic, curved sides discourages early climbing by the more energetic puppies and yet allows easy entry for cleaning and assisting in whelping (you know how bitches like to plant their rumps in the most inaccessible corner for that final push). The bottom is rippled for better footholds at the "milk wagon." These wading pools are tough, durable, sanitary and as an added benefit, may be used later as a summer play pool for older pups. They make great extra whelping boxes.

When my girl whelped her (and my) first litter of puppies, everything went off without a hitch. But a week later she came down with mastitis. I caught the problem quickly, but the discomfort it caused made her reluctant to stay in the puppies' box even when her absence was loudly bewailed. I work all day and couldn't always be there to make her responsible. In desperation, I placed a children's collapsible wading pool inside my exercise pen and covered the floor with an old blanket. Clothespins helped hold the collapsible sides against the pen walls. It worked beautifully. My girl could move around when she needed to and her hungry puppies were close to her when they wanted dinner. The only problem I encountered was locating a wading pool during January.

When whelping a litter, a great aid in helping to eliminate those knees from becoming creaky is to use a large airline shipping crate. I use a crate large enough to hold a German Shepherd when whelping my Sheltie puppies. I put the upper half of the crate so its open side is down on the floor and its lower half has its open side up (with the door facing towards the front). I sit on an ottoman in front of the crate while awaiting the next delivery. After all is done, one person lifts the top and another person removes the lower and it then becomes a puppy bed. After about one-and-a-half weeks a higher lip may be taped in place (to keep the puppies inside a little longer). I now have a bitch who dislikes anything tied or taped to her crate so I devised an A-frame of plywood which I may insert and remove with no alteration to the crate. Also, there isn't a problem of finding a place to store a large whelping box when using an airline crate (since you may add bedding and use the same crate for a sleeping adult dog). You may also nest several crates together when putting them back into storage. Then a crate is available for whelping as long as you have sterilized that crate before using it again. I bought one of these crates at the airport because it was damaged and I was able to purchase it at a discount.

When whelping litters, I use the smallest Doskocil crate, (#1911, as an incubator). My heating pad fits into it perfectly and with a towel to cover the crate and the pad on low heat, I place each puppy into the crate to keep him warm and out of the way when the bitch is whelping another puppy. For the first week or so (when the bitch gets her periodic breaks out of the whelping box) I turn the pad on and place the puppies inside until their mother is ready to get back into the box with her babies. These newborns stay warm and asleep which eliminates any worry of puppies becoming chilled while mother is out of the whelping box.

〰〰〰 ≫ ≪ 〰〰〰

Feeding

Containers—Food, Water, Etc.

A feeding pan is created by mixing the puppies' food in a glass pie plate which may then go into the microwave to be warmed. I place a 16-ounce glass soda bottle (filled with hot water) in the center. The bottle keeps the puppies feeding in a neat circle, not walking into the dish, and the hot water keeps the food warm until the last laggard has finished eating. In addition, the glass pie plate can go into the dishwasher easily.

A frisbee makes a fantastic dish for puppies just starting to eat.

A good idea for watering those dogs who like to take a swim in their regular-sized dog dishes is to use galvanized, rounded-edged metal three-gallon hog pans. These may be purchased at your local farm store.

Being busy and not having enough time to hold a dish for young puppies who are just starting to eat, I've found an alternative. Feed your puppies in an 8" cake pan which has been nestled into a large stainless steel 2-quart feeding dish. This will raise the meal up to their level. The pups don't seem to wade through their food quite as much.

For feeding litters of pups who are being weaned, try metal ice cube trays (without the dividers, of course). Split the pups into groups and give them each a tray. These do not tip and spill as easily as metal pie plates and pups can line up on the sides of them. They are easily cleaned and scalded with no breakage.

For the determined dog who delights in tipping over water buckets in outdoor runs, buy some double-sided snap bolts and clip one side to the pail handle and the other to the fencing. They are inexpensive and most hardware stores and animal supply houses carry them.

For those who have tennis players in the family, the plastic lids that come on the cans of tennis balls fit perfectly on the tops of dog food cans (and other human food cans). This comes in handy when you are using a special canned food, for whatever reason, when you normally use dry food.

If you're tired of having those aluminum clip-on water dishes knocked over by active puppies, find some smooth, round or oval palm-sized rocks and put them in the dishes before adding water. They clean easily in soapy water with a potato scrubbing brush and fit in the cutlery section of most dishwashers. The rocks I've been using weigh approximately 1/2 pound to 3/4 pound and are about 1" thick and 3" oval/round. You'll get used to the strange looks and remarks from visitors after awhile but it really does help.

I have found that hanging an animal-drinking bottle (the kind used for rabbits and other small animals) on the pen when puppies are just beginning to move around allows them to quickly learn to drink from the stainless steel tube. This helps keep the puppies more content when they're thirsty and also keeps them drier (since they can't spill pans of water).

I use a 12-ounce Cool Whip container for a food bowl whenever I need to warm dog food in the microwave. A Cool Whip bowl may be substituted for the 12-ounce stainless steel coop cup and it fits into its holder. The bowl is easily washed and ready to use again.

Many clip-on food/water dishes do not fit snugly on wire

crates and play pens. Decide where you want to put the dishes. In puppy pens, put the dishes toward the back to keep the little darlings' feet out of them as they stand and jump to greet you. With masking tape or adhesive tape, circle the wire a few times until the clips fit tightly. The tape is easily removed (especially masking tape), and the tape and dishes may then be raised as the puppies grow.

Need a puppy feeding pan? I mix their food in a glass pie plate which can go into the microwave to be slightly warmed. Then place a 16-ounce glass soda bottle (filled with hot water) in the center. The bottle keeps the puppies feeding in a neat circle and not walking into the dish. The hot water keeps the food warm until the last puppy has finished eating, plus the glass pie plate can go into the dishwasher easily.

Shower curtain rings are very handy to a dog owner. These shower curtain rings hold water buckets on the fences (we use the relatively light two-quart stainless steel type). Some are attached to the Space Blankets we use to cover the exercise pens at outdoor shows. They are light, easily opened, not prone to rust and are inexpensive.

Store large bags of pet food in clean plastic pails with lids. This keeps food fresh and makes it easy to dish out.

The dogs I show are crated for short periods of time during the day in my dog room. Unfortunately, there is no available running water in this room. Rather than run three or four times a day to fill their water bowls, I use a 5-quart thermos with a spigot. I fill the bowls from the thermos and save myself time and it also eliminates spilled water.

The heat-sealing gadgets (like Seal-A-Meal) are great for us doggy folks. They are perfect for cooking ahead and freezing home-cooked meals for the family to then simply plop into boiling water and "presto," Mommy is not missed quite so much while she is off to the shows.

The large 32-ounce plastic water bottles used in rabbit cages work great for medium-size dogs. Just hang them on the outside of your exercise pen or kennel run. I do not use them as a sole source of water for adults as I also provide a bucket. But for puppies and supplemental water for the adults they work great. *They are not to be used in sunshine.* Follow the directions on the bottle to prevent excessive dripping. They keep puppies from getting wet, from playing in their water buckets, along with having hair, dust and shavings not falling into the water. Puppies and adults both seem to catch on right away regarding how to use them, and they enjoy the noise the roller makes as they lick the bottle. To teach your dog how to drink from them, first make sure your dog is thirsty. Put your finger where the bottle is dripping very slightly. Your dog will lick your finger with water on it and then start licking the spout. A bit of peanut butter on the tip of the spout could be used for very slow learners. Puppies seem to catch on all by themselves about four weeks of age. I have tried Farnam, Lixit and Oasis brands and they all seem to work equally well. They are available in most pet shops. I use a large, #500 crate for whelping so I also fasten one of these water bottles to the outside of the crate door so the bitch has unlimited water always available to her.

The next time you have a litter ready for their first pan feeding try using a 12-section muffin or cupcake tin instead of your regular food dish. With a four- to six-puppy litter, you put the food in every other section, allowing an empty section in between for that unsteady puppy foot that invariably steps into the food for balance when first starting out at the dinner dish. I always have a separate bottle of warm goat's milk on hand to warm up the food as I train each pup to eat. Also, a slow starting pup may be encouraged to eat by holding him in your arms and raising the muffin tin up to his mouth. The puppy's chin can rest on the edge of the tin for balance until he gets the idea. This is an especially easy way to train the really young ones who you may have been hand raising or supplementing up to this point.

This is so simple that probably everyone else does it too and yet sometimes we overlook the simple things. When traveling to shows or wherever with my dogs, I pre-measure their individual meals into Ziploc sandwich bags. They are on a carefully calculated formula of dry food, K-Zyme including a biscuit. Pre-measuring ahead of time makes feeding time easy and stays consistent with feeding at home. Each dog's daily rations are then dropped into a large Ziploc with his name on his Ziploc bag. At meal time, the contents of one bag are simply dumped into each dog's bowl and mixed with the moist additives. There is no having to remember who gets what amount, and the dogs will attest to it being a faster process as they don't like to wait while I fumble for measuring cups and feeding charts.

This tip is for those who are always worried about their *dogs getting into the kitchen trash basket or garbage container and eating chicken bones or any type of dangerous bones.* We save spaghetti sauce jars (any type of jar will work) and put all bones inside those jars (with their lids securely closed). Then we throw away the jars. No need to be paranoid anymore about the dogs getting into any type of cooked bones.

To keep ants out of your pet dishes, place the food dish inside a pie pan of water.

To make doggy iced tea: take beef bouillon (cubes or granules) and place it in hot water, stirring until dissolved. Use five to ten times more water than you would use if making bouillon broth for yourself. Pour the broth into ice cube trays or other small plastic containers and freeze. Pop out when needed.

To prevent your dog from scooting his food or water dish across the floor, glue a rubber ring to the bottom of the bowl.

To provide water for bitches and/or puppies while in a crate, kennel or in a exercise pen, we use large rabbit bottles. Just hook the bottle to the outside with the spout pointing into the enclosed area.

To save multiple trips into a dog run, I hang a two-quart stainless steel bucket on a light chain to hold the water bucket. By doing this, I just need to go up to the fence, raise the pail, rinse and fill it up with clean water and then lower it back into its original position. I keep the chain's length just long enough to let the pail rest on the ground. It then cannot be tipped over. I have another pail set up in the same manner which I fill with dry kibble when my dogs are on a self-feeding plan.

To stop annoying bowl pushing on slippery floors, I spray Firm Grip on the bottom of the bowl (before putting any food or water into that bowl). It prevents food or water bowls from getting pushed and then spilled.

Try using rabbit water bottles for your dogs instead of bowls. Even five-week-old puppies quickly learn to drink from the bottles. These bottles hang on the side of the pen and water is dispensed by the puppy licking the spout located on the bottom. The water stays fresh and sanitary which is always a problem with puppies. No more wet pens from water being dumped over (thus eliminating crusted feet and bleeding pads). No puppies right now? Don't pack that bottle away. Take it with you to the shows. No more accidental spills just as you have gotten everybody groomed and they are calling your first class. Rabbit bottles may be purchased at any feed store. Oasis also makes a one-quart "pet bottle" which is great for large breeds. Since it is glass, dogs cannot puncture it.

Warning—don't store dog food in plastic "garbage" bags because the plastic will give off toxic fumes (which may then be absorbed by the food). Plastic "food storage" bags are all right to use for storage of dog food as are metal cans, paper bags and plastic containers.

We buy Pet Tabs in the 500 container. This large plastic container, when empty, is perfect to contain dry dog food during travel. They hold about eight cups of food. We keep about eight of them stocked and labeled all the time and when we pack for a show, we just grab a couple of regular dog chows, one puppy chow, etc. They fit easily in all sorts of vehicles no matter how little space you have.

When feeding puppies being weaned, I use a six-muffin tin. Then I know how much each pup is eating and which ones I need to watch as some puppies eat much faster than others. It also cuts down on those messy paws.

When I start to feed young puppies for the first few times, I use paper plates. Instead of having to clean out the dish after they get finished walking through it, etc., I just pick the paper plate up and throw it away. Seeing that paper plates have no sides, it doesn't discourage the little ones from reaching in and trying some food.

When I start to wean my puppies, I add a "liver cube" to one meal a day. To make these, I put equal amounts of raw beef liver and water in the blender and liquefy it. I pour it into ice cube trays and freeze. Then I pop them out and store in a plastic bag. This adds terrific additional nutrition, plus taste, and my pups are always fat with big healthy coats.

When starting young pups on their first solid meals, try holding the dish up to their faces rather than pushing their heads down into the dish.

When weaning puppies, I have found that banana split dishes are the perfect feeding dish. The dishes are long and puppies can line up on either side. They are very inexpensive and some ice cream parlors will even give them to you.

You can get excellent water buckets for your kennel runs from restaurants, pizza parlors, etc. These establishments receive large, white plastic buckets filled with mayonnaise, salad dressing, sauces, etc., which are usually thrown away. The buckets hold about eight gallons of water, clean well and are far less expensive than galvanized or rubber horse buckets. They also have seal-tight plastic lids which make good containers when traveling with dry dog food.

Your pet's dish will stay put while he is eating if placed on a rubber mat or a rubber ring (such as those rings used when canning).

Daily Feeding

A cheap substitute for hamburger meat for your dogs is beef kidneys. They are equally high in protein, about one-third the price, and the dogs just love them. Boil them, cut into small pieces and then pour both broth and meat over your dogs' kibble. Watch their food disappear.

Don't let uneaten moist dog food stand in your dog's bowl longer than 5 to 20 minutes. *This is due to the fact that bacteria may develop quickly in food that is allowed to stand unrefriger-*

ated.

Instead of feeding your dog canned commercial dog food, (which is approximately 70 percent water), try inexpensive meats such as chicken livers and gizzards, beef liver and cow's heart. Since dogs are carnivores, mixing these different tidbits (already cooked, of course) into their kibble is very satisfying and healthy for your dog.

The easiest way to chop up liver is to freeze it, let it thaw just enough to cut. Then cut it up using a serrated knife.

Tired of lugging big 50-pound sacks of dog food from car to house or garage every time you stock up? Next time bring out your dog show crate dolly. You may load four to six 50-pound bags on it and roll them anywhere you wish without any stress or strain.

To supplement my dry kibble, I have found most of the supermarkets in the area were selling chicken necks and backs inexpensively. When I find them, I stock up and freeze. To use, I cook them in my pressure cooker for one hour at 15 pounds of pressure. This will cook bones and all into a thick chicken broth. Allow three to four ounces per dog (before cooking) and add broth to the kibble. I have no problem eaters or stool problems and their coats are looking great.

Dangerous Foods For Dogs
(See "WARNINGS"—"Foods Dangerous To Dogs")

Healthy "People-Food" For Dogs

Chicken is a favorite of dogs, but they will enjoy nearly any type of meat.

Dogs are omnivores, yet dogs often enjoy being given vegetables. These vegetables might include broccoli, asparagus, spinach and green beans. If your doggy eats grass, he might also eat parsley and that parsley will freshen his breath.

Don't toss out the giblets when you roast your turkey since tongue, heart, liver and gizzards are loaded with vitamins and minerals which help support your dog's organs.

Feeding firm beef can scrub your dog's teeth since much chewing is required.

Holistic veterinarians state that raw beets provide a powerful punch for cleansing the liver. Dogs may enjoy receiving small amounts of cooked beets as a treat.

Turkey contains tryptophan so feeding your dogs turkey would help with their sleeping and would calm down an overly-anxious or excited dog.

"In Whelp" Bitches

Do you find in your large litters that you have one weak puppy or that your older bitch's puppies have one weaker one even though it is a smaller litter? We have found that by feeding an additive to all our pregnant bitches from the time they are bred until whelping, we have never lost a small one nor have we had to help a pup. The product is called Stress and is an excellent product. It is made by the makers of Vetzyme products.

Like to give your pregnant bitches raw liver but hate the mess and waste? Partially freeze it, then use a sharp knife to cut it into 1/2-inch strips. Refreeze it. When you need a little, take out a strip, cut it while frozen into tiny pieces and add to regular food with a little water. It will defrost immediately and you have no waste, no odor and it's very economical. «»Editor's note: based on nutritional biochemistry, use calves' livers because these livers are basically clean livers whereas, livers from older animals are filled with impurities.«»

One of my brood bitches stopped eating completely three to four days prior to whelping. Because she has reasonably large litters (five to seven pups), I was concerned about her having enough energy to whelp. To provide enough calories and yet not to overburden her digestive tract, I gave her Nutrivit during the period of non-eating and also between puppies while she was whelping. Nutrivit is a paste available in tube form from your vet and is designed for convalescing dogs to stimulate appetite. I've be pleased with the results.

Raspberry leaf tea is a good aid for a bitch due to whelp. Read the ingredients and make sure the tea only contains pure, dried herbs. Tear open a tea bag and sprinkle on the dog food. Measuring the amount isn't really necessary because being a little bit off with herbs won't harm your dog. When using raspberry leaf, start giving it when you're sure your bitch is "in whelp." I give herbs to all my dogs, pups and adults, and I am happy with the results.

We feed Shaklee's Vitamin B-Complex to our show dogs. We find that some of our bitches become edgy when they are "in-season" and being shown at the same time. Vitamin B-Complex is a natural relaxant. From what we understand, you can't overdose your dog as the unneeded excess is passed through the urine. We begin giving these vitamins two days before the show (once the night before and once more in the morning of the show). We feed 3 to 5 tablets (250 mg.) each time (depending on the individual dog).

When new puppies are "on their way," I make sure that I have purchased fresh goat's milk and freeze it in ice-cube trays. I then store those frozen cubes in a Ziploc bag and place the bag in the freezer. If a puppy needs a boost, I can take out one cube of goat's milk and mix it with equal parts of Pedialyte. It seems to work great. If there are leftover cubes, I mix them in with the puppy food during their weaning time.

Newborns

A few drops of room temperature liver blood when puppies are first whelped gives puppies an extra shot of energy for a good start.

A new device (designed by a veterinarian to save lives of baby pigs) may help save puppies, too. Called a Pig Resuscitator, this device pumps air into the lungs of non-breathing newborns. If the animal is not breathing, first clean out his mouth and then tilt his head back in order to open his air passage. Slip the mask over his nose. Then compress the bellows to force air into his lungs. Next, pull off the mask (to allow fresh air to enter). Repeat until the animal breathes on his own. It's available from Joseph Magrath, D.V.M., Box 148, McCook, NE 69001.

A product called Probiocin (live culture Lactobacillus) is excellent for enteritis in newborns and to fight E. Coli. Definitely use this if any antibiotic is given. Also, give it to the bitch. «»Editor's note: based upon reading and research in nutritional biochemistry, Natren Acidophilus and Life Start are excellent (1/2 teaspoon of each in 1 ounce of lukewarm water for adults and especially for the new mother).«»

As the best substitute for bitch's milk, I use the following recipe: 1/2 cup of water, 1/2 cup of Carnation Evaporated Milk (canned), 2 teaspoons white Karo syrup and 1 raw egg yolk. Mix well. It is quite simple to make, and I have gotten better results with this than from powdered or prepared varieties. «»Editor's note: based on reading and research in nutritional biochemistry if

the puppy is orphaned before nursing is completed, bifido bacteria or bifidobacteria (1/8 teaspoon into warm formula) should be supplemented. Based upon further reading and research, goat's milk works well and is less upsetting to a puppy.«»

A tube of Nutri-Cal is a necessary item in my dog supplies. A tiny bit in the mouth of a weak newborn puppy is usually all that is needed to strengthen him. Since dogs love the taste, it is also a handy tool in teaching puppies to bait. Nutri-Cal may be purchased through veterinarians and many supply catalogs.

Do you find in your large litters that you have one weak puppy or that your older bitch's puppies have one weaker one even though it is a smaller litter? We have found that by feeding an additive to all our pregnant bitches from the time they are bred until whelping, we have never lost a small one nor have we had to help a pup. The product is called Stress and is an excellent product. It is made by the makers of Vetzyme products.

Esbilac cocktail may be made by mixing (in a blender): 3 Dixie paper cupfuls (kitchen size) Esbilac to 1 paper cupful of water. Add 1 tablespoon honey, 1 tablespoon lactobacillus acidophilus and 1 tablespoon Pepto-Bismol. Not only does this recipe produce better puppy stools, but it seems to stick to their ribs better as well.

Extra tiny newborn puppies dehydrate very easily especially when subjected to the artificial heat sources (which are sometimes vital to keep them from becoming too chilled and subsequently dying). I have found that keeping a very close watch on them for the first several days is vital and checking several times daily for any signs of dehydration (like pinching up the skin on the back). *If a pup's skin stays up at all, dehydration is beginning.* I keep a bottle of Ringers Solution (purchased from my vet) at home at all times. At the very first sign of dehydration, I give subcutaneous (under the skin) injections of the Ringers using an allergy syringe and needle. You may purchase allergy syringes at many pharmacies (without a prescription), or you can simply get a prescription from your vet or physician. Remove the Ringers from the bottle with one of your regular-size needles, then replace the regular-size needle with the very fine allergy needle (which will be used for the actual injection). I also heat the solution in the syringe by holding it under hot water for a bit or putting it in the microwave oven for a split-second *(without the needle). Test the heat on the inside of your wrist as you would a baby's bottle.* Body-temperature Ringers eliminates the shock to the body that cold solution would cause and it saves puppies.

For weak puppies, we have found that Diamino 4x Vitamins may bring around a weak puppy in 24 hours. We usually use the vitamins for about a week and assist the puppy when he's nursing. These vitamins are available from veterinarians.

From working in a hospital with premature infants, I have learned when tube-feeding to always let the fluid drain into the stomach by gravity flow *(not by force of the plunger). That way, when the flow stops, you'll know that the puppy's tummy is full and you'll prevent the risk of overflow and aspiration.*

Here's a liver-water recipe for fading puppies. Put a large piece (or pieces) of calves' liver in a little bit of water and boil slowly (about five minutes) until the blood comes out. Let it cool, and then drain and save the liquid. Put four drops into an eyedropper and give to a weak puppy. At first, you give four drops to the puppy every two hours for 12 hours, and then every four hours. You may do this for however long you need to until you feel that the puppy is thriving. «»Editor's note: based on nutritional biochemistry, use calves' livers because these livers are basically clean livers whereas, livers from older animals are filled with impurities.«»

I needed to tube-feed my last litter. My bitch had produced a huge litter of ten puppies and she and I were both exhausted. In my befuddled state, I wasn't sure that I would reset the alarm correctly. How could I get up in time for the next feeding? While sleepily waiting for the milk to become warm, I drank a large glass of water and drinking that water turned out to be the solution to my problem. Later, I urgently woke up without an alarm in time for the next feeding. Because bladder capacity varies, you may need to try drinking between one-half to two glasses of water. Then time your awakening before you have a tube-feeding problem. For me, drinking a glass of water was a simple solution to my dilemma of waking every few hours without an alarm.

Like to give a new mother or your pregnant bitch raw liver but hate the mess and waste? Partially freeze it, then use a sharp knife to cut it into 1/2-inch strips. Refreeze it. When you need a little, take out a strip, cut it while frozen into tiny pieces and add to regular food with a little water. It will defrost immediately and you have no waste, no odor and it's very economical. «»Editor's note: based on nutritional biochemistry, use calves' livers because these livers are basically clean livers whereas, livers from older animals are filled with impurities.«»

One helpful hint I might pass on is an "Orphan Puppy Formula." Here's the recipe: 1 can Carnation milk, 2 cans warm water, 2 tablespoons table cream, 2 tablespoons honey, 2 egg yolks, 1 envelope unflavored gelatin and 1 dropperful Vetamino 4x. I heat up small portions in the microwave at medium power for 35 seconds. It seems to be well tolerated and weight gain is noticed quickly when fed through preemie nipples. «»Editor's note: based on reading and research in nutritional biochemistry if the puppy is orphaned before nursing is completed, bifido bacteria or bifidobacteria (1/8 teaspoon into warm formula) should be supplemented. Based upon further reading and research, goat's milk works well and is less upsetting to a puppy.«»

Pedialyte is an oral electrolyte solution (which you may keep on hand) for both newborns and for older dogs. Give a weak newborn puppy a dropperful every hour. Pedialyte is found in the canned milk section of the baby department. It comes in several strengths so *check with you vet for the best strength to use for your pup or older dog.*

The fastest and safest way to warm a puppy (if he is small, weak or cold) is to carry that pup in the front of your blouse or shirt (making very sure that he can't slip out while your carrying him). I had to prove it to myself with two small premature puppies weighing only 3 1/2 ounces. They wouldn't nurse so I carried them around all afternoon in the front of my blouse and, presto ,they are now three weeks old, fine and healthy. «»Editor's note: based upon reading and research, handling puppies in this manner will also help their temperaments when it comes to bonding with humans and wanting to be cuddled.«»

This recipe came from a nurse who works in a hospital. It is useful for weak puppies or finicky eaters: 1 can Carnation, 8 ounces water, 8 ounces plain yogurt, 3 or 4 egg yolks and 3 tablespoons of Karo syrup.

We had a puppy who I had to supplement feed. Although he seemed strong enough, he did not want to even try nursing from his dam again. By putting some honey on a nipple which another puppy had already started, the weaker puppy was able to latch right on and begin nursing.

New Mothers

During whelping when my bitch goes into a rest period, I wait no longer than one hour. Then I fill a dish with ice cold milk and torn-up white bread. Then I offer this to the bitch. More often than not, she will drink the cold milk which seems to prompt labor once again. Those bitches who don't eat the bread will usually go back and gobble that up, too (once they have finished whelping). I have used this method from my first litter and ever since that litter. Several other breeders (who have called me desperately in the middle of the night) tried my somewhat old-fashioned method have told me that this method worked for them. The vet, of course, is the last resort if labor does not start up shortly.

Have you ever had a bitch who, for any reason, has been unable to nurse her babies? Unfortunately some of us have. We have a solution for allowing the mother to clean up her babies without allowing the babies to nurse. We put a baby's sleeper (30-pound size) on the dam. When its been altered, place the bitch's front legs through the sleeves, snap the snaps down her back, cut the feet out. You'll need to put a hem with an elastic piece inside each leg, and then sew or move the snaps in the crotch area so that the pups cannot sneak inside. The sleepers are cotton and, therefore, are cool. The mother cleans the puppies and you feed them. This way is much easier for both of you.

Here's a super stew recipe for whelping bitches: combine one pound stew beef, one large beef kidney and one pound of calves' liver. Simmer along with two sliced onions and two or three carrots. Flavor with 1/3 package dried onion soup. This will take about three hours of cooking time. Feed this to bitches for three to four days after they have whelped. It seems to help clean them out and bring in your bitch's milk. Feed it several times a day and begin to add kibble by the morning of the third day.

If a bitch goes for more than an hour between whelping puppies (but isn't in trouble otherwise), I always give her ice-cold milk (some like it with torn-up bread mixed with the milk). She gobbles it up and labor usually starts again very shortly after drinking the milk.

If you have a first-time mama who is less than enthusiastic with diaper duty, try spreading a little peanut butter on the new puppies' tummies and bottoms. Mom should get the idea in one or two applications of the peanut butter.

If your bitch has just had a litter and does not have enough milk for the new arrivals, give her a few swallows of beer. This will bring on milk in abundant quantities. This small amount of alcohol will not affect her puppies.

Like to give the new mother or your pregnant bitch raw liver but hate the mess and waste? Partially freeze it, then use a sharp knife to cut it into 1/2-inch strips. Refreeze it. When you need a little, take out a strip, cut it while frozen into tiny pieces and add to regular food with a little water. It will defrost immediately and you have no waste, no odor and it's very economical. «»Editor's note: based on nutritional biochemistry, use calves' livers because these livers are basically clean livers whereas, livers from older animals are filled with impurities.«»

To get a C-sectioned bitch to accept her pups, use your fingers and gather the discharge from her vulva and smear it on her pups. One sniff will tell mom that these puppies are hers.

When a brand-new mother lets me know that she doesn't want to eat, I mix one tablespoon of canned cat food well into her food. Few dams will refuse that fishy treat and I figure it's got to be full of extra goodies.

Puppies

All of us at times wake up to screaming six-week-old pups who want their food right now. With my last litter I found a secret on how to soften puppy food in seconds instead of soaking it for 15 minutes. Just pop it in the microwave oven for 45 seconds, soaking it in water. It cools rapidly and shuts up those screaming pups.

A tube of Nutri-Cal is a necessary item in my dog supplies. A tiny bit in the mouth of a weak newborn puppy is usually all that is needed to strengthen him. Since dogs love the taste, it is also a handy tool in teaching puppies to bait. Nutri-Cal may be purchased through veterinarians and many supply catalogs.

Banana Flakes (Karena brand) are excellent for diarrhea and are easy to digest when a puppy or a baby is not eating well. «»Editor's note: based upon reading and research in nutritional biochemistry, Natren Acidophilus and Life Start are excellent (1/2 teaspoon of each in 1 ounce of lukewarm water for adults and especially for the new mother).«»

Esbilac formula or recipe: in a blender mix 3 Dixie paper cupfuls (kitchen size) Esbilac to 1 paper cupful of water. Add 1 tablespoon honey, 1 tablespoon lactobacillus acidophilus and 1 tablespoon Pepto-Bismol. Not only does this recipe produce better puppy stools but it seems to stick to their ribs better as well.

For weak puppies, we have found that Diamino 4x Vitamins may bring around a weak puppy in 24 hours. We usually use the vitamins for about a week and assist the puppy when he's nursing. These vitamins are available from veterinarians.

For your older puppy "problem" eaters, try a name-brand soup. Cream of Chicken is one of our favorites. It may be diluted with water and mixed in with your regular dry dog food. One can adds flavor to many feedings, and what is not used may be stored in the refrigerator without spoiling for several days.

Here's a liver-water recipe for fading puppies. Put a large piece (or pieces) of calves' liver in a little bit of water and boil slowly (about five minutes) until the blood comes out. Let it cool, and then drain and save the liquid. Put four drops into an eyedropper and give to a weak puppy. At first, you give four drops to the puppy every two hours for 12 hours, and then every four hours. You may do this for however long you need to until you feel that the puppy is thriving. «»Editor's note: based on nutritional biochemistry, use calves' livers because these livers are basically clean livers whereas, livers from older animals are filled with impurities.«»

If you have a puppy who is a finicky eater and you cannot afford to feed him the high-priced canned dog food, try making gravy for his dry food. Blend a can of the "yummy" dog food with water (you may also add cottage cheese, cooked egg, liver, etc.). Pour this over his dry food. It goes a lot farther and your dogs will love it.

I have developed a schedule for weaning my litters to solid food in a gradual, smooth way. At three weeks of age, I introduce them to Esbilac in a pan (once a day). They learn very quickly and all pups will be eating within two days. At this time, I add High Protein Baby Cereal to the Esbilac and increase their feedings to two times a day. At four weeks of age, I like to add a half of a jar of baby food meat to the High Protein Baby Cereal and the Esbilac (well mixed). The puppies devour this mixture with relish. Since baby food meat comes in several flavors, you may vary them. By

four-and-a-half weeks of age, I decrease the cereal and the meat and add chopped-up Puppy Chow to the mixture. I also increase their feedings to three times a day. I let the mother decide when she wants to wean them and the pups adjust with very little trauma because they were already eating so well.

I have found that giving my dogs ice cubes (from the time they are young) is something my dogs seem to relish since they act as though the ice cubes are pieces of steak. A big plus is that these ice cubes come in handy when any dog is going through a period of dehydration (vomiting, diarrhea, etc.) because he will still chomp down the ice cubes. In this situation, we freeze Pedialyte to help stabilize the dog's system. The only down side is that you have a lot of company when you open the freezer.

Instead of paying twice the price for puppy meal, put your food blender to some excellent use. Make puppy meal by putting dry dog food in the blender and turning it on. By doing this and as long as you have dog food around, you may always make your own puppy meal.

I start teaching my puppies "to come" at three weeks of age. The day I start feeding them, I push their noses down to the food and make what is best described as "repeated kissing" sounds. I do this every time they are fed. People are always amazed that my six-week-old pups obediently run to me when I call them. Once this is learned, they never forget it.

My puppies are self-fed and I found that the adults were getting too "porky" with their constant access to the puppies' food. I solved this problem without having to separate them. I made a creep-feeder (a pen so constructed as to exclude larger animals while permitting young animals to enter and obtain feed) out of a Kennel Aire crate. I used a rubber bungee strap or a piece of heavy wire to tie the crate door open and block off most of the crate entrance with an extra door that I had from a plastic crate. This was fastened, too, with rubber straps. The entrance is vertical and just wide enough for the pups to enter and "pig out" on the bowl of food placed inside to the back of the crate. (You could use this same procedure with an exercise pen with a door.) The adults can't fit through the entrance and have to wait until feeding time for their measured portions.

Now that enteritis in puppies is less of a problem, I have not had to worry as much about dehydration due to diarrhea, however I've learned some tricks and I will share one with you. If the pup is not having problems with vomiting (or, it has been controlled) and it is too early to feed the pup solid food, I use Pedialyte (by Ross Labs), either with a feeding tube or in their water bowls. It may be purchased in any pharmacy over-the-counter. Normally, it is used for fluid and electrolyte replacement in young children with severe diarrhea, but it also works very well for young puppies (especially those who are still too sick to get up and drink but to whom you don't want to give the fluids intravenously or subcutaneously).

Spray a cookie sheet with Pam to cook golf ball-sized hamburger meatballs. When cool, place the cookie sheet and meatballs in the freezer. When they're frozen, remove the balls and store in a Ziploc bag in the freezer for those special hot-weather treats. They are extra special for teething puppies. You may also microwave the balls for a few seconds and hide pills in them when medication is necessary.

This recipe came from a nurse who works in a hospital. It is useful for weak puppies or finicky eaters: 1 can Carnation, 8 ounces water, 8 ounces plain yogurt, 3 or 4 egg yolks and 3 tablespoons of Karo syrup.

When feeding puppies being weaned, I use a six-muffin tin. Then I know how much each pup is eating and which ones I have to watch as some puppies eat much faster than others. It also cuts down on messy paws.

When I start to feed young puppies for the first few times, I use paper plates. Instead of having to clean out the dish after they get finished walking through it, etc., I just pick up the paper plate and throw it away. Seeing that paper plates have no sides, it doesn't discourage the little ones from reaching in and trying some food.

When weaning my puppies, I put about a cup of dry dog food in my blender and grate it. This makes a fine, dry (inexpensive) meal that I offer free choice starting at about three weeks of age. My puppies are never screaming and wean easily.

When weaning puppies, I have found that banana split dishes are the perfect feeding dish. The dishes are long and puppies may line up on either side. They are very inexpensive and some ice cream parlors will even give them to you.

When we start weaning puppies, we feed each puppy separately and this continues until they leave for their new homes. This way we may keep track of the amount of food consumed by each pup, and it makes it easier for the puppies when they leave since they do not need the rest of the litter to be with them during feeding time.

When starting young pups on their first meals, try holding the dish up to their face rather than pushing their heads down into the dish.

Show Bait

Always rushed to find time to cook bait before a show? I now keep a Ziploc sandwich bag in my freezer compartment tossing in that one leftover chicken breast, the remaining slice of meat loaf, whatever. I am no longer tempted to eat those unneeded calories when I think of the time saved and when I remember how much better those leftovers will look on the dogs rather than on me or in the garbage. The morning of the show, I simply remove the frozen bag and let it defrost en route.

Before cooking my liver (as show bait), I sprinkle a little garlic powder on the liver. My dogs love this.

Boiling liver for shows is a messy job, but you will have a lot less scum in the pot it you rinse the liver thoroughly before boiling.

Boiling liver? I microwave it and have one tenth of the odor. To microwave, I chop it into bite-size chunks, place it in a baking dish, then cover and microwave it.

Boil your show bait (liver) with a dash of vinegar in the water and watch your dog take your hand off in the ring trying to get at it.

Here are two easy ways to cook liver and a suggestion for getting bait to the ringside fresh, easy to handle and without stained, smelly pockets. First, here are two easy ways to cook liver: 1) put it in a microwave bowl or pan and "nuke" it until it's thoroughly cooked, or 2) bake it on a cookie sheet or roasting pan, covered with aluminum foil, while roasting chicken or something similar on another oven shelf (I wouldn't recommend doing this while cooking cake because the cake could come out with a liver smell). It saves time and money on gas or electric bills.

Here is a recipe for liver treats: 1 pound of liver, 4 raw whole eggs, 1 tablespoon of garlic, 1 cup of self-rising flour, 1 cup of cornmeal, 1/2 teaspoon of salt and 1/2 teaspoon of pepper. Blend the raw liver in a blender until it is totally blended, add the eggs and blend well. Mix all dry ingredients in a large bowl, add the blended liver and eggs and mix well. Spread in a microwave pie dish and microwave for 2 1/2 minutes on high. Cut into small squares, put into Ziploc bags and freeze until needed. «»Editor's note: based on nutritional biochemistry, a diet which contains an excess of raw egg whites quickly and almost invariably leads to a biotin deficiency. In raw eggs, biotin is typically bound to a sugar-protein molecule (the glycoprotein called avidin) and cannot be absorbed into the body unless the egg is cooked, allowing the biotin to separate from the avidin protein.«»

If you have trouble getting your dog to bait using the normal goodies, try deer liver. The wild flavor or scent usually gets an immediate reaction.

If you're tired of making smelly, messy liver (as bait for a dog show), try Bonkers Cat Treats. They are bit-sized chunks that come in liver or chicken flavors. They won't crumble like Redi Liver (or Redi Pro Treats—100% Freeze Dried Liver For Dogs) and they don't require refrigeration like liver does. They are packaged in a 4-ounce reclosable box (like a little milk carton) and are available at most grocery stores. Dogs love them.

If you sprinkle your liver heavily with both salt and garlic salt, it will keep better for your dogs.

Tired of cooking liver? I've found something my dogs like even better. It's a cat treat called Pounce (by Puss N Boots). A 3-ounce can has lots of bite-size pieces. It comes in liver, chicken and kidney flavors. Even finicky eaters will go crazy over it's taste and most of our kennel club members use it now. Try it and you may never want to cook liver again.

To prepare liver for the show, I cut it into quarter-size pieces once it has been thoroughly cooked and cooled. Then I take one or two small handfuls and place them into a Baggie. After filling each Baggie, I get out all the air before sealing it tightly and then I pop each Baggie into the freezer. Basically I've made my own freeze-dried liver but when thawed, it is soft and very tasty (to my dogs, that is, along with being very convenient to reach. Whenever I go to a one-day show or match show, I pop one or two Baggies into my show bag and they thaw out on the way to the show. In winter (or, if I'm in a hurry), they thaw out on my dashboard with the defrost going. For longer weekends, the Baggies may be kept frozen and cold in a thermal bag or thermos and taken out each day as needed. Having the bait in Baggies is also very neat as all you'll need to do is to remove the twist-ties (or unzip the Ziploc) and pop the whole bag into your pocket. They are the perfect size (because you control the size of each bag) and the Baggie protects your pocket to keep it from getting stained and smelly.

To preserve liver for use on long circuits or for around-the-house training, pack it in rock salt. It will keep for weeks. The dogs seem to really like it. For storage, try a Tupperware container or an empty coffee or shortening can with a plastic lid.

When that (ugh!) smell of boiling liver invades your house, try sprinkling a little cinnamon right out of its container directly onto the electric burner. It burns up almost immediately and leaves a wonderful smell that seems to displace the liver smell. If you have a gas stove, you may put about a teaspoon of cinnamon and a few cloves into a pot of water and boil it for a few minutes after you finish cooking and cooling the liver.

Supplements

After adding a new supplement, not one of my dogs would touch their food. Out of desperation I reached into the refrigerator and grabbed the cheese for my spaghetti and sprinkled it over the food. Even my most finicky eater wolfed his food down.

A little grated (not shredded) carrot in your dog's daily diet is said to help prevent roundworm infestation.

An easy way to keep from forgetting to give medications is to keep each medication in a little crate watering cup. I use the cups designed for birds (plastic with wire holders) as the wires may be bent to accommodate any crate or pen. Attach the cup to the outside of the crate or pen. This way the pills are always handy and you can't forget them since they're right under your nose. Naturally, this is for indoor use only. It's perfect for visiting bitches' heartworm medication, vitamins, etc., and for keeping vitamins handy in the maternity ward.

A product called Probiocin (live culture Lactobacillus) is excellent for enteritis in newborns and to fight E. Coli. Definitely use this if any antibiotic is given. Also, give it to the litter's dam. «»Editor's note: based upon reading and research in nutritional biochemistry, Natren Acidophilus and Life Start are excellent (1/2 teaspoon of each in 1 ounce of lukewarm water for adults and especially for the new mother).«»

Banana Flakes (Karena brand) are excellent for diarrhea and are easy to digest if a puppy or a baby is not eating well.

Do you have the problem with light rims around your dog's eyes? We put powdered Vitamin C in our dog's dinner (approximately 1000 mg.+ each day for a medium-sized dog) and the rims return to their natural dark color.

Dried blueberries firm up loose stools and diarrhea and are mild enough to feed even to young puppies. Our dogs eat them happily. They are available in the dried fruit section of natural food stores or in supermarkets.

Eggs are an excellent source of protein and calcium. When cracking eggs (for dogs or yourself) save the eggshells and grind them up using your food processor or by using a rolling pin, and then add them to your dogs' food. You'll find that the dogs like them, and they are a good and cheap source of calcium (especially for pregnant and lactating bitches). «»Editor's note: based on reading and research in nutritional biochemistry, eggshells may be placed in a small amount of vinegar. The shells will dissolve completely, thus avoiding the possible complications associated with ingesting the sharp-edged eggshell fragments, although dogs consuming vinegar wasn't discussed.«».

Every summer my dog would chew holes in his coat. It would sometimes happen at the back of his tail (his anal glands were removed when he was very young so that wasn't the problem) and some places along his legs, etc. Our vet called it a seasonal skin allergy possibly due to fleas and/or grass allergies. The vet prescribed some flea medications which helped. Benadryl cream on the chewed places also helped. The yard was treated to kill fleas. But my dog still sometimes chewed. Then at a show, my mother talked to someone who recommended flax seed oil (100 mg. capsules are available at health food stores). At first, one per day was given and that helped. He stopped chewing his coat. Eventually, the one per day regimen proved an overdose. Now, we just give him one every other day. So far, he has quit chewing.

For diarrhea, feed canned pumpkin (not pumpkin pie mix).

For weak puppies, we have found that Diamino 4x Vitamins may bring around a weak puppy in 24 hours. We usually use the vitamins for about a week and assist the puppy when he's nursing. These vitamins are available from veterinarians.

If your dog is overactive and will not calm down, try mixing thyme in with his food. Thyme may also improve his coat and help slow down any hair loss (by improving superficial blood vessels of the skin-feeding hair root).

If your dog's coat is looking dull and dry after a hot summer or any other time, I put 1 tablespoon of Brewer's Yeast and 1 tablespoon of vinegar (cider) in his food daily. It puts a nice healthy shine into the coat and gives his coat a better texture.

I have found a product call Super-14 (made by Farnum products) has really helped to put coat on my dog. It is a coat supplement designed mainly for horses and which also works for dogs.

I have found that giving my dogs ice cubes (from the time they are young) is something my dogs seem to relish since they act as though the ice cubes are pieces of steak. A big plus is that these ice cubes come in handy when any dog is going through a period of dehydration (vomiting, diarrhea, etc.) because he will still chomp down the ice cubes. In this situation, we freeze Pedialyte to help stabilize the dog's system. The only down side is that you have a lot of company when you open the freezer.

I think I've found a solution for that awful habit of stool eating. One tablespoon of crushed pineapple or pureed pumpkin given daily has stopped my medium-sized dog from eating stool.

Peanut Butter is a universal food many a child would gladly live on, and it's not a bad choice considering it's high protein and energy content. Now, peanut butter has also entered the world of veterinary medicine as an effective method of getting nutrients into a debilitated or anorexic dog or cat. Just smear peanut butter on your animal's nose and paws. Your dog or cat will automatically swallow this sticky food as it goes about getting the mess cleaned up. The high fat content of peanut butter (about 50 percent) will also encourage your pet to eat.

Put freeze-dried liver (available at pet-supply sources) into the blender and use this powder as a flavor-enhancer in food for your picky eaters, or try sprinkling Parmesan cheese into your dog's food.

Spray a cookie sheet with Pam to cook golf ball-sized hamburger meatballs. When cool, place the cookie sheet and meatballs in the freezer. When they're frozen, remove the balls and store in a Ziploc bag in the freezer for those special hot-weather treats. They are extra special for teething puppies. You may also microwave the balls for a few seconds and hide pills in them when medication is necessary.

The easiest way to administer a vitamin tablet (when it is in human form) is to crush it with a pill pulverizer which is available at drug stores.

To make dog iced tea: take beef bouillon (cubes or granules) and place them in hot water, stirring until dissolved. Use five to ten times more water than you would use if making bouillon broth for yourself. Pour the broth into ice cube trays or other small plastic containers and freeze. Pop out when needed and give to your dog.

To put a stop to that canine "poop-scooper" in the back yard, try sprinkling Accent on his food. This seems to discourage him from eating any of his stools.

Want natural vitamins that usually cost less? Try including herbs in your dog's food. You may grow your own herbs or purchase them from your supermarket. Look in the herb tea section. Read the ingredients and make sure the tea only contains pure, dried herbs. Different herbs contain different vitamins so your best buy is a mixture of herbs. Raspberry leaf tea is a good aid for the bitch due to whelp. To administer, I just tear open a tea bag and sprinkle an estimated amount on your dog's food. Measuring the amount isn't really necessary because being a little bit off with herbs won't hurt your dog. When using raspberry leaf, start administering it when you're sure the bitch is "in whelp." I give herbs to all my dogs, pups and adults and I am happy with the results.

We feed Shaklee's Vitamin B-Complex to our show dogs. We find that some of our bitches become edgy when they are "in-season" and being shown at the same time. Vitamin B-Complex is a natural relaxant. From what we understand, you can't overdose your dog as the unneeded excess is passed through the urine. We begin giving these vitamins two days before the show (once the night before and once more in the morning of the show). We feed 3 to 5 tablets (250 mg.) each time (depending on the individual dog).

When I start to wean my puppies, I add a "liver cube" to one meal a day. To make these, I put equal amounts of raw beef liver and water in the blender and liquefy it. I pour it into ice cube trays and freeze. Then I pop them out and store in a plastic bag. This adds terrific additional nutrition, plus taste, and my pups are always fat with big healthy coats.

When new puppies are "on their way," I make sure that I have purchased fresh goat's milk and freeze it in ice-cube trays. I then store those frozen cubes in a Ziploc bag and place the bag in the freezer. If a puppy needs a boost, I can take out one cube of goat's milk and mix it with equal parts of Pedialyte. It seems to work great. If there are leftover cubes, I mix them in with the puppy food during their weaning time.

Travel and Feeding

Always rushed to find time to cook bait before a show? I now keep a Ziploc sandwich bag in my freezer compartment tossing in that one leftover chicken breast, the remaining slice of meat loaf, whatever. I am no longer tempted to eat those unneeded calories when I think of the time saved and when I remember how much better those leftovers will look on the dogs rather than on me or in the garbage. The morning of the show, I simply remove the frozen bag and let it defrost en route.

Be sure to pack your dog's own food and water to avoid upsets on a trip because some animal's stomachs will become upset with new food and/or water.

Dried blueberries firm up loose stools and diarrhea when traveling and are mild enough to feed even to young puppies. Our dogs eat them happily. They are available in the dried fruit section of natural food stores or in supermarkets.

Fireplace tongs make great arm extensions for reaching over exercise pens to either place or to retrieve food bowls.

For you wine-drinking dog exhibitors: after finishing your wine-in-a-box, carefully remove the inner metallic bag, pry off the spout, rinse out the bag, fill to the desired size with water, replace the spout and freeze. This makes a terrific cooler for your ice chest and will easily last throughout an entire weekend circuit. Just re-freeze the bag when you get home and it is ready to use again on your next circuit.

Going to a weekend dog show? Measure each day's ration of dog food, place it in an individual size Baggie and close. Next, go to your vet and ask to buy some disposable paper feeding trays (if you are a regular client, he will probably give them to you). This eliminates packing a dog food sack and worrying about it getting spilled. It is more sanitary and neat. You take only the amount of food needed, and it leaves room for all the trophies you are going to win over the weekend.

I freeze 1/2-gallon milk cartons (filled with water) to use in the dogs' crates as I travel during hot weather. Also, this is an easy way to transport water to the shows and matches. Put a few cartons out in the run during the hot summer and see the dogs all crowd around it at nap time.

If you are going to be traveling in the summer's heat without benefit of air conditioning, freeze a large, covered container of water (plastic milk jugs work great) ahead of time. The jug may then be placed right into the crate with your dog. Not only will the crate be kept cooler, but the cold water (which condenses on the jug) will provide welcome refreshment. If you're going on a longer trip, bring extra jugs in a cooler.

If you plan to travel with your dog, start out with small trips before going on longer trips.

In very warm weather I take one of my six-pack ice chests with a Ziploc bag full of ice and lay a folded dish towel on top of that. Then, after making a slight crease in the towel, I lay anything which needs to be kept cool on top of it. I now have one of the eight-pack-type coolers which has a refrigerated motor in the lid and I can plug this into the cigarette lighter. This provides me with a refrigerator everywhere I go.

It is recommended that you keep your dog's food to a minimum during travel. Be sure to feed him regular dog food and resist the temptation to give him some of your fast food burger or fries as that's not good for any dog.

The heat-sealing gadgets like Seal-A-Meal are great for us doggy folks. This is especially true when preparing each dog's meal required for a dog show circuit. They are also perfect for cooking ahead and freezing home-cooked meals for the family (so they may simply plop each meal into boiling water and "presto," Mommy is not missed quite so much while she is at the shows). These bags work well to hold those "spillables" that we must have while traveling (like our cosmetics and any grooming goo which might leak). Also, shipping labels may be sealed in these containers if your shipping your dog to a handler or to a dog show.

This is so simple that probably everyone else does it too and yet sometimes we overlook the simple things. When traveling to shows or wherever with my dogs, I pre-measure their individual meals into Ziploc sandwich bags. They are on a carefully calculated formula of dry food, K-Zyme including a biscuit. Pre-measuring ahead of time makes feeding time easy and stays consistent with feeding at home. Each dog's daily rations are then dropped into a large Ziploc with his name on his Ziploc bag. At meal time, the contents of one bag are simply dumped into each dog's bowl and mixed with the moist additives. There is no having to remember who gets what amount, and the dogs will attest to it being a faster process as they don't like to wait while I fumble for measuring cups and feeding charts.

When traveling to other areas with your dogs, carry along a Real-Lemon. A couple of drops in their drinking water neutralizes strange water and it will not upset them. I have yet to run into the new water malady (from which so many dogs suffer) when I have my trusty Real-Lemon along.

When traveling with my dogs, I measure out each meal in a

zippered sandwich bag. I also put their supplements right in (and label either "a.m." or "p.m.") so while on the trip I won't need to check which bags contain which supplements. The bags keep their meals super fresh and also water-proof and spill-proof.

Treats

Croutons make a great crunchy treat for puppies and dogs alike. The cheese-flavored ones are a favorite at my house.

For a fun, healthy game for your dog, try slicing up a banana. Freeze the sliced pieces and then hide the frozen banana chips around the yard. The banana doesn't freeze solidly so it won't hurt your dog's teeth.

I have found that giving my dogs ice cubes (from the time they are young) is something my dogs seem to relish since they act as though the ice cubes are pieces of steak. A big plus is that these ice cubes come in handy when any dog is going through a period of dehydration (vomiting, diarrhea, etc.) because he will still chomp down the ice cubes. In this situation, we freeze Pedialyte to help stabilize the dog's system. The only down side is that you have a lot of company when you open the freezer.

I keep a stock of chew sticks by my telephone because that's when my puppies (and some juvenile delinquents) decide to chew on everything they know they shouldn't. If I can't leave the phone, I may divert their attention with a bribe they love.

I used to throw away my pizza crusts (which I didn't want to eat) but I discovered a way to recycle them. I use them as "bones" for puppies who are too young to eat them (around five to eight weeks of age). The puppies love to play with the crusts and after they've had fun for a while, I throw the crusts away.

Spray a cookie sheet with Pam to cook golf ball-sized hamburger meatballs. When cool, place the cookie sheet and meatballs in the freezer. When they're frozen, remove the balls and store in a Ziploc bag in the freezer for those special hot-weather treats. They are extra special for teething puppies. You may also microwave the balls for a few seconds and hide pills in them when medication is necessary.

Tube-Feeding Newborns

A product called Probiocin (live culture Lactobacillus) is excellent for enteritis in newborns and to fight E. Coli. Definitely use this if any antibiotic is given. Also, give it to the bitch. «»Editor's note: based on reading and research in nutritional biochemistry, an effective anti-diarrhea mixture (Bifidobacterium infantis) for puppies is Natren's Life Start (1/8 teaspoon in 1/2 ounce of lukewarm water and 1/2 teaspoon of each in 1 ounce of lukewarm water for adults and especially for the new mother).«»

As the best substitute for bitch's milk, I use the following recipe: 1/2 cup of water, 1/2 cup of Carnation Evaporated Milk (canned), 2 teaspoons white Karo syrup and 1 raw egg yolk. Mix well. It is quite simple to make, and I have gotten better results with this than from powdered or prepared varieties. «»Editor's note: based on nutritional biochemistry, if the puppy is orphaned before nursing is completed, bifido bacteria or bifidobacteria (1/8 teaspoon into warm formula) should be supplemented. Based upon further reading and research, goat's milk works well and is less upsetting to a puppy.«»

From working in a hospital with premature infants, I have learned when tube-feeding to always let the fluid drain into the stomach by gravity flow *(not by force of the plunger). That way, when the flow stops, you'll know that the puppy's tummy is full and you'll prevent the risk of overflow and aspiration.*

Hand-raising a newborn litter? Tube-feed them. It's the safest, most efficient and quickest method. To make those feedings in those wee hours of the morning easy for myself, I keep two to four 30 cc syringes in the refrigerator (filled with enough formula for the entire litter). When awakened by the alarm, I simply put hot tap water in a tall glass or other container. Then I place the feeding tube on the syringe and place the syringe (tube down) into the glass containing hot water. The hot tap water warms the formula without making it too hot and also softens and warms the tube. Then I simply depress the plunger to dispense the prescribed amount of formula to each pup. After a few practices, you will hardly even remember you had to get up. This method requires no measuring, filling or thinking.

I needed to tube-feed my last litter. The bitch had produced a huge litter of ten puppies and she and I were both exhausted. In my befuddled state, I wasn't sure that I would reset the alarm correctly. How could I get up in time for the next feeding? While sleepily waiting for the milk to become warm, I drank a large glass of water and drinking that water turned out to be the solution to my problem. Later, I urgently woke up without an alarm in time for the next feeding. Because bladder capacity varies, you may need to try drinking between one-half to two glasses of water and time your awakening before you have a tube-feeding problem. For me, drinking a glass of water was a simple solution to my dilemma of waking every few hours without an alarm.

We use a syringe (with a feeding tube attached) to medicate young puppies. Medicine may be measured correctly and put directly into a puppy's stomach.

Water

For you wine-drinking dog exhibitors: after finishing your wine-in-a-box, carefully remove the inner metallic bag, pry off the spout, rinse out the bag, fill to the desired size with water, replace the spout and freeze. This makes a terrific cooler for your ice chest and will easily last throughout an entire weekend circuit. Just refreeze the bag when you get home and it is ready to use again on your next circuit.

I freeze 1/2-gallon milk cartons which have been filled with water to use in the dogs' crates as I travel in hot weather. Also, this is an easy way to transport water to the shows and matches. Put a few cartons out in the run during the hot summer and see the dogs all crowd around it at nap time.

I found shower curtain rings handy in my kennel runs. Fasten one to the wire outside the run and hang a little dishwashing brush from it. I now always have the brush handy to give a quick wipe around the water buckets every time I water. This keeps them clean and sparkling, and the brush goes easily back on the ring after use (avoiding the usual fate of somehow becoming misplaced).

If you are going to be traveling in the summer's heat without benefit of air conditioning, freeze a large, covered container of water (plastic milk jugs work great) ahead of time. The jug may then be placed right into the crate with your dog. Not only will the crate be kept cooler, but the cold water (which condenses on the jug) will provide welcome refreshment. If you're going on a longer trip, bring extra jugs in a cooler.

If you have one of those dogs who is extra-finicky about drinking "strange" water at out-of-area events, try adding a few drops of wine or apple cider vinegar to his home water every day. Do the same when away from home and out-of-town water will seem properly familiar. I have also heard that it keeps down the bacteria count in standing water, and it is a folk-remedy for arthritic joints.

If you're tired of having those aluminum clip-on water dishes knocked over by active puppies, find some round or oval palm-sized rocks (relatively smooth surfaced) and put them in the dishes before adding water. They clean easily in soapy water with a potato scrubbing brush and fit in the cutlery section of most dishwashers. The rocks I've been using weigh approximately 1/2 to 1 pound and are about 1 inch thick and 3 inches in diameter. You'll get used to strange looks and remarks from visitors after a while, and it really does help.

I have found that giving my dogs ice cubes (from the time they are young) is something my dogs seem to relish since they act as though the ice cubes are pieces of steak. A big plus is that these ice cubes come in handy when any dog is going through a period of dehydration (vomiting, diarrhea, etc.) because he will still chomp down the ice cubes. In this situation, we freeze Pedialyte to help stabilize the dog's system. The only down side is that you have a lot of company when you open the freezer.

I have found that hanging an animal-drinking bottle (the kind used for rabbits and other small animals) on the pen when puppies are just beginning to move around allows them to quickly learn to drink from the stainless steel tube. This helps keep the puppies more content when they're thirsty and also keeps them drier (since they can't spill pans of water).

In many parts of the West and Southwest, the water has a high mineral content and is quite alkaline. It tastes terrible. A few drops of lime juice added to a glass of water may make the taste similar to delicious spring water. The amount of lime you add depends on how hard the water is and your personal taste. Start with about three or four drops squeezed into a glass. Limes are small, seedless and easy to carry.

In the heat of the summer, freeze blocks of ice to add to water bowls. I use tupperware square plastic containers as they fit easily into my water dishes. The article from which I got the idea suggested using ice cream cartons. In the heat of the summer, this will keep the water at least somewhat cold.

To give my dogs something to help cool them off at those hot summer shows, I take a frozen plastic bottle of water with me when I leave in the morning. By the time I get to the show and get all set up, the ice is melting and I've got some nice cool water to refresh my dogs.

Try using rabbit bottles in your puppy pens. These bottles hang on the side of the pen and the water is dispensed by the puppy licking the spout from the bottom of the rabbit bottle. The water stays fresh and sanitary. No more wet pens from water being dumped over and it eliminates those crusted feet and bleeding pads. No puppies right now? Don't pack that bottle away. Take it with you to the shows. No more accidental spills just as you have gotten everybody groomed and they are calling your first class. Rabbit bottles may be purchased at any feed store.

When traveling to other areas with your dogs, carry along a Real-Lemon. A couple of drops in their drinking water neutralizes strange water and it will not upset them. I have yet to run into the new water malady (from which so many dogs suffer) when I have my trusty Real-Lemon along.

Weight Problems

Add interest to your dog's dinner by mixing in a bit of "liver dust" with your dog's meal along with sprinkling some over the top. "Liver dust" is made by putting freeze-dried liver chunks into the blender for a few seconds. "Liver dust" is very fine so that your dog can't pick through and just eat the "goodies."

After adding a new supplement, not one of my dogs would touch their food. Out of desperation I reached into the refrigerator and grabbed the cheese for my spaghetti and sprinkled it over the food. Even my most finicky eater wolfed his food down.

Do you have picky eaters or are you having trouble putting weight on a dog? I have found mixing a couple of spoonfuls of junior baby food with the dog food works wonders. I use either the meat/vegetable blends or the vegetable jars.

Dyne is a wonderful product that I learned about in the '60s when I was working for veterinarians. They used it in their practice and I've found it extremely useful to put quick weight on dogs, maintain weight and cut down on stress to puppies during weaning, etc. It's very palatable and very high in calories and vitamins. It's a thick liquid and easy to administer orally with a syringe or add to the dog's food. I had a very skinny, picky eater who got to a good show weight (in one month by giving 12 cc three times a day for that month). The dog was not force-fed and ate little else. Dyne may be ordered from Omaha Vaccine Co. Write for their free catalog: P.O. Box 7228, 3030 "L" St., Omaha, NE 68107-0228.

For an easy way to make your dog's food more appealing, save the water in which you boil your liver. This makes a great tasty treat for finicky eaters when poured over dry food. I have had great success putting weight on a dog when I have done this consistently for a period of time. Refrigerated, this "liver water" may be kept for several days.

For the finicky eater, we've had great success with Squeeze Parkay liquid margarine. You may use quite a bit at a time. It mixes right in the food (we add a little extra just to sit on the top). It won't give the dogs the runs, it's good for the coat and has a good amount of calories to help with the weight gain.

For your problem eaters, try a name-brand soup. Cream of Chicken is one of our favorites. It may be diluted with water and mixed in with your regular dry brands of food. One can adds flavor to many feedings, and what is not used may be stored in the refrigerator without spoiling for several days.

If weight gain is a problem with your Shelties and some other breeds (even though they receive enough exercise and they are not being overfed), the problem may be inadequate iodine. The Sheltie, being a native islander, was often fed fish. Try supplementing your dog's diet with fish or kelp.

If you have a dog who eats the meat and leaves his kibble, try putting the dry kibble into a blender first and then mixing this powdered kibble into the meat.

If you have a finicky eater, try sprinkling Parmesan grated cheese over your dog's food. I found that it helped my finicky eater improve his appetite tremendously.

In an effort to control my dog's extra weight, I feed him french-cut green beans. I place them in a strainer and run hot tap water over the beans to make them warm. This helps my dog feel full without overeating.

My puppies are self-fed and I found that the adults were getting too "porky" with their constant access to the puppies' food. I solved this problem without having to separate them. I made a creep-feeder (a pen so constructed as to exclude larger animals while permitting young animals to enter and obtain feed) out of a Kennel Aire crate. I used a rubber bungee strap or a piece of heavy wire to tie the crate door open and block off most of the crate entrance with an extra door that I had from a plastic crate. This was fastened, too, with rubber straps. The entrance is vertical and just wide enough for the pups to enter and "pig out" on the bowl of food placed inside to the back of the crate. (You could use this same procedure with an exercise pen with a door.) The adults can't fit through the entrance and have to wait until feeding time for their measured portions.

My young bitch had coccidiosis. Then, some time later, she picked up a liver virus (both of which disturbed her digestion). She absolutely refused to eat and I would need to force-feed her. Then her tummy would just rumble. After trying several things (none of which worked), Geritol came to the rescue. She loved it. Apparently, it soothed her stomach. After a month of a teaspoonful twice a day on her food, she became her normal self. With a great deal of trepidation, we decided to breed her. She breezed through her pregnancy, fed and cleaned her puppies and actually became fat by the time her three babies were weaned. Now we have to limit her food.

Put freeze-dried liver (available at pet-supply sources) into the blender and use this powder as a flavor enhancer in food for your picky eaters, or try sprinkling Parmesan cheese into your dog's food.

This recipe came from a nurse who works in a hospital. It is useful for weak puppies or finicky eaters: 1 can Carnation, 8 ounces water, 8 ounces plain yogurt, 3 or 4 egg yolks and 3 tablespoons of Karo syrup.

To get that skinny, bag-o-bones, picky eater to eat more, take 1/2 can of dog food and mix with your kibble until combined. Then place food in the microwave and warm. This makes it like their favorite...people food. Try it, as it really works.

To put weight on a dog fast, mix: 2 cups pure cream, 2 tablespoons brown sugar and 2 tablespoons suet. Heat cream only to melt suet. Give at night and leave with the dog so he may drink during the night.

To stimulate a lagging appetite (especially in an older dog), I administer B-12 injections (subcutaneously with 1 cc every third day). Besides sparking the appetite, it has a soothing effect on a dog's overall restlessness.

Whether for rapid weight gain or adapted for maintenance, this recipe approximates the fresh frozen foods that are, for some, difficult to obtain. Quantities may be halved or doubled accordingly. This is a supplement which should be accompanied by at least: 1 cup of dry kibble, 5 pounds of cheap hamburger (higher fat content), 10 tablespoons unflavored gelatin, 10 egg yolks, 1 12-ounce jar wheat germ, 1 regular-size box of Total cereal and 1 cup molasses and 1 cup corn oil. Do not cook. Mix very well with hands or food processor. Form into 1/2-cup balls, place in individual plastic bags and freeze (0° F to destroy any bacteria). Thaw as needed. Feed two daily for weight gain or one daily as a supplement. «»Editor's note: based on reading and research in nutritional biochemistry, corn oil is deficient in omega-3 fatty acids (whose end chain products are essential for brain development and function), however corn oil is very rich in omega-6 fatty acids (which will help produce a luxuriant coat and healthy skin). Further reading suggested that 1 to 2 teaspoons daily of corn oil and 1 teaspoon daily of a fish oil would strike a better balance. These oils must be added after thawing since freezing oils and fats may significantly change their structure.«»

Whelping and Feeding

(Also see "BITCHES"—"Whelping Bitches"
and "Bitches With Puppies")

During whelping when my bitch goes into a rest period, I wait no longer than one hour. Then I fill a dish with ice cold milk and torn-up white bread. Then I offer this to the bitch. More often than not, she will drink the cold milk which seems to prompt labor once again. Those bitches who don't eat the bread will usually go back and gobble that up, too (once they have finished whelping). I have used this method from my first litter and ever since that litter. Several other breeders (who have called me desperately in the middle of the night) tried my somewhat old-fashioned method have told me that this method worked for them. The vet, of course, is the last resort if labor does not start up shortly.

Here's a super stew recipe for whelping bitches: combine one pound stew beef, one large beef kidney and one pound of beef liver. Simmer along with two sliced onions and two or three carrots. Flavor with 1/3 package dried onion soup. This will take about three hours of cooking time. Feed this to bitches for three to four days after they have whelped. It seems to help clean them out and bring in your bitch's milk. Feed it several times a day and begin to add kibble by the morning of the third day.

One of my young bitches refused to eat after whelping her first litter. Normally she's a glutton, however I couldn't tempt her to eat anything...even her favorite cheese. I offered her many food goodies with no success. Then I stumbled upon beaten raw egg mixed with a little milk. She loved it. Soon she was accepting her dry food with the egg mixed in and later she ate the dry food only. «»Editor's note: based on nutritional biochemistry, a diet which contains an excess of raw egg whites quickly and almost invariably leads to a biotin deficiency. In raw eggs, biotin is typically bound to a sugar-protein molecule (the glycoprotein called avidin) and cannot be absorbed into the body unless the egg is cooked, allowing the biotin to separate from the avidin protein. «»

Misc.

Tired of lugging big 50-pound packs of dog food from car to house or garage ever time you stock up? Next time bring out your dog show crate dolly. You may load four to six 50-pound bags on it and roll them anywhere you wish without any stress or strain.

Grooming

Bathing and Conditioning Dog's Coat

A capful of liquid peppermint (Castile) soap in a quart of warm water should be kept handy to clean spots when your dog has an accident. Pour this mixture on a sponge and go over the entire spot. Then flush the sponge and repeat the process. No rinsing is necessary. This will not only neutralize the ammonia odor and remove the stain but will leave a fresh, natural smell in its place. Two or three capfuls in a bucket of water cleans linoleum, tile and other no-wax floors. A capful in the final rinse of washing dog blankets cleans and deodorizes them and helps repel fleas. Bathing your dog in this soap leaves the coat shiny and smelling nice longer than special dog shampoos. Liquid peppermint soap is sold at most health food stores.

A conditioner which dissolves easily in water and is great to add to your spray bottle of water is Unicure. You may be able to find it at a drug store or a beauty supply store. It's colorless, odorless and tasteless.

Afro-Sheen works wonders on black coats and produces a nicely set-up coat for the shows. Results vary on different dogs so some experimentation is necessary, but the "look" is worth the effort.

After trying innumerable coat conditioners I tried Vidal Sassoon's Conditioner. I put about one teaspoon in a spray bottle of water. A light mist does wonders for texture and shine in a damaged, dull coat.

A good, concentrated shampoo which lathers (even in hard water), rinses easily and really gets the white areas white is Orvus Concentrated Shampoo by Farnam. It may be found in livestock supply stores.

A great coat conditioner for a dry coat is a product made by Jafra called Precious Protein.

A groomer shared this neat trick with me. Palmolive Liquid Dish Soap is an excellent flea shampoo. I tried it and it works. It will soften coats a bit but it's fine for those dogs not being shown. It's cheap and it's great not to use chemicals.

A product I have found that really works for easier brushing of long skirt hair on bitches and long belly hair on males is Johnson's No More Tangles. It may be found at any drugstore or supermarket and costs a lot less than similar grooming products.

Baking soda in the rinse water will leave your pet's coat odor free, plus softer and shinier.

Before or after bathing a heavy-coated dog, if you need help in brushing through the thick or matted coat, spray first with Show Sheen. Show Sheen is a product made and used by horse people. It helps in removing and brushing through the tangles.

Dry clean your pet instead of washing by rubbing baking soda into his coat thoroughly and then brushing off. This will deodorize as well as clean his coat.

During flea season, my dogs get dipped about every 80 days and are then drip-dried. There is nothing like being sprayed when they shake off this excess dip. This solution has worked very well for me: as soon as they are dipped, I put on one of my husband's old T-shirts. They may shake all they want and I don't get wet.

For rapid cleaning of muddy feet we have found that a section of loofah dipped in warm water cleans all mud and stones, even between toes (with a minimum of effort). Just scrub the foot with a flipping motion and all the debris comes right out. A loofah may be purchased at most department or grocery stores in the bath soap section.

Hair-So-New cream rinse is a nice product to keep at home and in your grooming box at the shows. Not only is it a great coat spray for your dog but it is also perfect for touch-up misting on your own hair before entering the ring.

I fill two small spray bottles with water. To one, I add two tablespoons of shampoo and shake. I wet down my dog and mist him using the shampoo bottle. This process, although slower, provides even distribution of shampoo and facilitates rinsing. I use the second bottle to mist my dog's head so it's clean of shampoo.

If you bathe your dogs in the sink and have trouble with them slipping, buy one of the bath mats with suction cups on the bottom. Cut this bath mat in half and place a piece in each side of the sink. No more battles with scared puppies during bath time.

If you cannot find a shower hose to fit an odd-sized faucet, change the faucet to one with a pull-up cutoff for a shower. Instead of switching to the shower, it switches to a shower-hose attachment on the faucet. Presto...you will have a handheld shower at your dog's level. These faucets are at a plumbing supply stores, and you may change them yourself. Dog baths are no fun for the dog or the owner. One way to make it ten times easier on yourself is to buy a handheld "Water Pic" shower massage. They are easy to install and are inexpensive. You may even find your own shower more fun.

If you hate bathing dogs as much as I do, then this helpful hint may work for you. I purchased a plastic baby's bathtub at a local Kmart. I ran the garden hose from the house (that way I could regulate the temperature of the water). I set up an exercise pen in the sun and the baby tub on my grooming table. I was able to wash, rinse and drip-dry four dogs in less than an hour. By the time the fourth dog was washed, the first was dry enough to begin brushing.

If your dog's coat is looking dull and dry after a hot summer or any other time, I put 1 tablespoon of Brewer's Yeast and 1 tablespoon of vinegar (cider) in the food daily. It puts a nice healthy shine into the coat and gives it a better texture.

I have a product I just used on my blue merle's coat that I would like to pass on to other people who own a dog who's white coat is looking too yellow. My blue merle's blue was getting old and yellowing on the ends by the time he had finally grew enough coat to be shown. I hated the idea of trimming off any of his coat, but the ends of his hairs on his back were yellowing and almost starting to become tinged with a light brown. I found a great shampoo in my neighborhood drugstore. It's called Jhirmack's Silver Fox. It is a shampoo that stops yellowing and brassiness for people who have gray hair. I used it once and there was a noticeable difference. I bathed him once a week for three more weeks and his yellowing was 98 percent gone. Though I wouldn't use "people" shampoo on him all the time, I am certainly going to continue using the Silver Fox shampoo every few times I bathe him. The shampoo holds true to its name since he, once again, looks fabulous.

I have found a shampoo that intensifies coat color better than anything else I've tried. It is called Quik Silver and is a color-intensifying horse shampoo. It makes colors just glow but works especially well on blues. This is also excellent in removing stains or yellowing in the whites of the coat.

I'm always running out of dog shampoo when I need it. So, I made my own just for quick baths. In an empty 32-fluid-ounce bottle with a squirt top, I combined 1 tablespoon Dawn dishwashing detergent (makes white bright), 1 tablespoon Bio-Groom Super Coat Conditioner and 1 teaspoon Vet-Kem Paramite dip. I filled the rest of the bottle with warm water and shook it well. I used this "witches' brew" on my dogs last summer with very good results.

Instead of bathing or cutting off the skirts of bitches after whelping (in order to remove the blood), wipe the blood off by using straight hydrogen peroxide and then dry with a towel or paper towels. Pour or sponge the hydrogen peroxide through her skirts and then squeeze out with a dry towel. Her skirts will become beautifully clean. *Be sure to completely dry everything before returning mom to her pups.*

My favorite doggy perfume is St. Aubrey's Coat Dressing. We especially like it for a final touch-up when returning visiting bitches and for puppies who are leaving for their new homes. It has such a light clean smell and I have even used it in the house for room spray.

Sam's Wholesale Club sells (in its automotive department) packages of small hand-size white towels for washing cars. They come in packages of 12 towels, and they are excellent when washing your pet and during whelping of puppies.

The Absorber is a chamois sold in the auto section of Walmart and some auto parts stores. Use it after you bathe your dog instead of using a towel. You may have to wring it out several times. It pulls the water out of the coat and shortens drying time tremendously. Only the Absorber is recommended for this. Loose hairs do not stick to it as hair does with other chamois. I do not store it in the packing tube (as recommended) because it tends to get a moldy smell. Hang it out to dry and throw it in the washer periodically.

There was a discussion on the internet as to whether it was okay to bathe a bitch who is "in whelp" and due in about a week-and-a-half. When my bitches are pregnant and too big to pop in the tub, I spray Self Rinse Plus where the bitches are dirty and then wipe clean. It's very easy and less stressful on the mother-to-be.

To deodorize a dog who has rolled in filth, rub his shoulders and back with a damp sponge sprinkled heavily with baking soda. Then rinse off with clean water.

To improve a damaged coat or the looks of a sparse coat, apply a neutral henna. This may be purchased at beauty supply stores and it's fairly easy to apply. The neutral henna adds no color and adds body and shine to a lifeless coat.

Use a large trash bag as a cover-up when you bathe a dog. Poke your head through the bottom and your arms out the side. Also, carry a trash bag in your car or grooming box so it could become an emergency raincoat. You could also cover the dog with it.

Use an empty and rinsed one-gallon fabric-softener bottle to mix the proper dilution for your economy-size shampoos and conditioners. The contents are visible in the clear bottles and easy to label with a marking pen. When you need it, you always have a gallon ready to use on hand.

Wash your pet in salt water to kill the fleas on them, *but be sure to rinse thoroughly since salt water may irritate your dog's skin.*

We use an inexpensive hose with a spray head (purchased through a mail-order catalog) to wash our dogs. Simply take the hose and a wrench in the grooming supply box to remove the shower head and slip the nozzle over the shower pipe. Then rinse. Just don't turn the water pressure too high. It works great in our deep sink, too.

When bathing your dog, place a rubber mat in the bottom of the tub for a more secure footing for your pet. He will feel safer and be more relaxed.

When giving a bath during those times when your dog's shedding, place a tea strainer (or steel wool pad) in the drain. It prevents the hairs from clogging up the drain.

When washing a tri-color dog or a black dog (the day before a dog show) much of your dog's natural luster is lost and you may see that his coat has become dull-looking. I've found that if you put a little squirt of baby oil on your hands and then rub your oiled hands through your dog's coat, it will bring back the beautiful shine without leaving any trace of the oil when the judge examines your dog.

When washing your dog or cat, a cream rinse is helpful for those who have hair which tangles.

When washing your dogs, place a tea strainer or a piece of large steel wool (large enough to fill the opening of the drain) in the tub's drain to keep pipes from clogging up with your pet's hair. When your dog is dry, simply remove the tea strainer or steel wool and throw it away...along with your pet's hair. Your drain will avoid becoming clogged up with dog hair and you have saved yourself a plumber's bill.

You can save on laundry bills for your towels and cut drying time after bathing your dog by using The Absorber instead of a towel. The Absorber sucks water out of the coat. They are sold in Walmart's auto section and in some auto supply stores.

You will get more baths per bottle if you mix your shampoo half and half with water and put it into a spray bottle. You get a more even distribution of the shampoo and work up a better lather.

Cleaning

An easy way to remove tree pitch from a dog's coat is to rub vegetable oil into it until all the pitch is gone. Then wash the oily area with regular soap and water.

Ever have a dog get into cockleburs? Cover the cocklebur and the surrounding hair with baby powder and the cockleburs will come out a lot easier. Also, if the cockleburs stick into your hands or fingers, rub powder all over the palms of your hands and all around your fingers. The cockleburs don't attach themselves as easily to your fingers.

Have you ever brought your dog in from a romp in the yard only to find bubble gum entwined in his hair? No need to cut it out. Just add a glob of peanut butter and work it in well. Add soap and water and out it comes. Some spots may need more peanut butter added but it will come out. Not only does this work on hair, but it also works on clothes.

Instead of bathing or cutting off the skirts of bitches after whelping (in order to remove the blood), wipe the blood off by using straight hydrogen peroxide and then dry with a towel or paper towels. Pour or sponge the hydrogen peroxide through her skirts and then squeeze out with a dry towel. Her skirts will become beautifully clean. *Be sure to completely dry everything before returning mom to her pups.*

Make your own Handi Wipes for dog show trips or summer travels. Cut a roll of heavy paper toweling such as Bounty or Viva into pieces which will then fit into a Tupperware or Rubbermaid type of covered container. Whip the following liquid ingredients and pour over the paper towels. The liquid ingredients are: 2 capfuls of rubbing alcohol, 2 squirts of baby oil, 2 squirts of baby soap and 1/4 cup of water. Keep in covered container.

Remove burrs from your dog's fur by working oil into the tangle or by crushing the burrs with pliers. You can comb out crushed burrs as the burrs lose their holding power.

Rubbing alcohol removes pine sap from dog fur or from the hood of your vehicle if you make the mistake of parking in the shade of a pine tree at a dog show.

Sam's Wholesale Club sells (in its automotive department) packages of small hand-size white towels for washing cars. They come in packages of 12 towels, and they are excellent when washing your pet and during whelping of puppies.

The Absorber is a chamois sold in the auto section of Walmart and some auto parts stores. Use it after you bathe your dog instead of using a towel. You may have to wring it out several times. It pulls the water out of the coat and shortens drying time tremendously. Only the Absorber is recommended for this. Loose hairs do not stick to it as hair does with other chamois. I do not store it in the packing tube (as recommended) because it tends to get a moldy smell. Hang it out to dry and throw it in the washer periodically.

To deodorize a dog who has rolled in filth, rub his shoulders and back with a damp sponge sprinkled heavily with baking soda. Then rinse off with clean water.

To remove excessive hair from clothing, dampen a sponge and briskly rub clothing. Hair should ball up and you'll then be able to pick off the hair balls.

To wash away strong odors and cut soap film, add vinegar or lemon juice to the rinse water.

We use Baby Wipes for a multitude of reasons: a quick ear cleaning before a show and for wiping grooming materials from our hands. The least expensive ones contain more moisture, and you'll be surprised how many uses you'll find for them.

You can save on laundry bills for your towels and cut drying time after bathing your dog by using The Absorber instead of a towel. The Absorber sucks water out of the coat. They are sold in Walmart's auto section and in some auto supply stores.

Cleaning Your Hands

This is for those groomers who have dry hands and broken nails: an excellent product to use to grow nails and soften hands is called Hoofmaker. This may be purchased through Omaha Vaccine and other places. A nice smelling white cream, it is also very healing for cuts and abrasions.

When grooming at shows, I normally don't find the time to wash my hands as often as I'd like. For instance, after using mousse or gel and before chalking, rather than taking numerous trips to the rest room, I carry moist towelettes, (available at most stores) or Baby Wipes. Once I wipe my hands clean, I just throw it in my disposable grocery bag and I'm ready to show.

Equipment, Products and Supplies

Add something new to your grooming or tack box and throw away that old writing pen. Invest in one of the easy-to-adjust digital time readout pens (or a digital time pen). When placed on the corner of your grooming table, the time is always there at a glance.

A neat way to protect the sharp points on your grooming scissors and dewclaw removal scissors (with the added benefit of no holes poked in clothing or your hand) is to take plastic aquarium tubing and cut it into one-inch lengths. These sections of tubing will stretch and slip snugly over the points. Some tubing may even be steam-sterilized (if you autoclave your instruments).

An empty Kleenex box (I use the square Kleenex boxes, but I suppose the oblong ones would do, as well) makes a wonderful disposal for hair when grooming. It's amazing how much hair you can stuff in that box and the hair stays put. When finished, just toss the box into the trash.

A nifty towel rack may be made from a dry cleaner's wire hanger which has a cardboard tube attached. Remove one end of the tube and insert your roll of paper towels. Presto...you have a towel rack that travels to shows and which you may hang on a grooming table, in the car, in the kennel house, etc.

Any time you stay in a motel which offers free shower caps, be sure to save them. They take practically no space in your purse, glove compartment or grooming box and may come in very handy during those unexpected rain showers (when you're at dog shows and you must be out in the rain to exercise, groom or even to show

your dog...if you're braver than I am).

Carry a trash bag in your car or grooming box so it could become an emergency raincoat. You may even cover your dog with it.

For those who have wire handles on crates or exercise pens, make it easier on your hands. Get an old piece of hose (a garden hose works well) and measure the amount of hose you'll need for the handle where your hand will grip it. Slice the hose on one side from one end to the other. Slip it onto the handle and then tape the hose shut with tape. (I find friction tape works well.) Wrap the tape around the length of the hose several times. It makes crates and pens so much easier to carry.

I bought an Air Force blow dryer, but it stayed on the floor in its shipping box and was getting in my way. I was going to buy the carrying case when my husband suggested I use my old bowling bag. The cord fits in the side pocket, the hose and attachments fit under the ball rack and the dryer fits perfectly on top of the rack. It's hidden, easy to carry and it's simple to get in and out.

I cleaned and dried a (human) shampoo bottle with a flip-top pour spout and filled it with white powdered chalk. It is very handy when applying chalk to the white ruff. There is also less waste when chalk is applied in this manner.

If you've ever strained your wrist and find it too painful to brush through those heavy coats, try this: take a piece of white adhesive tape and wrap one strand around your arm halfway between the wrist and the elbow. This taping provides support to the tendons and helps in preventing further injury.

I guess I am a bit of a neatness freak when it comes to cupboards, closets and drawers and tack boxes are no exception. While trying to find something in which to store my mat comb (mat splitter) which would neither dull the blade nor be cut through, I decided that one of our numerous glasses' cases (the kind eye doctors give out when you buy a new pair of glasses) worked well. These may be written on (using a permanent marker if they are the vinyl type) and work to hold the many small items which seem to "float" around inside a tack box. All of my family wear either contacts or glasses so our eyeglass supply is pretty steady. Perfect vision? Lucky you! Ask a four-eyed friend to share their cases.

In an attempt to keep my tack box somewhat organized, I ran across a nifty piece of equipment to have handy: a shower curtain ring (the metal kind). That little "goodie" is perfect for hanging all my dog collars in a single place. Held up in the air, the correct length collar is more easily determined than by picking them up one at a time and comparing the length of each collar. It is easily unfastened when removing the collar of choice and when refastened, it may be put down with all the other collars still neatly joined on the shower ring.

Instead of purchasing a roller base for hauling all your equipment and dogs to your grooming area, a dolly or hand truck combination is available for less money. Use it horizontally and attach a rope or lead to pull it easily. It has wheels large enough to go over curbs and bumps. The front wheels swivel for turning with ease. It will stand up (out of your way), or it may be used for hanging your outfit (to keep your clothes wrinkle-free before ring time).

It is very easy to make a container which will hold all the hair from a shedding, long-haired dog. Take a waxed carton (the round kind such as an ice cream container) and put a round hole approximately 1 1/2" wide in its top. Push the combings inside as you remove them from the dog. They will scrape off easily on the edge of the hole. When you're through, throw the whole carton away into a trash can. For a more lasting container (which may be used over and over again...at shows and at home), use one of the plastic containers in which moist tissues are packed (such as Wet Ones). You may buy these at supermarkets or drugstores. They have a nice strap with a ring attached which you may hang on your grooming table.

Looking for a good pin brush that's inexpensive? I bought a wig brush at Kmart for less than one dollar. It looks just like the brushes you'd buy at a dog show.

Metal Band-Aid boxes make good storage containers for your solid chalk as well as for small combs.

Most of us set up next to friends at shows and in the course of everyone grooming his own dogs and sometimes others' dogs, it's easy to misplace or mix up grooming tools. So, I have put a tiny piece of adhesive tape on every single grooming item I own and printed my name or initials on it. This identification has proved handy a number of times.

My local photo shop, "Photo Pro" (who processes photos in-house rather than sending them out) gives away small plastic film holders for free. Sometimes they will give away a whole sackful of black and clear plastic holders. These have any number of uses. You may write on them with waterproof, small-tipped marking pens to indicate their contents. Put about three small pebbles in one and put it in your pocket when taking dog photos. When the dog is in place (if all else fails to get him to use those ears), take it out, shake it once and throw it far in front of him so it rolls and bounces.

One of the best purchases we've ever made was an adjustable mechanic's seat which is a small padded stool that is adjustable in height and mounted on swivel casters (allowing it to roll easily from one spot to another). This rolling stool has been invaluable in saving my knees and back while grooming and when assisting in natural breedings or collecting semen from stud dogs for artificial insemination (AI). The swivel casters allow me to move around with the dogs so they are always within my reach. We bought ours from Northern Tool and Equipment, 800-533-5545, 800-221-0516 or www.northerntool.com.

One of the handiest tools we own is an electric engraving pencil. It's the kind police suggest you use to mark all your personal possessions like TVs, stereos, etc. With it, my husband has put our name and our kennel name on each piece of grooming equipment (from scissors to combs, even wood brushes, etc.). He also tastefully decorated and engraved my metal tack box. This way when a group of us groom together and often trade equipment, mine doesn't get mixed up with theirs.

Remove your pet's hair from your clothing by using masking tape. Roll the tape out and attach the tape backwards on the roll so the sticky side is out. Roll the tape on your clothes and the hair will stick to the tape.

Rubbermaid Sure Grip (for drawer lining) is great for lining puppy pens, tubs, tops of counters and any surface which you may use for measuring, grooming, etc. It's inexpensive, comes in great colors and you just throw it in the washer when it needs cleaning.

The plastic shampoo bottles (with the flip-up spouts) are wonderful to use with chalks and powders. With a little practice, you can aim and shoot the powder, getting as little or as much as you need right where you want it and without tons of excess which may dull the rest of the coat.

There are a lot of handy uses for your spray bottle besides misting when line-brushing. With the bottle always full of water

and water only, set the nozzle on "stream." It will squirt across a room. My aim is not that good but I can generally get a barking dog's face and/or mouth very wet from across the room. Even if you just hit the body or dampen an ear, you do get their attention. If you don't think it shuts them up, try it. Also, my dogs are not afraid of the spray bottle, they merely respect it because they drink from it at shows. At hot outdoor shows, you may not have a bowl of water handy but you probably have a spray bottle within reach. My dogs love to have this water sprayed into their mouths, however you need to *make sure the nozzle is reset to "spray" (so it's not too strong) and that they do not receive too much, too rapidly because they might then vomit.* If you have sloppy drinkers and you are ready to go into the ring, but "Superdog" looks like he could use a drink, a squirt in the mouth is a lot neater than water slurped all over his ruff. I also use the spray bottle to rinse chalk off my hands when I'm in a hurry or off my shoes, clothes, etc. Believe it or not, I have been known to squirt the thing in my own mouth or at my nervous husband.

The soft insulators which go around pipes are great for the tops of exercise pens. Just pop them on and the metal ex-pen will not mark or scratch your walls or anything they touch.

To identify my grooming tools and other supplies, I write my name on each item with bright fingernail polish. By doing this, whenever someone borrows one of them, I am able to easily see it and then retrieve any of those missing or mislaid items.

When combing out dogs who are "blowing coat," try using a clean, dry milk jug. This milk jug will hold a ton of hair. Just clean the hair off your brush, roll the hair in a ball and then just poke it into the opening of the jug. This is much cleaner and less messy than putting the hair in a grocery bag. For easy access, hang the milk container from the handle on your grooming arm. When you are done, just toss out the jug.

You may use the plastic tubs that peanut butter or butter come in as feeders and water pails which may then be attached to your exercise pen or wire crate. Also, they store grooming powder safely.

Grooming Boxes and Tack Boxes

A Rubbermaid (hard plastic) filing container makes a great grooming box. Since it's made to hold files, this container is high enough for bottles to stand upright and everything can be kept in one place. Use smaller Rubbermaid containers inside this one to keep all the little things handy.

For better organization when going to the dog shows, I use a plastic laundry basket which has a hard plastic lid. This works well to hold everything that your tack box doesn't hold (like towels, newspaper, dog food, shoes, show clothes, picture albums, etc.). The plastic lid keeps everything in the basket so its contents don't get crushed.

For those of us with a heavy tack box, a Coleman camp stove stand supports it at the right height so we save our backs and crates. It folds up small.

One of the lightest and least expensive grooming cases you can purchase may be found in the automotive department of many stores. They are tool cases which are plastic and are on wheels. They come in various styles and are inexpensive. Many have a top part (with a handle) that disconnects from the bottom. They have large areas for towels and compartments to hold anything you want. I know several show people who use them all the time. Being on wheels, they can be very easy to move about and since they are plastic, they are light in weight.

Rubbermaid Sure Grip (for drawer lining) is great for lining tack boxes, tubs, tops of counters and any surface which you may use for measuring, grooming, etc. It's inexpensive, comes in great colors and you just throw it in the washer when it needs cleaning.

Some open tool caddies at a dollar store may hold all of your combs and brushes on your grooming table.

Grooming Tables

A non-slip surface (for grooming or for stacking your dog) is a Rubbermaid bath mat. The suction cups on the back of the mat hold firmly to any slippery surface.

A piece of plastic (clear polyethylene as sold in hardware stores) may be used on top of your towelled grooming table while chalking. Any fallen chalk may be neatly channeled back into the chalk container. Best of all, there will be no more loose chalk being shaken out those towels.

For a grooming table at home, I use either a card table or a utility table. Either one may be obtained less expensively than a grooming table and they may be larger. You may even attach your grooming arm to these tables. I glue Velcro around the edges of the table and, therefore, I'm able to attach towels to the table top (for easier cleanup).

For an ideal grooming table, try a baby-changer with a non-skid mat glued to its top surface. Not only is it the right height for our tired backs, it has safety side rails and back rails (for timid puppies) along with loads of shelf space for grooming supplies.

For table training my young puppies for future grooming, I use a little one-step stool with a rubber vinyl top. They work great for stacking puppies and for getting puppies used to being on a table. The rubbery top feels like a real table. You may even sit down on the floor or in the yard while stacking the pups. I have even stacked puppies on the stool in order to take their pictures, shoot videos and to measure them.

Having a baby? Don't rush out and buy a changing table. If you won't be needing your grooming table for a while, use your grooming table as a changing table. Buy fabric (which appeals to you and your future baby) and elastic so you may make a skirt to wrap around the table. Then push the grooming table against the wall. Presto, you now have a changing table for the newest member of your family.

If anyone in your family is even a little bit handy with a screwdriver, you can make your own grooming table very inexpensively. Buy a piece of 3/4-inch-thick particle board from your local hardware or building supply store. The store will probably cut it to size for you. If not, you may do it yourself easily. Cut it to 2' by 3'. Order a length of rubber runner from Sears (it comes in 2-foot widths). Cut off 3 feet off the runner and glue it to one side of the particle board with any strong glue. Order a pair of their folding, tubular metal legs (also from Sears) and attach them to the board. My husband finished off the table by putting a strip of 3/4-inch-wide metal stripping around the edge of the board. It screws on. The table will be the perfect size and height for grooming.

I have a card table in my grooming room situated right next to my grooming table. On top of the card table I keep all the items I use frequently (such as ear cleaner, cotton balls, coat spray, etc.). Rather than keep these items in my tack box, I keep them out on the card table on a large Rubbermaid "turntable" (available in most retail stores). This way I have easy access to them and I don't have to rummage around inside my tack box.

I have had some puppies who hated the grooming table. By placing the grooming table in front of the TV and giving them little tidbits while on the grooming table, I have alleviated this problem. They distract themselves with the noise and the tidbits help as well. They soon learn that the grooming table is not as bad as they thought.

I like to use Astroturf (artificial grass carpet) on the top of my grooming table. The non-slip surface is rubber-backed and is easily hosed off and sterilized. I also use Astroturf in my breeding pen as it provides excellent footing.

Just starting out? To make an inexpensive but sturdy grooming table, buy Banquet Table Legs. These are sold at discount department stores (Kmart, Zayre's, etc.) at a reasonable price and are foldable. Attach them to a 24" x 36" piece of plywood or waferboard (greater than 1/2" thick is best). Round the corners uniformly by using a bowl as a template. Cover with indoor/outdoor carpeting for a nonslip surface. Attach with a good glue and/or with carpet tacks. Remember to cover with a large towel when chalking. It may be vacuumed for cleaning.

My ironing board (which is up most of the time) makes an ideal and quick substitute for a grooming table (to prepare small puppies for the Conformation ring table). It is higher than most grooming tables for better eye-to-eye contact. It provides great footing, is adjustable as needed and is generally close to the kitchen for that quick treat. *(Never leave your puppy's side while he's on the ironing board.)* I use this all the time and it really works great.

Rubbermaid Sure Grip (for drawer lining) is great for covering grooming tables, lining tack boxes and any surface which you may use for measuring, grooming, etc. It's inexpensive, comes in great colors and you just throw it in the washer when it needs cleaning.

Tired of having your towel or newspapers blow off your grooming table at those windy outdoor shows? Try plastic snap-on tablecloth clips made by the Wecolite Company. They are effective on even the windiest days. Inexpensive, two sets are usually sufficient to protect any size grooming table. They may be found at some supermarkets (Eagle) or where picnic supplies are sold or contact Wecolite Company, 699 Front Street, Teaneck, NJ 07666.

When grooming puppies or unsure adults, I place a bath mat (the kind with carpeting on one side) on the grooming table. You may find them in any department store in various colors. The bottom of the mat secures nicely to the grooming table and the dogs feel more comfortable with the better footing. After each grooming session, I shake it outside and it's usually as clean as it was when it was new. You may also drop it in the washer and dryer. They are also great mats for the dog's crates.

Wooden bar stools are perfect to use as a convenient chair when sitting at a grooming table. Use a saw to cut off the extra length of the legs and the stool will be a custom-fit for you. Not only will sitting at the grooming table help relieve any back strain, but you will have a better eye-level view when grooming.

Nail Trimming

A little peanut butter spread on a ferret's tummy (or, possibly, other pets' tummies, too) may distract him long enough for you to clip his nails. You may use a nail file to file down the sharp ends on a frisky animal's nail. Use the metal nail clippers for bigger animal's and emery boards for smaller animals. No more bleeding nails.

An addition to my grooming supplies has been the Sears Cordless two-speed rotary tool. This is an excellent way to trim toenails without leaving jagged edges. Sanding bits for this tool are much cheaper at Walmart.

A nice way to smooth your dog's toenails without the expense of a professional dog nail grinder is to use the "coarse" nail attachment on those battery operated manicure sets for people. The one I like best is by Norelco's Nail Dazzler because it has a sturdy clear plastic case to hold the whole thing.

A quick alternative to clipping sharp nails on wiggly nursing pups is to let the pups scramble around briefly on a piece of fine sandpaper. This results in nice smooth nails with no rough edge to scratch mom's tummy. Be sure to use fine sandpaper as this does not seem to hurt the pads.

Do your dogs dislike having their nails trimmed? This may be caused by using dull nail clippers in which case the nail is actually crushed before it is cut off. To prolong the life of your clippers and make it more pleasant for your dog, keep your clippers sharp by using a chainsaw file. These are long, thin filing rods which work well on both guillotine and scissor-type clippers. They usually cost less than a new set of clippers and are found where chain saws are sold and serviced.

Do your puppies wear you out when you try to trim their toenails? I have learned a simple form of restraint used on children in the emergency room. Wrap your puppy in a sheet or large towel, leaving his head exposed. Pull one leg, flexed at the elbow, through the opening so that only his paw sticks through. Your puppy will probably scream and fight for a while, but soon he will wear himself out and you will be fresh as a daisy. Now...go ahead and cut those nails.

For cutting nails, I use a small flashlight held close to each nail. After locating the quick, I place my fingernail against the dog's nail to mark how far down to cut. Then I put down the flashlight, pick up the clippers and cut. This method makes even black nails easy to cut.

From the time my puppies are about a week old until they are about three weeks of age (while Mom is still cleaning up after them), I do the following while cleaning out the whelping area. I hold the pup for Mom, placing her pup upside down on my lap and let Mom clean this puppy. Of course, I am seated on the floor. Mom seems to appreciate this and does a thorough job since she has no squirming puppy to contend with. It is also a good way to get puppies familiar with being handled at an early age (which we should be doing anyway). Puppies don't mind it a bit as Mom is tending to them. It seems to form a bond between all of us. This is, also, how I begin cutting each puppy's toenails.

I discovered a secret for easing the task that everyone dreads (dog and owner)...toenail clipping. One day while trying to cut the nails on a very stubborn puppy, I tried blindfolding the pup using a long (loosely knit to allow breathing) stocking cap. I simply and gently pulled the hat down over the head of the puppy and, low and behold, the puppy remained still for the entire procedure. I have used this method on some stubborn adults with the same results. Wish I had discovered this helpful hint years ago.

If you're the crafty type and own a motor-tool for wood carving and other craft purposes, you also own an excellent nail trimmer. We use the soft sanding attachment to grind down our dog's toenails and it really works. You also save big bucks by not buying the expensive nail-care units.

I have one dog who fights nail trims even at the vet's office. After two and a half years, I have found two tricks that work well for me. First, do not trim the toenails during the grooming session before the bath. Instead, just before you have finished washing your dog, trim his nails while he is still standing in water. He is too busy keeping his balance and worrying about getting out of the bath. The water seems to soften the nails so he will not feel the nail trimmers as much. The other trick is to stand your dog on the grooming table and take each foot individually and turn it up so that you can see the pads (i.e., front feet toward the underbelly, back feet toward the tail tip the way a farrier would hold a horse's hoof). This way you may see the hollow of the nail and may clip accordingly. Never trim below the hollow part. My dog didn't flinch once. I find this especially helpful with black toenails when you cannot see the quick.

Is nail trimming a problem? Not at our home. We teach all our puppies to lie on their backs between our legs while they are very young. Play with them until they relax. Now, down to the business of cutting nails. Take a front foot and press the center pad and up pop the nails. Trim one foot, then praise the puppy. Repeat after each trim. Our oldest dog is 11 years old and still lies as quiet as a church mouse at nail time.

My little black-coated puppy was the wiggliest little pup I ever had. Needless to say, cutting those puppy nails was a chore. In an effort to distract him, I placed my grooming table in front of a window which looked out onto the street. He was fascinated by the cars, bikes, people and the occasional dog or cat. Now I have a well-groomed pup who loves to be up on the grooming table. Before you know it, those nails are clipped.

Nails are neglected by many dog owners. Pull back the hair that has covered the nails of your adult dog. See those long claws? Can you visualize a breed like a Doberman walking into the ring with claws like that? Yuck! A breed with short hair has the nails constantly in view. It is easy to tell when they need shortening. Because some dogs' nails are hidden from view, it is easy to neglect them. I cut all the dogs' nails in the kennel once a month and very young pups once a week. If the procedure is done on a regular basis (say the first Tuesday of the month), nails are less likely to be neglected. I have started writing an "N" on the calendar on the day I do them. This helps me to cut them on a regular basis.

The secret to avoid digging is simple: no toenails means no digging. If toenails are trimmed every week or filed very gently every few days with a roto-tool, they will remain so short that your dog cannot grab with them. Trimming must be constant to maintain a short toenail.

To help cut or grind black nails without hitting the quick, try putting a small flashlight behind them. The light helps the insides (the quick) show up better.

You may use a nail file to file down the sharp ends on a frisky animal's nails. Use the metal nail clippers for bigger animal's and emery boards for smaller animals. No more bleeding nails.

Removal of Skunk's Smell

Has your dog met a skunk? Try rubbing Crest toothpaste in his coat, moisten to a foam, then rinse out.

Here is a de-skunking tip that has really worked well for me and for several friends: if your dog gets too friendly with a skunk, wash the dog with soda water instead of tomato juice. It works even better.

If your dog has an encounter with a skunk, wash your dog in

tomato juice while you're both in a well-ventilated area. Then wash with shampoo and water. Rinse with a gallon of water to which a few tablespoons of ammonia have been added. Thoroughly rinse your cat with clear water.

Show Grooming and Preparation

A good coat spray, especially in summer, is a mixture of half a bottle of Listerine and half a bottle of water. The Listerine deodorizes the coat and cools the skin.

A good way to dry an oily coat (when there is no time for a bath) is to rub some of the chalk (that you put on the dog's legs) into the coat. Brush out thoroughly before entering the ring and the dog will look great.

An item I have found very effective for cleaning puppies before prospective puppy buyers come to my home and, also, for cleaning my show dog's ears before going into the ring is Diaparene Baby Wash Cloths. They are safe to use on young puppies and on ears because they are fast drying (since it's solution is alcohol based). They are easy to use, easy to take to a show and easy to throw away.

As our climate (West Australia) is very hot and dry, we are always looking for something to help the long-haired dogs' coats. I have used this for over ten years and find it much better than any of the commercial products. On a coat which is already split, mix equal amounts of glycerine and vinegar. I apply this mixture using a cotton wool swab (cotton ball) and then brush thoroughly. Reapply and when it's absorbed into the coat (every two or three days) and continue to reapply until your dog's coat is repaired. This should only take a week or two. Then, for everyday use, mix 1 tablespoon of glycerine and 1 tablespoon of vinegar with 1 cup of water. Shake well before using on the coat. This mixture is also my choice for use just prior to going in the ring. The coats hold up much longer.

Baby powder behind your dog's ears and in their petticoats will provide a nice light fragrance and will also keep the hair from matting. If you are traveling to the southern part of the United States, purchase some Brown Sugar Baby Powder. It is light brown in color which is perfect for sable-colored dogs.

Before or after bathing a heavy-coated dog, if you need help in brushing through the thick or matted coat, spray first with Show Sheen. Show Sheen is a product made and used by horse people. It helps in removing and brushing through the tangles.

Despite popular opinion, the best way to trim hocks is not with thinning shears. Usually you only end up trading long, dense hair for long, straggly hair. Instead, hold a pair of straight shears parallel to the hock and make one decisive cut to leave a flat ridge of hair. Then use the thinning shears to blend and shape for a natural look. This way you may keep the "fluff" and get rid of the length.

Do you have the problem with light rims around your dog's eyes? We put powdered Vitamin C in our dog's dinner (approximately 1000 mg.+ each day for a medium-sized dog) and the rims return to their natural dark color.

Do your hands get cramped from pulling the trigger on your water bottle to dampen your dog's coat? There is now out a spray bottle of compact size that you pump to pressurize. Just pull the trigger and out comes a soft, continuous spray of water. You will find it at your co-op in the section for spraying insecticides. Mine is the one-liter size.

Dry clean your pet instead of washing by rubbing baking soda into his coat thoroughly and then brushing off. This will deodorize as well as clean his coat.

Due to much winter sinus trouble from the dry air and wood heat, I have been forced to use a house humidifier and cold air vaporizer in my home. To my delight, I have found that the mist from these not only helps me, but helps keep my dogs' coats lustrous and glowing during this dry season and they have yet to have troubles with dry broken coats.

Fuller's Earth Powder is an easy and dry way to get rid of that "stringy" or "raggedy" look behind the dog's ears. Fuller's Earth is a very fine-grained astringent powder that is beige in color. It is perfect for sables. Since it may be completely brushed out, it is also usable on other colors. Sprinkle in behind the ears. I use a soft plastic salt shaker. Rub the powder in with your fingertips and use a flea comb to get most of it out. Then brush with a pin brush or a clean chalking brush.

I bought an Air Force blow dryer, but it stayed on the floor in its shipping box and was getting in my way. I was going to buy the carrying case when my husband suggested I use my old bowling bag. The cord fits in the side pocket, the hose and attachments fit under the ball rack and the dryer fits perfectly on top of the rack. It's hidden, easy to carry and it's simple to get in and out.

I cleaned and dried a (human) shampoo bottle with a flip-top pour spout and filled it with white powdered chalk. It is very handy when applying chalk to the white ruff. There is also less waste when the chalk is applied in this manner.

If your dog has an oily coat from too much oil or coat conditioner and you need to get it off quickly, try putting a hairbrush inside a nylon stocking and then brushing the dog with it. It works wonders.

If your dog needs more "feathering," try spraying with cold water every day. Brush and follow with a light oil dressing.

If you really want to put fluff in your dog's coat without extensive brushing and your dog readily accepts a hair dryer, use one of the small model electric (never gas) wind brooms or leaf blowers to dry or groom your dog. The powerful wind will line blow the coat without breaking the hairs. For extra effect, spray water or light body spray into the coat as you go. *Caution: avoid using this technique on your dog's head, ears, etc.*

If you've been using white chalk or white baby powder on the brown parts of your dogs, consider switching to Brownn Sugarr. This is a slightly beige baby powder designed for use on darker complexioned babies. It is available in the Midwest in large metropolitan areas and is made by Day Labs in Milwaukee, WI 53223.

If you've ever strained your wrist and find it too painful to brush through those heavy coats, try this: take a piece of white adhesive tape and wrap one strand around your arm halfway between the wrist and the elbow. This taping provides support to the tendons and helps in preventing further injury.

Keep a bar of white grooming chalk with your white show leads in a plastic Baggie. Tucked in your grooming bag, they will always be super white and ready to use.

Looking for a good pin brush that's inexpensive? I bought a wig brush at Kmart for less than one dollar. It looks just like the brushes you'd buy at a dog show.

My expensive pin brushes and slickers often start coming apart at the seams soon after purchase. The rubber portion pulls out from under the rim. To fix them, I buy a tube of silicone caulking, remove the rubber part completely, then run a heavy bead of caulking all along the inside rim and work the rubber section back into the frame. You may wipe off any excess caulking on the outside, although I leave it "as is" on my brushes to seal from the outside as well. Let the brush set for 24 hours. I find that the brushes I've fixed stay fixed and they're better than new.

My vet suggested a remedy for dry and sunburned coats which is also effective as a grooming aid. The product is called Derma Oil and is available only from vets. I take one to two capfuls since it is expensive and add it to a spray bottle filled with water. Shake well and spray on the coat. Then massage into the coat. Follow this with a thorough deep brushing. If this is done three times a week, it may really improve the looks of a dry coat.

Rather than buying the expensive commercial varieties of coat conditioners, I make my own and it only costs pennies. I use 1/2 tablespoon of Avon's Smooth As Silk bath oil with water in a pint spray bottle. Giving it a slight shake before using readily emulsifies the oil in the water. It gives a sheen to the coat with a light spraying. More heavily sprayed coats need a day or two to absorb the oil.

Save those yellow plastic squeeze-type containers. They're great for dispensing pumice (just squeeze onto the ears), kennel dust (squeeze into the corners of the crates) or for holding other powders.

Since I couldn't find any Brownn Sugarr at local drugstores, I decided to make my own. At a show, I bought a brown chalk stick. I ground it into as fine a powder as possible, put it into a bowl and started adding my regular white powder to it. I mixed it thoroughly until I got just the shade of brown I wanted.

There are a lot of handy uses for your spray bottle besides misting when line-brushing. With the bottle always full of water and water only, set the nozzle on "stream." It will squirt across a room. My aim is not that good but I can generally get a barking dog's face and/or mouth very wet from across the room. Even if you just hit the body or dampen an ear, you do get their attention. If you don't think it shuts them up, try it. Also, my dogs are not afraid of the spray bottle, they merely respect it because they drink from it at shows. At hot outdoor shows, you may not have a bowl of water handy but you probably have a spray bottle within reach. My dogs love to have this water sprayed into their mouths, however you need to *make sure the nozzle is reset to "spray" (so it's not too strong) and that they do not receive too much, too rapidly because they might then vomit.* If you have sloppy drinkers and you are ready to go into the ring, but "Superdog" looks like he could use a drink, a squirt in the mouth is a lot neater than water slurped all over his ruff. I also use the spray bottle to rinse chalk off my hands when I'm in a hurry or off my shoes, clothes, etc. Believe it or not, I have been known to squirt the thing in my own mouth or at my nervous husband.

To cut down on mats behind the ears or any static electricity in the coat, spray with Static Guard. It makes brushing a breeze and fine hair will not mat as fast.

To improve a damaged coat or the looks of a sparse coat, apply a neutral henna. This may be purchased at beauty supply stores and it's fairly easy to apply. The neutral henna adds no color but adds body and shine to a lifeless coat.

To remove dead undercoat without pulling and causing pain to your long-hair dog, try using a grooming comb with rotating teeth. We use the 7-inch size. They are available from most vet supply houses.

We use Baby Wipes for a multitude of reasons: a quick ear cleaning before a show and for wiping grooming materials from our hands. The least expensive ones contain more moisture, and you'll be surprised how many uses you'll find for them.

When a walk past the family dog gives your clothes a new mohair look, you may be certain the season is finally changing. Pets may lose hair throughout the year but when a thick, winter coat gives way to a sparser summer coat, the results may be hairy. You may help prevent your pet's hairs from sticking to your clothes, carpeting, draperies and furniture by spraying each pet with Static Guard (the odorless anti-static spray made by the Alberto Culver Company). Stray hairs may also be removed by spraying lightly with Static Guard, and then brushing or vacuuming pet hairs away. This Static Guard won't stain, discolor or build up and is safe for most colorfast fabrics. You may also use Static Guard as a grooming aid for your pet. If you've been tempted to wear a mask to protect your nose from airborne hairs as you brush your pet, try spraying your grooming tools and you'll find it easier to keep excess hair where you want it. You'll also be able to control your pet's hair and keep it from standing on end. Controlling loose animal hairs is just one handy way to use Static Guard. Since it neutralizes electricity, applying it to your clothing prevents static cling and lint build-up. In dry weather, spraying your carpets and the soles of your shoes eliminates static electric shocks when you touch metal or another person. And you may apply it to your own brush or comb to keep your hair from flying away as you groom.

Whitening White Parts of Dog's Coat

Everyone is always looking for a good whitening shampoo and a good one for blue dogs, also. I found a shampoo for horses (paints, greys, etc.) which contains no harsh bluings. It will make coats softer as it is Color Bright horse shampoo so I use it for regular bathing but not for show bathing. Since I don't know if this company is still in business, you might try using White N Brite shampoo.

For an economical self-rinsing shampoo (for last minute cleaning of white coat areas such as ruff, feet, etc.), try this mixture: 1 teaspoon Ivory liquid (or any shampoo), 1 teaspoon glycerin, 2 teaspoons white vinegar and enough water to make a quart and laundry bluing, if desired, for color.

Here's a new chalk tip: mix your chalk, whiting, cornstarch, or whatever, with enough water to make liquid. The night before the show, spray the whitener into the dog's coat. The morning of the show, just brush it out.

If you need a super vibrant white coat or part of a coat, use a small amount of concentrated liquid bluing (Mrs. Stewart's Bluing). Mix with water in a separate cup, then shampoo as you normally do. Be sure to wash out thoroughly or you may end up with a blue dog.

I have a product I just used on my blue merle's coat that I would like to pass on to other people who own a dog who's white coat is looking too yellow. My blue merle's blue was getting old and yellowing on the ends by the time he had finally grew enough coat to be shown. I hated the idea of trimming off any of his coat, but the ends of his hairs on his back were yellowing and almost starting to become tinged with a light brown. I found a great shampoo in my neighborhood drugstore. It's called Jhirmack's Silver Fox. It is a shampoo that stops yellowing and brassiness for people who have gray hair. I used it once and there was a noticeable difference, so I bathed him once a week for three more weeks and his yellowing was 98 percent gone. Though I wouldn't use "people" shampoo on him all the time, I am certainly going to continue using the Silver Fox shampoo every few times I bathe him. The shampoo holds true to its name since he, once again, looks fabulous.

I learned about this one year ago at horse shows. To whiten the socks on horses, we mixed cornstarch and water into a paste, rubbed it on the socks, let it dry (didn't take long) and brushed it off. It takes out the dirt and leaves the socks white. The same thing works on the legs of my dogs. The mixture dries hard and brushes off easily and there's no chalk powder which might cause choking or coughing. I use it on the legs only, as collars and ruffs take much longer to dry, although it also may be used on dirty spots on collars or ruffs.

Is your Foo Foo powder bill too high? If so, try using a mixture of 1/2 Foo Foo powder and 1/2 cornstarch for excellent and economical results.

Keep a bar of white grooming chalk with your white show leads in a plastic Baggie. Tucked in your grooming bag, they will always be super white and ready to use.

My color-headed white Sheltie developed a habit of constantly licking his front legs while I was away. It probably occurred from him being bored. This compulsive habit stained the fur on his white legs with a faint, but very noticeable, pink. Application of Bitter Apple to his legs stopped his bad habit, but none of the shampoos developed for white dogs or those formulated to take out coat stains was able to remove those unsightly discolorations. The product I found which work wonders is Diamond Eye by Vitacoat. This is a product which is made to remove those dark tear stains Poodles and other breeds sometimes get under their eyes. I applied the Diamond Eye on a cotton ball a couple of times a day to my dog's discolored white leg hair and the saliva stains started to disappear within a week. This same dog also loves to "groom" my double merle bitch when I'm not around, leaving those ugly pinkish stains on the fuzzy white hair around her ears. Diamond Eye made those disappear, too. If your dogs sometimes get discolorations on their white areas, you might give this product a try. A bottle of Diamond Eye is always on hand in my grooming supplies now.

The plastic shampoo bottles (with the flip-up spouts) are wonderful to use with chalks and powders. With a little practice, you can aim and shoot the powder, getting as little or as much as you need right where you want it, without tons of excess which may dull the rest of the coat.

To bleach the yellow-gray stain out of the white of your pets white areas of hair, mix one pint Hydrogen Peroxide (20 volume) with enough Roux Fanci Full hair coloring rinse (Number 52) to turn the peroxide sky blue. Add about one box of corn starch to thicken. Put on the white areas. Leave this mixture on for a couple of days and then brush it out.

To get your dog's white markings really white, try Absorbine Mane and Tail Whitener. Available at most feed stores, I use it according to the directions for horses. It really removes stubborn stains and may be used on blue merle coats to remove "rusting" due to the sun, however on brown and black coats, I would use it on white areas only.

To help whiten those white areas in your dog's coat, try using Nolvasan Solution as a rinse after your dog's bath. It comes in a concentrated form. Dilute to five tablespoons per gallon to make a light blue solution. After shampooing, pour on liberally. Wait one minute and then rinse off. It has a natural bleaching agent, is harmless to a dog's coat and skin and repeated uses help whiten

even yellowed, stained areas. It will not affect colored areas of the coat (I've used this on black, brown and blue merle coats). It is a disinfectant/virucidal wipe used by veterinarians to clean surgical tables and may be obtained from your vet. It's also excellent to use as a kennel disinfectant. (Nolvasan also makes a shampoo but the whitening effects do not seem to be in it.)

To make your dog's white whiter, I have tried almost everything and finally found something that really works. The little blue jug is Dynamo. It is highly concentrated, but I use it full-strength on the white areas. Rub, rinse and repeat. It is time-consuming to rinse out so I dilute it to bathe the rest of the body. It works.

To whiten the yellow-stained ruff and collar on your dog who has a white ruff and collar, mix a 50:50 ratio of 3 percent peroxide and water. Moisten stained areas with the mixture, leave on for 5 to 10 minutes or longer (depending on the degree of the stain). Shampoo in the usual way. It will not harm the coat.

We have found a terrific shampoo which whitens whites and brightens colors all in one step. It's called Orvus. It is a highly concentrated paste and is sold at most farm-and-feed stores. Horse owners found it long ago.

When dogs lick or chew their feet, the white hair often turns pink or rusty looking. To stop the chewing and allow the feet to get pretty and white again, apply Dr. Scholl's Athlete's Foot Spray liberally once a day.

Misc.

We moved to West Germany. We were here less than two months when our six-month-old puppy decided that grabbing on to our older dog's tail and yanking on it for long periods of time would be great fun. Since I didn't know how to say "Bitter Apple" in German, I was at a loss as to what to do. Finally an idea came to me. The juice from a jar of jalapeno peppers applied liberally to our older dog's tail put a stop to the problem in short order.

Health

The 24/7 Animal Poison Control Center's phone number is 800-213-6680. If you're calling from the Caribbean or US Virgin Islands for poisoning assistance 24/7, you may call them (toll-free) at 877-416-7319. Other Caribbean islands may reach them at (011)-1-952-853-1716.

Arthritis

«»Editor's note: the following information (covering "Arthritis") is not in alphabetical sequence and has been divided into separate paragraphs only for easier reading. «»

· If your dog is slowly being crippled with arthritis, the following information explains the various forms of arthritis. Arthritis, in virtually all of its forms, is acknowledged to be a degenerative disease. Many clinical nutritional experts would concur that nearly all degenerative diseases originate from problems in the diet or in digestive disorders. The three most common forms of arthritis are: 1) osteoarthritis, 2) gouty arthritis and 3) rheumatoid arthritis. The nutritional treatments for osteoarthritis and gouty arthritis are fairly well-known whereas rheumatoid arthritis treatment is much more complex and is not well-established. Check with your vet to determine which form of arthritis your dog has and listen to his or her opinion as to what is occurring with your dog.

Osteoarthritis (OA) —

· In comparing these three forms of arthritis, osteoarthritis is the most common and generally occurs due to loss of bone. The cause may be inadequate mineral intake or a digestive or immune function disorder as well. Typically, inflammation of the joint and arthritic deformities may be seen, and there will be substantial bone loss and low levels of ionized calcium in the blood. This degenerative form of arthritis, caused by digestive disorders, is usually seen as a dog grows older...just as in humans, because their capacity to produce digestive enzymes and, in particular, stomach acid (hydrochloric acid and pepsin) diminishes dramatically. If dogs continue on a relatively high-protein diet and eat substantially more protein than needed (two to four times bodily requirements), a process occurs whereby protein combines with calcium in the blood and has the effect of drawing calcium from the bone. Usually increasing dietary calcium in young animals resolves such problems, but this is not really the answer. Increasing dietary calcium often will not resolve the problem completely, especially in older dogs and is not the best long-term solution. The solution is: 1) control the total amount of protein and be sure that the dose of protein is reasonable for your dog (probably less than 20 percent of the total food intake which does not cause weight gain); 2) provide your dog with adequate amounts of calcium, phosphorus, magnesium, Vitamin D and copper and 3) be sure your dog has adequate digestive enzymes, in particular, hydrochloric acid and pepsin.

· If you dog has been on dog food which contained virtually no magnesium, he might then have experienced bone spurs as a consequence. It is difficult for any one brand of dog food (a single source) to provide all the nutrients your dog requires for his best health throughout his life. Calcium, phosphorus, magnesium, Vitamin D and copper are essential for good calcium metabolism. You may be sure your dog has all the nutrients required for good calcium metabolism by feeding him two to three ounces of liver once a week (in order to provide adequate copper and by making sure he receives enough magnesium and calcium). A good amino acid chelated multiple mineral for humans (containing calcium and magnesium—with 50 to 70 percent as much magnesium as calcium) which has been dose-adjusted to your dog's size should be given. To dose-adjust for a typical medium-size dog (weighing about 20 pounds), multiply your dog's weight by five. This translates the dog to a comparable human size. Typical supplements for humans are designed for a 158-pound person. For example, if a multiple mineral supplement recommends six tablets per day, use four tablets per day of that supplement for your dog's weight (20 pounds dog weight x 5 = 100 pounds). Multiply the total pounds by the total supplements needed (100 pounds x 6 supplements = 600). Divide the total supplements' figure by its designed human weight (600 divided by 158 pounds = 3.8 supplements for your dog who weighs about 20 pounds or four supplements per day).

· If your dog's condition is complicated by bone (calcium) spurs, magnesium orotate may be used to dissolve these spurs provided his liver function is good. Clinical experience has proven this to be an extremely effective therapy. Typical use is 210 mg. or more per day of magnesium orotate for 158-pound person for six to 12 months. Then ordinary magnesium may be used.

· By using a good multiple mineral supplement and by controlling the total amount of protein (so it is not excessive for your dog's body size) one may gain control of osteoarthritis in many situations. In some instances, a digestant will be necessary and in other situations immune function support may also be required. If you suspect your dog falls into this group, you will need help to safely and effectively treat his condition.

Gouty Arthritis (GA) —

· Gouty arthritis is triggered by elevated levels of uric acid. Uric acid may cause painful swelling and stiffness of the joints. Actual dagger-shaped uric acid crystals lodge at the joints causing pain, swelling and inflammation. This may be caused by an error in metabolism, but most often it is a degenerative disease which occurs as a result of very high levels of organ or glandular meats or other high-purine-based proteins fed to the dog in large quantities. Some examples of these are sardines, salmon, organ or glandular meats or just red meat, in general.

· To treat gouty arthritic symptoms, the first goal would be to substantially reduce red meats (especially organ or glandular meats) along with any other sources of purine-based proteins. Even cheeses should be kept to the very minimum. To bring down uric acid, the appropriate supplementation is a very high dose of folic acid. In a medium-size dog who weighs about 20 pounds (treating the dog as approximately a 100-pound human), 5 mg. to even 10 mg. (not mcg.) folic acid have been demonstrated to be fairly effective when in conjunction with the reduction of the purine-based proteins in the dog's food. More complex therapies are also available in very stubborn situations.

Rheumatoid Arthritis (RA) —

· This form of arthritis (rheumatoid arthritis) is the most complex. Generally speaking, the blood test conducted by your veterinarian will show a positive reading for the RA factor in the blood if rheumatoid arthritis is present. RA causes the destruction of the protective sheathing around the joints (the material which keeps bone from rubbing on bone). The RA factor seems to literally destroy this sheathing and thereby causing tremendous pain and inflammation of the joints. Medical therapies have proven reasonably ineffective until 1971 when it was shown that histidine (an isolated free-form amino acid) could be used to stop the RA factor from attacking the bone sheathing. An effective dose for a 158-pound person was found to be approximately three grams per day, so you may adjust the dose to fit your medium-size dog who weighs about 20 pounds. About two grams per day would be administered to a 20-pound dog to stop the destruction of the bone sheathing until the RA factor in the blood may be cleared.

· Rheumatoid arthritis may be similar to an allergic process. Dogs showing the RA factor may have induced this disease condition by consuming one particular brand of dog food over a very long period of time. Try removing that single-source food and switching dog foods. Be sure that the major protein source is different in the new dog food.

· It may be extremely effective to treat RA by stimulating the immune function. Many times a dog may have low thyroid output. Stimulation of the immune function and the thyroid (with nutrients, not hormones) is often enough to clear the RA factor from the blood. Once the RA factor is cleared from the blood, histidine therapy may be discontinued.

• You should check for rheumatoid arthritis on a regular basis. If RA is permitted to continue for even one or two years, progressive damage to the bone sheathing occurs. This may leave your dog crippled even after the RA factor has been cleared from his blood. It is very important to monitor your dog on a regular basis. The test for RA is a very simple blood test which your veterinarian can run for you.

Drugs For Treating Arthritis —

• Most drugs used in the control of arthritis merely mask the pain but they do not deal with the root cause. The American Medical Association's articles, relative to osteoarthritis, urge the use of nutritional therapies as the treatment of choice. Drugs used in osteoarthritis merely kill pain and are hard on the liver. Relative to rheumatoid arthritis, critical health care approaches have seemed to ignore the use and importance of histidine (in particular, the fact that histidine halts the destruction of the bone sheathing) despite New York State University's findings and publications in *Medical World News* in January 1971 and also in other publications. Drugs used to control uric acid may sometimes cause other side effects on the kidneys and the rest of the body. The logical treatment for any form of arthritis would seem to be to stop the disease at its root cause which is faulty nutrition and/or faulty enzymatic function. The ideal treatment should deal with the root cause without creating any side effects, without making another part of the body pay and without masking the disease while it continues to progress.

Breathing Difficulties In Newborns

From a nutritional standpoint when a newborn encounters difficulties with breathing, one capsule of 200 IU d-Alpha tocopheryl succinate (a form of Vitamin E) may be most helpful. It is best administered in this form because it is easier for a newborn to absorb. Crush a tablet or empty the powder from capsule and place it under his tongue and hold it there as long as possible. If relief does not follow, one to two Vitamin B6 (100 mg. tablets) may be crushed and placed under the tongue and held there for a moment. Many times just this bit of help may make a difference between the life and death of your puppy.

If your newborn puppy is gasping and can barely breathe, first make sure that there is no physical obstruction to his breathing. Refer to the book *Sheltie Talk* (re: shaking fluid out of breathing passageways). In addition to using a breast pump to suck out any fluid from the puppy's breathing passageways, you may use an ear syringe or a baby aspirator.

Sometimes, by pushing a small catheter tube down the newborn's throat you may dislodge mucous from the puppy's wind pipe.

Care During Cold Temperatures

«» Editor's note: since almost all of the following hints contained a warning, the previously-included italics for those warnings were removed.«»

Antifreeze (which is put into a car during colder weather) may be fatal to a dog and other pets even in small amounts. Any pet who has ingested antifreeze will need immediate emergency care. Symptoms of antifreeze poisoning include: drunk-like behavior, vomiting, excessive urination, drinking and depression. Pets may

appear to recover within a few hours, but the antifreeze will continue to poison their systems and is often fatal.

Dogs and other pets, like people, are vulnerable to hypothermia and frostbite. Immediately take your pet to a vet if he is shivering, disoriented and lethargic or if his hair is puffed out and standing on end. Frostbite may turn his skin bright red, pale or black. Skin at tips of his ears and on his extremities (including reproductive organs) are particularly at risk.

Dogs kept outdoors should have a dry, draft-free dog house which is large enough for the dog to both sit and lie down in comfort but still small enough to maintain his body heat inside the dog house. The floor should be a few inches off the ground and covered with cedar shavings or straw. The house should face away from wind and the doorway should be covered with waterproof burlap or heavy plastic.

Dogs, outdoor cats and wildlife often will sleep under hoods of cars when it's cold. Bang on the hood of your car before starting the car to give that animal a chance to escape.

Dogs who are shivering uncontrollably or who have blue tongues could be experiencing hypothermia. Don't bathe this dog since a warm bath may make the dog lose more body heat and a hot bath could cause the dog to go into shock. Instead, take as many towels and blankets as you possibly can and wrap them around the dog. Position the dog near a heat vent or a small light bulb. If this dog doesn't return to normal within five minutes, call the vet or emergency pet clinic.

Don't ever leave any pet unattended in a car. The vehicle may act like a refrigerator by holding in the cold and freezing your pet to death.

During an outing to the beach or lake (either during chilly or hot weather), make sure that hypothermia doesn't occur in your dog. Bring lots of towels that you wrap him in and remove any excess cold water. This will warm him up quicker and it also helps in removing any sand and salt water from his fur so he won't be in danger of shaking off on someone else.

If you think that your dog has hypothermia, take the following actions immediately. Wrap your dog in towels and blankets which have been warmed by the sun or by having been put into a warm clothes dryer. Bring extra fresh water in bottles and leave them out in the sun as this warm water may be applied to your dog to bring his body's temperature back up. If your dog has still not stopped shivering and has continued lethargy, take him to the nearest vet.

Keep your dog leashed when he's in the snow, and make sure he has an ID tag since dogs may lose scents in snow and then become lost.

Keep your dog's coat longer for warmth. If you have a short-haired pet, get a coat or sweater with a high collar or turtleneck which covers him from the base of his tail to his belly.

Puppies may be difficult to housebreak during winter. If weather bothers a puppy, try paper training indoors.

Make sure your dog has a warm place to sleep (away from drafts and, if possible, off the floor).

Use pet-friendly versions of products which melt the ice on steps, driveways and sidewalks. Products such as Safe Paw Ice Melter and Safe-T-Pet Ice Melt avoid chemicals which irritate dogs' paws and their stomachs, if they lick their paws. These pet-friendly products are usually colored so you can also see where you've sprinkled them.

Use plastic food and water bowls instead of metal because

your cat's tongue may stick and freeze to metal when it's below freezing and you're feeding your cat outdoors.

Care During Hot Temperatures

«» Editor's note: since almost all of the following hints contained a warning, the previously-included italics for those warnings were removed.«»

Carry a spray bottle containing cool water (for spraying your dog). This will cool him down and reduce his temperature.

During an outing to the beach or lake (either during hot or chilly weather), make sure that hypothermia doesn't occur to your dog even though the outside temperature is hot. Bring lots of towels that you wrap him in and remove any excess cold water. This will warm him up quicker and it also helps in removing any sand and salt water from his fur so he won't be in danger of shaking off on someone else.

During travel, being confined in a crate or animal carrier for long periods of time during the hottest months of the year is potentially dangerous for your pet and may lead to dehydration and heatstroke. In addition, certain breeds such as brachycephalic (snub-nosed or flat-faced) dogs and cats are susceptible to pulmonary distress when temperatures are extreme.

Heat stroke at the beach may be avoided by providing lots of fresh, cool water so your dog may drink at any time.

Heat stroke may be prevented during a hot day. Observe how your dog is acting since he could suffer from either heat stroke or hyperthermia.

Here are some signs of heat stroke in a dog: rapid panting, bright red tongue, thick, sticky saliva, weakness, vomiting and/or diarrhea, lethargy, shivering, muscle stiffness, difficulty breathing, fixed and/or dilated pupils.

If you think that your dog has hypothermia (even though it's a hot day) while you're at the beach, take the following actions immediately. Wrap your dog in towels and blankets which have been warmed by the sun. Bring extra fresh water in bottles and leave them out in the sun as this warm water may be applied to your dog to bring his body's temperature back up. If your dog has still not stopped shivering and has continued lethargy, take him to the nearest vet.

If you think that your dog might be exhibiting signs of heat stroke during a hot day, move him into the shade and apply cool (not cold) water all over his body. This will gradually lower his body's temperature. Apply ice packs or cool towels to your dog's head, neck and chest only. Allow your dog to drink small amounts of cool water or to lick ice cubes. Take him to the nearest vet.

I have found that giving my dogs ice cubes (from the time they are young) is something my dogs seem to relish since they act as though the ice cubes are pieces of steak. A big plus is that these ice cubes come in handy when any dog is going through a period of dehydration (vomiting, diarrhea, etc.) because he will still chomp down the ice cubes. In this situation, we freeze Pedialyte to help stabilize the dog's system. The only down side is that you have a lot of company when you open the freezer.

It might be best to leave your dog at home when going to large outdoor events, parties and/or gatherings. A large crowd may become overwhelming to your dog. This type of outing increases the opportunity for injury, dehydration and exhaustion. Most likely, there will probably be a lot of unhealthy or even toxic food and trash on the ground which your dog might try to eat. Also, remember that fireworks and other loud noises may frighten your dog into running away and/or become injured. If you do bring your dog to outdoor events, keep him on a short leash and always be on watch for any potential dangers.

Keep fresh water with you when you go to the beach so you may wash off the sand and salt water which may cause irritation and dry out his sensitive pads.

Never leave your dog in the car unattended. Despite the many warnings about this, each summer brings numerous accounts of dogs who become sick or even die of heat stroke because they were left inside a car. Even though it doesn't seem that hot outside, the temperature inside the car may rise to dangerous levels within minutes. If you absolutely must bring your dog with you on errands, make sure you bring another person who will stay in the running, air-conditioned car with your dog, otherwise, leave your dog at home.

Stay near your dog when playing or swimming in a pool, lake, river or ocean. Contrary to common belief, not all dogs are skilled swimmers. Also, remember that even the most experienced swimmer may become a victim of an undertow, jellyfish or other hazard.

Steer clear of long walks and strenuous exercise on hot, sunny days to avoid prolonged sun exposure. Not only is there a risk of heat stroke, dogs may get sunburned. Consider sunscreen for your dog. If you are planning to spend time outdoors with your dog, find a shady spot and provide plenty of fresh, cool water. Try to take leisurely walks during the cooler times of the day (like during the morning or evening hours). Remember to protect your dog's feet from getting scorched from walking on a hot pavement or hot sand

Summer heat is very dangerous to a dog locked in a car, however this danger is actually present all year. A well-known champion sire and his daughter died tragically some years ago because the owners of these two dogs had left them locked in their car. Sadly, the owners did not realize that their brand-new car was airtight until it was too late. Avoid another such tragedy. If you must leave your dog in the car, always leave a window or vent open even during the winter. Sometimes leaving a window open isn't even enough to keep your dog from suffering or dying during those hot days. It's much safer to have one person stay inside the car because having someone with your dog will discourage anyone from stealing a dog who has been left alone in a car.

When at the beach, do not let your dog drink that salt water since salt water may cause dehydration, vomiting and diarrhea. Water in lakes, ponds and rivers may contain parasites and bacteria which may infect your dog. Always provide your dog with plenty of fresh, clean water for drinking which you've brought from home.

When going to the beach or a lake, you can't guarantee that you will have access to a shady area so take an umbrella so your dog may cool off under that shady covering.

Care During Illness and Injury

«» Editor's note: since almost all of the following hints contained a warning, the previously-included italics for those warnings were removed.«»

Before putting an ill or aged dog to bed, fluff a towel in the dryer and place it in the bed to make a cozy sleeping area.

Due to a family emergency, I was required to transport my

litter of very small (4 to 5 ounces) puppies. Since I was very concerned about them getting chilled (as it was cold and damp outside), I prewarmed a small ice chest and put the puppies in and covered them only with a towel. Do not put the lid on the ice chest as the puppies may suffocate. They stayed warm and cozy and the handle made carrying them easy.

If you need to make your pet vomit for some reason, put 1/2 to 1 teaspoon of salt on the back of his tongue and hold his mouth closed for a few seconds.

I have found that giving my dogs ice cubes (from the time they are young) is something my dogs seem to relish since they act as though the ice cubes are pieces of steak. A big plus is that these ice cubes come in handy when any dog is going through a period of dehydration (vomiting, diarrhea, etc.) because he will still chomp down the ice cubes. In this situation, we freeze Pedialyte to help stabilize the dog's system. The only down side is that you have a lot of company when you open the freezer.

To check your pet's pulse, feel on the inside of his back thigh where the leg joins the body. Normal for dogs is 70-150 beats a minute. Normal for cats is 110-170 beats a minute.

To keep our dog from biting at a wound, we used a people cervical collar instead of an Elizabethan collar. Since it was soft and pliable (foam rubber), it was more comfortable and allowed him to sleep. Also, it did not restrict his vision.

We had a litter that appeared healthy, however at six days of age one of the pups developed a rattle in his throat. As I am always leery of any medication for such a young, otherwise healthy puppy, I decided to try something a friend of mine had used on her canaries when they got pneumonia. She suggested filling a bowl with steaming water from the tap into which a glob of Vicks VapoRub had been placed. Let the bowl fill with rising steam while holding the pup upright over the sink so that the steam and the Vicks go into his nose and thus into his lungs. (It will really do wonders for your sinuses, too.) This pup would start to cry out and wriggle uncomfortably so I knew it was reaching him. Do this for about five to ten minutes several times a day to start, decreasing as needed. Within two to three days, I noticed a vast improvement in his condition. I repeated this on and off (for at least a week) before he stopped rattling altogether. No medication was necessary. He was able to eat on his own and grew into a healthy, normal youngster with no side effects.

Car Sickness

Common signs of car sickness in your pet are: inactivity, restlessness, excessive yawning, whining, hyper-salivation (drooling) and vomiting. These symptoms will usually go away shortly after the vehicle stops.

Does your dog have incurable car sickness? Try placing an inexpensive static strip under the car.

For anyone who has a problem with drooling puppies and young adults and if you want to show those puppies at matches or point shows, you don't want to give them any tranquilizers, Dramamine or other remedies because then they won't want to show. I have tried everything to prevent them from drooling—to no avail. In order to keep them from getting themselves and the other puppies in the crate with them wet (because saliva takes forever to dry), I take old terry T-shirts and cut the arms out. The arm fits over the head and acts like a barber's bib. It catches and absorbs the saliva and keeps each puppy dry. Cut the length to reach to the pastern so the puppy may move around without stepping on the

bib. Keep the bib on when you get to the match as it takes them a few minutes to realize they aren't moving anymore. Then remove the bib and you'll have a dry puppy.

Here are some of the most common reasons for car sickness in puppies and dogs: 1) their ear structures used for balance aren't fully developed in puppies which may cause motion sickness, however, many dogs will outgrow car sickness; 2) stress may also add to travel sickness (for example, if your dog has only been in the car to go to the vet, he may make himself sick from the worry and apprehension from previously seeing the vet); or 3) if your dog has been nauseous the first few times when traveling in the car as a puppy, he may have conditioned himself to view car travel as a time when he will become sick.

Holistic treatments are an option for a dog owners to try. Some common holistic choices are: 1) ginger may be used for nausea (ginger snap cookies or ginger pills should be given at least 30 minutes before travel begins); 2) peppermint, chamomile and horehound naturally help calm the stomach of your pup; 3) massage helps to relax your pet before traveling. Before using any of these suggestions, discuss these holistic remedies with your veterinarian to make sure your dog is healthy, the dosage is correct and that the treatment won't harm your dog.

If your dog always gets carsick, fresh ginger root (Nature's Way) may be the answer. Give your medium-sized dog one capsule ten minutes before beginning each ride and continue every hour or when salivating begins.

I had a pup who became carsick each time he rode in a vehicle. I remembered that whenever I felt sick I would eat saltine crackers. Next time I took him for a ride, I gave him two saltine crackers before we left and small pieces of animal cookies on the way. Also, before we started the return trip, I gave him another cracker. Now when we go on a trip, there are no accidents and he looks forward to riding and getting his treats. He now gets a cracker before we go and before we return home and nothing in between. You could probably use the unsalted variety of cracker to cut down on the intake of salt.

Pack your dog's own food and water to avoid problems on a trip because some animal's stomachs will become upset with new food and/or water.

Reconditioning will sometimes help your dog relax in the car. This is needed if your dog associates riding in the car with something bad (like getting carsick or being taken to the vet). Reconditioning requires patience for both you and your dog. Here are some suggestions: 1) try putting your dog in a different vehicle because he may associate your vehicle with unpleasant memories; 2) take short car trips to places your dog enjoys; 3) begin reconditioning by sitting in the car with your dog with the engine off and do that for a few days; 4) when he seems comfortable with the car engine being off, sit in the car with the car idling; 5) after doing that, take a ride around the block; 6) then try a longer trip; 7) provide treats to make the car a fun place for your dog; and 8) bring along a special toy that he may only play with while he's in the car.

There are times when medications are necessary to help your dog when traveling. Some over-the-counter and prescribed medications are: 1) anti-nausea drugs to reduce vomiting; 2) anti-histamines to lessen motion sickness, reduce drooling and help him to be calm; 3) phenothiazine and related drugs to reduce vomiting and help to sedate. Always discuss any medications with your veterinarian before using (to make sure your dog is healthy, the dosage is correct and that the medication won't harm your dog).

Try these nine following treatments to help prevent car sickness for your puppy or dog: 1) face your dog forward in the vehicle because if your dog is facing forward he will see less movement and looking out of a side window causes objects to blur which may then cause or compound his motion sickness; 2) avoid letting your dog travel in the farthest backseat because that is where the most movement will occur; 3) opening the windows in the car (just a little bit) may help reduce air pressure inside the vehicle and will provide better ventilation; 4) don't give your puppy or dog any food for a few hours before getting into the car; 5) put him in a travel crate since, sometimes, this helps to keep him from looking outside too much and this will keep any unfortunate drool or vomit within his crate; 6) keep it cool in the vehicle because a hot, stuffy ride may make his car sickness worse; 7) toys may help distract and entertain your dog; 8) take frequent potty breaks; and 9) exercise your dog before getting into the car.

Ear Care and Ear Health

Consult a veterinarian immediately if your dog exhibits any of these conditions: 1) tilting, shaking, rubbing or scratching his head and ears more than usual; 2) hair loss around the ears as the result of excessive scratching; 3) excessive oily or waxy debris in the ear canal; 4) black debris that looks like coffee grounds in the ear; 5) discharge of any kind; 6) redness or inflammation; 7) foul-smelling ears; or 8) soreness to the touch.

Debris which looks like coffee grinds in a dog's ear usually indicates that he has ear mites. These microscopic parasites cause severe itching and require medical treatment. A vet will usually treat the infestation with an insecticidal ointment for at least ten days.

I once had a dog's ear split like a "V" by a cat, and the vet said he could not stitch it and it would not heal. I went home, clipped hair inside and out to the skin and applied solid tape on one side and butterfly tape on the other side in order to allow the air in. (Ask any nurse to show you the butterfly.) When the tape fell off, the ear was healed and when the hair came in, it was all normal.

Johnson's Baby Oil is good for cleaning inside your dog's ears. It may also be applied to small puppies who may have picked up fleas. The oil will be totally absorbed by the coat in a day or so and may be used on the head and face.

To clean a waxy or dirty ear: 1) dampen a cotton ball with a non-irritating ear cleanser (available in pet supply stores and/or ask your veterinarian to recommend one), and *do not use alcohol, especially in a red and inflamed ear since alcohol may cause severe irritation*; 2) wrap the cotton ball around your finger and insert your finger into the dog's ear canal and wipe, and *do not use cotton swabs because they could cause damage if used incorrectly*; 3) work from the inside out and if the ear is extremely dirty you may need more than one cotton ball; 4) clean the folds, crevices and the inside the ear flap; 5) wipe thoroughly but gently; and 6) ask your vet what would be best for your dog.

To keep your dog's ears clean, odor-free and healthy: 1) place your dog on a grooming table or have him lie his head in your lap (if the dog has floppy ears, fold back the flaps since cropped or naturally erect ears are easily visible); 2) look carefully to see if your dog's ears are pink because redness could be a sign of infection or inflammation; 3) check both ears for something in one ear but not the other (for example: a discharge, dirt or other particles or even objects...as even a tiny foxtail bristle may cause major discomfort); 4) check for excessive amount or change in color or

consistency in earwax; 5) smell each ear and if the ears have a strong odor or unusual smell; or 6) if your normally cooperative dog whines or pulls away when you touch his ears, health problems such as infection or allergies may be to blame.

You may use hydrogen peroxide to remove a foreign object from deep in your dog's ear providing you *first check with you vet to make sure the hydrogen peroxide is appropriate. Also, check with your vet for the correct percentage of hydrogen peroxide for this purpose.* Even foxtails may be bubbled out. You may use an ear syringe or just gently pour the peroxide right from the bottle into the ear. Hold the dog's head, fill the ear with peroxide and then hold the base of the ear between your fingers and gently move it about. The peroxide will begin to bubble to the surface bringing the object with it. You may need to repeat the process several times to get results.

Your dog's ears may be washed out with a drop of vinegar in water. Mix in a small bottle. This is the same thing many vets use except it doesn't have any coloring.

Epilepsy

«»Editor's note: the following information (covering "Epilepsy") is not in alphabetical sequence and has been divided into separate paragraphs only for easier reading. «»

· If your dog has epilepsy, the following information may offer valuable nutritional insight. In addition to keeping your dog on a healthy diet, try adding lecithin to his food. Two tablespoons of lecithin granules added to his food daily would be needed for the rest of his life.

· Additionally, research suggests seizures may be prevented with the addition of a free-form amino acid know as taurine. Five hundred to 750 mgs. of taurine (as a powder) should also be given daily. After 28 days of this treatment, the dog should be seizure-free (if it is going to work). If your dog is old and has had these seizures for many years, chances are not as good as they would be for a young dog who may recover and then be symptom-free for life (without any need for medication).

· The problem with epileptic seizures in dogs may well have increased and entered into many breeding lines which previously had no such history of epilepsy. This may have occurred simply because egg protein (lactoalbumin) has become expensive and, therefore, is no longer being included...even in the best-quality dog foods. Eggs are the only rich source of taurine which might be used in dog food. A good preventative measure would be to give your medium-size dog (approximately weighing 20 pounds) an egg three or four times each week. Be sure to cook the egg white as the raw egg white contains avidin. Avidin destroys biotin in the bowels which could then trigger loss of coat. Cooking destroys the avidin.

· More may be done, but it should be carefully supervised. Check with a nutritional expert.

Equipment

A first aid kit should include: a pet first aid book, nylon leash, a muslin sling bandage, muzzle or strips of cloth to prevent biting (as long as pet is not vomiting, choking, coughing or otherwise having difficulty breathing), adhesive tape, antiseptic wipes, bandages, scissors, hydrogen peroxide, tongue depressor, tweezers, antibiotic ointment, alcohol prep pads, latex gloves, rectal thermometer, eye wash solution, instant cold pack, rescue blanket, diphenhydramine (abbreviated DPH, sometimes DHM—Benadryl) if approved by a veterinarian for allergic reactions (a vet must specify correct dosage for your pet's size). Also include a list of emergency phone numbers including those for your pet's veterinarian, an after hour's emergency veterinary hospital phone number and the National Animal Poison Control Center (1-888-426-4435). It's also a good idea to include the following items for each pet: copies of vaccine records, medical records and current photos of your pet.

An easy way to keep from forgetting to give medications is to keep each medication in a little crate watering cup. I use the cups designed for birds (plastic with wire holders) as the wires may be bent to accommodate any crate or pen. Attach the cup to the outside of the crate or pen. This way the pills are always handy and you can't forget them since they're right under your nose. Naturally, this is for indoor use only. It's perfect for visiting bitches' heartworm medication, vitamins, etc., and for keeping vitamins handy in the maternity ward.

A quick, easy way to take your dog's temperature is to use one of those new digital thermometers. You don't have to "shake it down." Instead, just press the button to turn it on and in it goes (we use one drop of K-Y jelly on the tip). About one minute later, it beeps and you're done. They're made of plastic and are almost unbreakable (a blessing which cuts down time on an unpleasant chore).

Clean old socks may be handy covers for wounds on a dog's legs or paws. They are flexible, comfortable and keep dirt off the bandages and the wound. When other bandages are removed, a sock may keep dirt off and help in keeping the dog from prematurely removing any stitches, yet the sock covering allows air to help heal the wound.

Due to a family emergency, I was required to transport my litter of very small (4 to 5 ounces) puppies. Since I was very concerned about them getting chilled (as it was cold and damp outside), I prewarmed a small ice chest and put the puppies in and covered them only with a towel. *Do not put the lid on the ice chest as the puppies may suffocate.* They stayed warm and cozy and the handle made carrying them easy.

End the struggle of administering medicines by using a curved syringe (all plastic) which you may get from your friendly oral surgeon. It is large and has a hooked end which fits in the space between the dog's teeth. The syringe should be pointed towards the dog's throat. Simply lift your dog's lip (without opening his mouth) and inject medication between his teeth.

If you need to bandage your dog's foot, look for a tubular knit gauze called Surgitube. Use the number 2 size (for large fingers and toes) as this size just fits a medium-sized dog's paw. Follow the package directions to put it on, and then take 10" to 12" of tape and wrap it around the dog's pastern making sure it contacts both layers of the bandage. On rear feet, you'll need to tape it to the hair, but this isn't necessary on the front feet. Plastic nurser refill bags may be taped over the bandage when the dog goes outdoors.

If your dog has hurt his foot, medicate and/or bandage it. Then cut the toe out of an old pair of hose or socks. Slip the sock over the foot and tape it snugly around the leg. It works well to protect the bandage and keeps the foot clean.

If you've never been confronted with a request from your vet to bring him a urine specimen from your dog, you've missed a rare experience. I won't go into my several abortive attempts to collect specimens but necessity forced me to be inventive. So if you ever face this task, here are some ideas that worked for me: 1) for a bitch—find a narrow, shallow container (such as the lid to an old butter dish or the narrow plastic foam container used in grocery stores). With wire cutters, cut the top off of a wire coat hanger and then straighten the hanger out. Bend one end of the hanger to make a holder for your container. Bend the other end into a loop for you to hold in your hand. With your collection device assembled, put the dog on lead and take her for a walk. Stay as near to her as possible so you don't have to make any sudden moves at a crucial time. When she starts to squat, calmly slip the container between her hind legs from the rear and voile...you've got it...before she even knew what was happening. Caution: don't get so excited over your success that you spill the container! Go straight back home and transfer the contents into a small, clean bottle with a lid. 2) for a dog (first technique)—again using a wire coat hanger, cut the top off and bend one end into a loop to hold in your hand. Bend the other end into another loop slightly smaller than the top of a styrofoam cup. Put the cup in the loop and push it down so that it fits securely. Then with the dog on lead, head for a clump of grass. Stay as close to his side as possible and make sure that you and the clump are on the same side. When he starts to lift his leg, quickly but calmly, position the cup under him at an angle so that he hits it, not the clump. If you're lucky, that will do it. If you're not, you may have a problem because now he's wise to what you're doing and next time he'll choose the clump, and it'll be on the other side of you and you'll never get to that side in time to do your thing. If that happens, go to this second technique for a dog—using the same styrofoam cup that you were unsuccessful with in the first technique, punch a small hole (with a turkey skewer or meat fork tine) in each side of the top (about 1/4 of an inch from the edge). Hopefully, you have one of those stretchy ties that stores use on their gift boxes because that works best, but if you don't have one, use a very narrow elastic. Cut the elastic into two pieces (the length of each being determined by the size of your dog's middle). Tie a knot in one end of each piece. Thread the pieces from the inside out through the holes in the cup (one on each side). Put the dog on lead, position the cup so that it covers his equipment, bring the elastic around each side of him and tie the apparatus securely by making a bow or knot on top of his back. Then head for a bush. He'll react instinctively and if you've positioned the cup properly, the cup will receive it instead of the bush. The instant it's over, go quickly to him and with one hand and grab the cup and with the other hand. Untie the bow (hold the lead in your teeth, if necessary). Carefully carry your trophy home and transfer the contents to a bottle (same as for bitches). Pat yourself on the back and take two aspirin and a nap until it's time to go to the vet to proudly present him with the hard-earned fruits of your labor.

I made a trip to the vet and asked him for a clean-out shot (oxytocin) for a bitch who was having her litter within a couple of days. The vet reminded me that the shot should be kept cold. Since I wasn't going directly home, I decided I better do some fast thinking about a way to keep it cool. I pulled into a Burger King and (along with my food order) asked for a small cup filled with ice and a lid. I placed the syringe (covered-needle-end first) into the cup through the straw hole. I made sure the barrel part of the syringe was not in the ice. (The cup should be a little more than halfway full of ice.) The cold air between the ice and the lid made a nice refrigerated area and when I reached home, the syringe was just as cool as when it was handed to me.

I save the plastic containers from my 35 mm film and other similar containers (such as empty and clean prescription bottles) and use them for liquid wormers when sending a puppy to its new home and for many other uses.

Necessity is the "mother of invention." At times, we all have our little problems and they may not necessarily warrant an immediate visit to the vet, but they do call for watchful and supportive treatment. Sometimes we find our dogs limping, down on pasterns, etc. I wanted to create a lightweight support for a puppy's leg and found a stock household item that would serve the purpose: the cardboard tube inside toilet paper. It works great as a temporary splint. Cut through the tube lengthwise from end to end. Measure the length of the leg you need to support and cut the tube to that length. Wrap the tube around the area of the leg needing support until it is snug but not too tight. Tape the ends down with surgical tape at top and bottom (partially sticking the tape to the hair on the leg) and once or twice around the middle. It is lightweight and I found that my puppy adjusted to it quickly. Of course, any chronic lameness should be checked by the vet.

One of my dogs sprained his front leg and needed to be in a splint for a time. It was crucial that the splint stay dry but the gauze wrapping soaked up water like a sponge. What was worse, the bottom of the splint was becoming badly abraded every time my dog walked outside. Everything I used to protect the splint quickly became scuffed to shreds (which then allowed moisture to sink in). If I put too many layers of protection over the splint, the poor dog could hardly maneuver that leg. After a new splint was put on, I hit upon a rather unorthodox but highly-effective solution. For the outer, scuff-proof layer, I purchased an extra-large doggy boot (the kind used on hunting dogs to protect their pads). I brought my dog into the store and tried various sizes over the splint. For the inner layer, I needed something that was snug-fitting (to slide into the boot which was both waterproof and also have the ability to protect all the way up the leg as we have tall, dew-covered grass near our place). It also needed to be cheap and easy to use. An non-lubricated condom did the job perfectly. Whenever there was any threat of moisture attacking the splint, on went the condom (if you're careful, you can use this on the dog more than once), then the boot, otherwise just the boot went on for our excursions outside. A little cornstarch or baby powder helped both protectors slide on easily. Warning—don't use the lubricated condoms for this as I doubt it's good for the oil to be near the splint and you don't want the boot to slide off. Send someone to the drugstore who won't get embarrassed (as I did...since I am a reverend in our town) especially if the sales clerk misplaces your money, insists loudly that you haven't paid, takes your driver's license information while I'm insisting that I'm really not cheating the store or anybody else, but that instead, this purchase is really for my dog! This is a true story and I was wearing my clerical collar at the time. Needless to say, after this adventure, I will never go into that drugstore again!

The best way I've found for collecting a urine sample (which works for both males and females) is to go to your personal doctor's office and pick up a pediatric urine collection pack for babies. They have a self-stick end that you attach over the bitch's vulva or the dog's sheath. Let the dog potty (preferably when on leash) and then collect the sample bag immediately afterward. This is easier than any other method I've tried, and it prevents adding any bacteria from the catheter while at the vet's office.

The new type of surface thermometer (such as Digitemp which may be found in the medical section of any store) would be a very valuable item for a pet owner to keep handy. The surface thermometers measure the surface temperature and not the internal temperature (as rectal thermometers do). The directions for them state that the surface temperature of humans (measured on the forehead) is five degrees below internal temperature. So when used on humans, normal would be approximately 94 degrees. Since a dog's internal temperature is normally 101 degrees, this thermometer should read about 96 degrees for his surface temperature. I have checked this temperature reading on my own dogs and found it to be accurate (at a normal 96 degrees surface temperature). I measure by holding the strip against the least hairy place on the inner thigh or belly of my dog and the whole procedure takes less than 30 seconds. Used as a quick check on a bitch close to whelping, you should be able to spot the temperature drop which would produce a reading of 94 degrees or below. Although it will not measure fractional changes, it is an easy-to-use tool to check for high or low temperatures when you are watching for a large deviation from normal.

To keep our dog from biting at a wound, we used a people cervical collar instead of an Elizabethan collar. Since it was soft and pliable (foam rubber), it was more comfortable and allowed him to sleep. Also, it did not restrict his vision.

We use a syringe (with a feeding tube attached) to medicate young puppies. Medicine may be measured correctly and put directly into a puppy's stomach.

We use Baby Wipes for a multitude of reasons: cleaning a "just-used" thermometer, any area that's been stitched or to clean our dog's ears, etc. The least expensive ones contain more moisture, and you'll be surprised how many uses you'll find for them.

With the threat of so many viruses affecting our dogs and puppies, we are all finding it necessary to take extra precautions. Aside from dog classes and shows from which we potentially track home the unknown, we also have three children and all their friends generate quite a bit of foot traffic throughout our home. I keep a spray bottle of Clorox and old carpet pieces in our garage. The children spray the soles of their shoes or take them off before entering the house. They always wash their hands before playing with our puppies. I also solved the dilemma of visitors coming into our house through the front door. I purchased a rubber-backed doormat (the kind with some type of material in the middle). I spray this heavily with Clorox and ask people to please wipe their shoes on the mat.

Eyes

Do you have the problem with light rims around your dog's eyes? We put powdered Vitamin C in our dog's dinner (approximately 1000 mg.+ each day for a medium-sized dog) and the rims return to their natural dark color.

Fungal Problems

If your dog is experiencing fungal problems, try the following: 1) use the topical treatment your vet recommends in order to clear the immediate problem; 2) make sure your dog is not overeating and do not permit unsupervised free-feeding; 3) once a day and away from all other food, empty the contents of 12 acidophilus capsules in lukewarm water and give that mixture to your 20-pound dog (dogs love acidophilus and therefore it will not be a problem for him to consume), continue for one month and repeat after any use of an antibiotic; and 4) if the dog is older, is not being overfed and has no history of antibiotic therapy, it may be necessary to feed one Nutri-Dyn's Pan-5-Plus tablet (a pancreatic enzyme) before each feeding to prevent further occurrences. There are occasional stubborn cases but most should yield to this approach. More can be done but again it would be necessary to carefully supervise that therapy.

Hyperactivity

«» Editor's note: the following information (covering "Hyperactivity") is not in alphabetical sequence and has been divided into separate paragraphs only for easier reading. «»

• If your dog is hyperactive, the following information might help resolve this problem. In humans, hyperactivity is treated first by removing all foods from the person's diet which are laden with chemical additives. In a dog, this should also be the first step. If a high-quality dog food is not already in use, switch and give the new dog food about a month to work. If there is no change, add about two tablespoons of lecithin granules to your dog's food daily.

• Also, free-form amino acids (taurine and tyrosine which are both available in health food stores) should be tried in order to gain immediate control. Add 500 mgs. to 750 mgs. of taurine (as a powder daily) along with 750 mgs. to 1,000 mgs. of tyrosine daily. It will take about 21-30 days to see a change. Most dogs will respond to this approach. Once you have control for about two months, experiment by removing tyrosine first. Remember, you should not make any other dietary changes for one month to see the full effect. If the symptoms return, resume the full dose for about a month and simply try cutting it to its lowest effective level (waiting about one month before making any other changes to your dog's diet). If you are able to cut back on the tyrosine, you may also be able to reduce the taurine.

• Even more (than the above) may be done, if necessary, but it would require expert nutritional supervision.

Lack of Coat Growth

«» Editor's note: the following information (covering "Lack of Coat Growth") is not in alphabetical sequence and has been divided into separate paragraphs only for easier reading. «»

• When you've made sure your dog has no parasites and that he's not on any medication (which might hinder his coat growth) and your dog still doesn't grow coat, here are some suggestions to encourage more coat growth. There are four common problem areas in which nutrition may be safely and effectively utilized. There is actually more that nutrition can do beyond these four areas but those require very careful supervision. Basically, these four involve: 1) inadequate, unsaturated fatty acids or an imbalance between saturated and unsaturated fatty acids; 2) digestive enzyme insufficiencies; 3) imbalances of bacteria in the bowels; and/or 4) certain hormonal imbalances.

• First, often in a dog's diet one may find far too much saturated fat (which is common in many dog foods) and a serious inadequacy of unsaturated fatty acids (such as lecithin). Many times the cheapest and simplest solution is to add lecithin (keep refrigerated). For a medium-size dog (weighing approximately 20 pounds) a heaping tablespoon of lecithin granules or one large 19-grain capsule (if you can get your dog to swallow it) should be enough to correct an imbalance between saturated and unsaturated fatty acids and/or enough unsaturated fatty acids. Certain dogs will have extraordinary needs and may even require double that dose. Administering this for a month may show real improvement in coat growth.

• Second, digestive enzyme insufficiencies (at least from the standpoint of pancreatic enzymes) may be checked by your vet. Should this be the case, obtain a good pancreatic enzyme preparation (made for humans from a health food store or a good preparation from your vet). Be sure this product doesn't have acid or bile in it if it is to be used for a young dog. Dosages should parallel a human (at about five times the weight of the dog). Always give the pancreatic enzyme to your dog *before* the dog begins to eat because studies have shown this is the most effective method. Feed a tablet or two ,or grind it up and put it on top of his food so it is eaten first or crush it between two spoons (whatever is necessary to make it into a form which will be easily absorbed at the start of your dog's meal).

• Before you add supplemental pancreatic enzymes, you may want to take a close look at the food your dog is being fed to be sure that his food doesn't contain any food antagonists or any foods which require a great deal of digestive enzymes. For example: 1) foods including sugar (fructose, dextrose, sucrose, maltose, lactose, corn sweetener, corn syrup, beet sugar, etc.); 2) extraordinary amounts of fat (much more than 35 percent of all calories); or 3) almost all meat foods which might be too difficult for your dog to digest and, in fact, may create an excessive burden for your dog's digestion. Foods which are best are those which provide a healthy mixture of foods and are not a single-source food such as meat, fish or chicken, etc.

• The third area of concern is a bacterial imbalance in the bowels. Make sure there isn't an excess of simple sugar in the dog's food or an excess of red meat and/or a deficiency in fiber. All of these could lead to problems with a bowel bacterial imbalance, not to mention inadequate hydrochloric acid (see your vet) and/ or inadequate pancreatic digestive enzymes (refer to the second problem area described above). In many cases, when there is a bowel imbalance, biotin (a very important B vitamin) is destroyed and when this occurs, a dog may begin to grow coat and then lose it. Most often adding biotin to your dog's diet will correct this problem (use three 300 mcg. tablets twice daily). At the root of its loss (which also needs to be corrected) is a problem with the normal balance of bacteria in the small bowel. Check your dog's food and limit the amount of sugar to as little as possible (avoiding foods with any added sugar or forms of sugar). Be sure the dog's food contains some fiber and is not a pure meat dog food.

• Additionally, a supplement of some form of acidophilus on a regular basis would be extremely effective in helping to normalize this bowel bacterial imbalance. Acidophilus should be given a couple of hours before or after food. For example: give four or five ordinary acidophilus capsules (keep refrigerated) just before going to bed on a regular basis (for a month or so). Have your vet check for digestive insufficiency problems and if the vet has the specific tests, check on stomach hydrochloric acid to be sure that your dog is capable of digesting his food. Also, your vet may run a stool or blood test as well (to see if your dog has adequate pancreatic enzymes). Checking these out and making sure your dog's body is working correctly is extremely important to your dog's overall health (which is many times reflected by the appearance of your dog's coat).

• The final problem area (hormonal imbalances) are sometimes the most complex because science may not be at the point where we can easily interfere with most of the hormone levels of an animal and continue it safely on a long-term basis. However, there have been some spectacular results when working with dogs and humans by providing them nutritional support for their glands and/or organs which have been distressed. Distress occurs when demands on an organ or gland exceed capacity (either because the animal is immature or the gland or organ is not developed sufficiently or as a consequence of disease or faulty nutrition). When all else fails, a good bet is to try a raw glandular supplement for situations where a hormonal imbalance is possible. Often tests will not suggest this is the problem but it is still worth a try. These compounds are nutrients and are harmless except when there is an allergy to the tablet source (beef or pork) or when the dog has very high uric acid. A recommended dosage for a medium-size dog (approximately 20 pounds) would be eight tablets per day of a raw gonad product for the male or a raw ovarian product for the female. A period of six weeks at this dose level should be maintained. If there is improvement, continue this regiment thereafter but cut the dose in half. This concept works simply by ingesting the ground-up raw source of the gland or organ. The nutritional priority seems to favor that gland or organ and, in many cases, is strengthened and its function is then either normalized or enhanced, and thus many times the problem is completely cleared.

• Other hormonal imbalances affecting coat growth may also be addressed with raw glandulars. When a dog lacks coat growth, there has to be some concern for pituitary function. If serum cholesterol is high and BUN and creatinine are also high with T4 low, even low normal nutritional support for the pituitary is indicated. Raw pituitary tablets may be obtained from health food stores and one to four tablets a day may be used. Please remember that if you have a small dog, it should be treated more or less like a human at five times the dog's weight (a 20-pound dog should be treated just as a 100-pound person). Assuming this, and knowing that most dose recommendations have been designed for humans who weigh 158 pounds, you would probably want to give 2/3 of the recommended dose to a medium-size dog (weighing about 20 pounds) in using any of these glandulars.

• Please remember that whenever you are dealing with meat, and in particular with organ or glandular meats, there is always a potential problem with an elevation of uric acid. If your dog has shown a high uric acid level (see vet), raw glandular dosages should be monitored to be sure that your dog's uric acid levels stay within a safe range.

• Nutritionally speaking, large doses of folic acid is often very effective in reducing serum levels of uric acid. Dosage will depend on severity, 2 to 25 mg. (not mcg.) may be required.

• If your dog still does not grow a coat, it might be beneficial to contact a clinical nutritionist. Present what evidence you have (blood tests, stool cultures and any other veterinarian information) to see if it would be worthwhile to pursue any further investigation into the cause of your dog's coat problem.

Medications and Shots

A cure or to relieve the discomfort from a bee or a wasp sting is first remove the stinger. Then apply uncut ammonia water or a paste of baking soda and water.

A hint on administering pills or capsules: try coating the medication with a bit of butter to help it slide down the dog's throat more easily.

An easy way to keep from forgetting to give medications is to keep each medication in a little crate watering cup. I use the cups designed for birds (plastic with wire holders) as the wires may be bent to accommodate any crate or pen. Attach the cup to the outside of the crate or pen. This way the pills are always handy and you can't forget them since they're right under your nose. Naturally, this is for indoor use only. It's perfect for visiting bitches' heartworm medication, vitamins, etc., and for keeping vitamins handy in the maternity ward.

A product called Probiocin (live culture Lactobacillus) is excellent for enteritis in newborns and to fight E. Coli. Definitely use this if any antibiotic is given. Also, give it to the bitch. «»Editor's note: based on reading and research in nutritional biochemistry, an effective anti-diarrhea mixture (Bifidobacterium infantis) for puppies is Natren's Life Start (1/8 teaspoon in 1/2 ounce of lukewarm water and 1/2 teaspoon of each in 1 ounce of lukewarm water for adults and especially for the new mother).«»

Are you bottle-raising a litter or do you have a puppy who eats too much or too fast and ends up with gas and a bellyache? Since bicarbonate of soda (household baking soda) is an antacid, mix according to directions on box (1/2 teaspoon per glass of water) and give two to three eye droppers-full to medium-sized puppy for instant relief. Gas and bloating may kill those wee ones, and I have saved several by using this remedy when a dam had unknowingly come down with acid milk.

A tube of Nutri-Cal is a necessary item in my dog supplies. A tiny bit in the mouth of a weak newborn puppy is usually all that is needed to strengthen a weak puppy. Since dogs love the taste, it is also a handy tool in teaching puppies to bait. Nutri-Cal may be purchased through veterinarians and many supply catalogs.

Banana Flakes (Karena brand) are excellent for diarrhea and are easy to digest if a puppy or a baby is not eating well. «»Editor's note: based on reading and research in nutritional biochemistry, an effective anti-diarrhea mixture (Bifidobacterium infantis) for puppies is Natren's Life Start (1/8 teaspoon in 1/2 ounce of lukewarm water and 1/2 teaspoon of each in 1 ounce of lukewarm water for adults and especially for the new mother).«»

Do you have the problem with light rims around your dog's eyes? We put powdered Vitamin C in our dog's dinner (approximately 1000 mg.+ each day for a medium-sized dog) and the rims return to their natural dark color.

Dried blueberries firm up loose stools and diarrhea and are mild enough to feed even to young puppies.

End the struggle of administering medicines by using a curved syringe (all plastic) which you may get from your friendly oral surgeon. It is large and has a hooked end (which fits in the space between the dog's teeth). The syringe should be pointed towards the dog's throat. Simply lift the dog's lip (without opening his mouth) and inject medication between his teeth.

Every summer my dog would chew holes in his coat. It would sometimes happen at the back of his tail (his anal glands were removed when he was very young so that wasn't the problem) and some places along his legs, etc. Our vet called it a seasonal skin allergy possibly due to fleas and/or grass allergies. The vet prescribed some flea medications which helped. Benadryl cream on the chewed places also helped. The yard was treated to kill fleas. But my dog still sometimes chewed. Then at a show, my mother talked to someone who recommended flax seed oil (100 mg. capsules are available at health food stores). At first, one per day was given and that helped. He stopped chewing his coat. Eventually, the one per day regimen proved an overdose. Now, we just give him one every other day. So far, he has quit chewing.

For diarrhea, feed canned pumpkin (not pumpkin pie mix). This is also good for constipation.

I am sure most breeders know that the best way to get a pill "down" is to enclose it in either a soft cheese, peanut butter or soft cooked liver. Pill time will become treat time. All dogs stand and "wait" for their pills. If you forget the pill, they don't. They will beg for it since it is a special treat.

If either you or your dogs are bothered by bites from mosquitoes or fleas, hydrocortisone cream or spray may be purchased in the pharmacy sections of stores without a prescription. If the bite is no more than an hour old, one application will take away the itching and swelling in a few minutes. Older bites require several applications. This cream is also great for any contact allergy like poison oak or poison ivy. Buy several tubes and keep one in your tack box, one with camping gear and another at home.

If you feed at night and need to give medications also in the morning, put the bottle on the kitchen table (or other conspicuous place) after the evening dose has been given. Place the bottle back with your feeding supplies after the morning dose. This not only helps you remember to give the dose but also indicates whether you already have given it that day.

If you have trouble using the spoon method to get liquid medication into your dogs, try a straw instead. Gently suck the measured amount of liquid up the straw (do not inhale too fast and "medicate" yourself!) and quickly place your finger over the top to hold it. Then, tip the dog's head up, pull the corner of the lips out to form a pocket and let a small amount of liquid dribble in. Release the lips to allow swallowing. Repeat until dosage is taken. It sure is less messy and the small amounts dribbled in the mouth in this manner are almost impossible to spit out.

If you need to make your pet vomit for some reason, put 1/2 to 1 teaspoon of salt on the back of his tongue and hold his mouth closed for a few seconds.

If you've tried disguising pills in cheese but your dog eats the cheese and spits out the pill, make up several dummy cheese bits and feed them to another dog. Then let the dog who needs the medicine grab the medicated one. If he thinks the other dog might get it, he won't pause to locate the pill. After a few weeks of this, my dog had learned to swallow his pills fast and no longer needed the stimulus of a rival dog.

I give my own puppy shots, for each puppy I peel off the label from the vials and place those labels on a sheet of paper. I also include (for each puppy) the date, weight, height, worming (date and type of medication), vet's physical date and any other pertinent data or information on this sheet of paper or "data sheet." When a puppy goes to his new home, his "data sheet" goes with him. By keeping this type of record, there is no question about the type of vaccinations or times given when the new family takes him to their vet for a physical.

I made a trip to the vet and asked him for a clean-out shot (oxytocin) for a bitch who was having her litter within a couple of days. The vet reminded me that the shot should be kept cold. Since I wasn't going directly home, I decided I better do some fast thinking about a way to keep it cool. I pulled into a Burger King and (along with my food order) asked for a small cup filled with

ice and a lid. I placed the syringe (covered-needle-end first) into the cup through the straw hole. I made sure the barrel part of the syringe was not in the ice. (The cup should be a little more than halfway full of ice.) The cold air between the ice and the lid made a nice refrigerated area and when I reached home, the syringe was just as cool as when it was handed to me.

I once had a dog's ear split like a "V" by a cat and the vet said he could not stitch it and it would not heal. I went home, clipped hair inside and out to the skin and applied solid tape on one side and butterfly tape on the other side in order to allow the air in (ask any nurse to show you the butterfly). When the tape fell off, the ear was healed and when the hair came in, it was all normal.

I save the "fines" (or crumbs) from my dry, poultry-based dog food and mix 1/2 cup of it with 1/2 cup of canned dog food, vitamins, minerals, Brewer's yeast and heartworm medication until it's of a doughy consistency. Then I make it into "meatballs." The older dogs love it (especially in hot weather as the canned dog food is cold). The fines are also mixed with buttermilk and yogurt for puppies' first meals. Nothing is wasted.

Maalox is terrific for drying up hot spots before they become infected.

Peanut Butter is a universal food many a child would gladly live on and it's not a bad choice considering it's high protein and energy content. Now, peanut butter has also entered the world of veterinary medicine as an effective method of getting nutrients into a debilitated or anorexic dog or cat. Just smear peanut butter on your animal's nose and paws. Your dog or cat will automatically swallow this sticky food as it goes about getting the mess cleaned up. The high fat content of peanut butter (about 50 percent) will also encourage your pet to eat.

Pedialyte is an oral electrolyte solution (which you may keep on hand) for both newborns and for older dogs. Give a weak newborn puppy a dropperful every hour. Pedialyte is found in the canned milk section of the baby department. It comes in several strengths so *check with you vet for the best strength to use for your pup or older dog.*

Sedatives from your veterinarian may be given to jittery pets for unavoidable traveling. Otherwise if your pet doesn't like traveling, it's better to leave him with a sitter.

Spray a cookie sheet with Pam to cook golf ball-sized hamburger meatballs. When cool, place the cookie sheet and meatballs in the freezer. When they're frozen, remove the balls and store in a Ziploc bag in the freezer for those special hot-weather treats. They are extra special for teething puppies. You may also microwave the balls for a few seconds and hide pills in them when medication is necessary.

To give pills or capsules, first cover them with a dab of Nabisco Snack Mate cheese. The cheese squirts out quickly and neatly to make the pill appetizing. It also does not stick to the roof of the mouth like peanut butter, nor can it spoil like liver sausage.

To temporarily distinguish very similar young puppies for whatever reason (medication, combining litters, etc.), simply color the tail tips with Magic Markers and make a note of which color belongs to the individual puppy or to each litter (if you need to distinguish which puppy is from which litter). You may need to recolor each tail tip every few days as the Magic marker colors do tend to wear away, but it is a good way to be sure you know which puppy is which.

We use liquid heartworm medication and place it right on the dog's food. To be sure it is consumed, squirt the liquid onto a small piece of bread. The preventative soaks right in and the bread is readily consumed.

When I have to give my dog any liquid medication, I use a disposable plastic syringe, *minus the needle, of course*. The small 3cc size is good for medium-sized puppies and the 12 cc syringe is right for the medium-sized adults. It is so easy to pull the liquid in, tilt the dog's head back, hold onto the muzzle and squirt the medication down his throat. You must put the syringe between the back teeth or just make the usual "pocket" (between the dog's lip and teeth). If they chomp on the syringe, no harm is done. The syringes are reusable and may be boiled to maintain some sterility and they are cheap.

When traveling, I tape a syringe to the side of any liquid medicines I have in my traveling canine pharmacy. Extracting liquid from the bottle and administering it into the side of the mouth is easier with the syringe *(minus the needle, of course)* with 5 cc = 1 teaspoon.

Newborns

A product called Probiocin (live culture Lactobacillus) is excellent for enteritis in newborns and to fight E. Coli. Definitely use this if any antibiotic is given. Also, give it to the bitch. «»Editor's note: based on reading and research in nutritional biochemistry, an effective anti-diarrhea mixture (Bifidobacterium infantis) for puppies is Natren's Life Start (1/8 teaspoon in 1/2 ounce of lukewarm water and 1/2 teaspoon of each in 1 ounce of lukewarm water for adults and especially for the new mother).«»

Are you raising a litter or do you have a puppy who eats too much or too fast and ends up with gas and a bellyache? Since bicarbonate of soda (household baking soda) is an antacid, mix according to directions on box (1/2 teaspoon per glass of water) and give two to three eye droppers-full to medium-sized puppy for instant relief. *Gas and bloating may kill those wee ones*, and I have saved several by using this remedy when a dam had unknowingly come down with acid milk.

A tube of Nutri-Cal is a necessary item in my dog supplies. A tiny bit in the mouth of a weak newborn puppy is usually all that is needed to strengthen it. Since dogs love the taste, it is also a handy tool in teaching puppies to bait. Nutri-Cal may be purchased through veterinarians and many supply catalogs.

Do you find in your large litters that you have one weak puppy or that your older bitch's puppies have one weaker one even though it is a smaller litter? We have found that by feeding an additive to all our pregnant bitches from the time they are bred until whelping, we have never lost a small one nor have we had to help a pup. The product is called Stress and is an excellent product. It is made by the makers of Vetzyme products.

Due to a family emergency, I was required to transport my litter of very small (4 to 5 ounces) puppies. Since I was very concerned about them getting chilled (as it was cold and damp outside), I prewarmed a small ice chest and put the puppies in and covered them only with a towel. *Do not put the lid on the ice chest as the puppies may suffocate.* They stayed warm and cozy and the ice chest's handle made carrying them easy.

Extra tiny newborn puppies dehydrate very easily especially when subjected to the artificial heat sources (which are sometimes vital to keep them from becoming too chilled and subsequently dying). I have found that keeping a very close watch on them for the first several days is vital and checking several times daily for any signs of dehydration (like pinching up the skin on the back).

If a pup's skin stays up at all, dehydration is beginning. I keep a bottle of Ringers Solution (purchased from my vet) at home at all times. At the very first sign of dehydration, I give subcutaneous (under the skin) injections of the Ringers using an allergy syringe and needle. You may purchase allergy syringes at many pharmacies (without a prescription), or you can simply get a prescription from your vet or physician. Remove the Ringers from the bottle with one of your regular-size needles, then replace the regular-size needle with the very fine allergy needle (which will be used for the actual injection). I also heat the solution in the syringe by holding it under hot water for a bit or putting it in the microwave oven for a split-second *(without the needle)*. *Test the heat on the inside of your wrist as you would a baby's bottle.* Body-temperature Ringers eliminates the shock to the body that cold solution would cause and it saves puppies.

Pedialyte is an oral electrolyte solution (which you may keep on hand) for both newborns and for older dogs. Give a weak newborn puppy a dropperful every hour. Pedialyte is found in the canned milk section of the baby department. It comes in several strengths so *check with you vet for the best strength to use for your pup or older dog.*

We had a litter that appeared healthy, however at six days of age one of the pups developed a rattle in his throat. As I am always leery of any medication for such a young, otherwise healthy puppy, I decided to try something a friend of mine had used on her canaries when they got pneumonia. She suggested filling a bowl with steaming water from the tap into which a glob of Vicks VapoRub had been placed. Let the bowl fill with rising steam while holding the pup upright over the sink so that the steam and the Vicks go into his nose and thus into his lungs. (It will really do wonders for your sinuses, too.) This pup would start to cry out and wriggle uncomfortably so I knew it was reaching him. Do this for about five to ten minutes several times a day to start, decreasing as needed. Within two to three days, I noticed a vast improvement in his condition. I repeated this on and off (for at least a week) before he stopped rattling altogether. No medication was necessary. He was able to eat on his own and grew into a healthy, normal youngster with no side effects.

The fastest and safest way to warm a puppy (if he is small, weak or cold) is to carry that pup in the front of your blouse or shirt (making very sure that he can't slip out while your carrying him). I had to prove it to myself with two small premature puppies weighing only 3 1/2 ounces. They wouldn't nurse so I carried them around all afternoon in the front of my blouse and, presto ,they are now three weeks old, fine and healthy. «»Editor's note: based upon reading and research, handling puppies in this manner will also help their temperaments when it comes to bonding with humans and wanting to be cuddled.«»

New Mothers
(Also see "BITCHES"—"New Mothers")

A product called Probiocin (live culture Lactobacillus) is excellent for enteritis in newborns and to fight E. Coli. Definitely use this if any antibiotic is given. Also, give it to the bitch. «»Editor's note: based on reading and research in nutritional biochemistry, an effective anti-diarrhea mixture (Bifidobacterium infantis) for puppies is Natren's Life Start (1/8 teaspoon in 1/2 ounce of lukewarm water and 1/2 teaspoon of each in 1 ounce of lukewarm water for adults and especially for the new mother).«»

Parasites

(See "PARASITE CONTROL")

Poisoning

(See "WARNINGS"—"Poisons and Poisonings")

Puppies

A tip for feeling testicles is to sit the puppy on your lap. Those questionable or disappearing lumps are much more easily palpated in this position than when the pup is standing. If the testicles are not down by four months, the pup should not be kept for breeding

A tube of Nutri-Cal is a necessary item in my dog supplies. A tiny bit in the mouth of a puppy is usually all that is needed to strengthen him. Since dogs love the taste, it is also a handy tool in teaching puppies to bait. Nutri-Cal may be purchased through veterinarians and many supply catalogs.

Banana Flakes (Karena brand) are excellent for diarrhea and are easy to digest if a puppy or a baby is not eating well. «»Editor's note: based on reading and research in nutritional biochemistry, an effective anti-diarrhea mixture (Bifidobacterium infantis) for puppies is Natren's Life Start (1/8 teaspoon in 1/2 ounce of lukewarm water and 1/2 teaspoon of each in 1 ounce of lukewarm water for adults and especially for the new mother).«»

Before putting a puppy or an ill or aged dog to bed, fluff a towel in the dryer and place it in the bed to make a cozy sleeping area.

Does your dog get sore or raw spots under his tail? An almost magic cure for small puppies who get sore and raw under their tails (from too much licking by the mother or from diarrhea) is to apply Fuller's Earth. The difference may be seen in 24 hours.

Dried blueberries firm up loose stools and diarrhea and are mild enough to feed even to young puppies.

For anyone who has a problem with drooling puppies and young adults and if you want to show those puppies at matches or point shows, you don't want to give them any tranquilizers, Dramamine or other remedies because then they won't want to show. I have tried everything to prevent them from drooling—to no avail. In order to keep them from getting themselves and the other puppies in the crate with them wet (because saliva takes forever to dry), I take old terry T-shirts and cut the arms out. The arm fits over the head and acts like a barber's bib. It catches and absorbs the saliva and keeps each puppy dry. Cut the length to reach to the pastern so the puppy may move around without stepping on the bib. Keep the bib on when you get to the match as it takes them a few minutes to realize they aren't moving anymore. Then remove the bib and you'll have a dry puppy.

I have found that giving my dogs ice cubes (from the time they are young) is something my dogs seem to relish since they act as though the ice cubes are pieces of steak. A big plus is that these ice cubes come in handy when any dog is going through a period of dehydration (vomiting, diarrhea, etc.) because he will still chomp down the ice cubes. In this situation, we freeze Pedialyte to help stabilize the dog's system. The only down side is that you have a lot of company when you open the freezer.

Now that enteritis in puppies is less of a problem, I have not had to worry as much about dehydration due to diarrhea, however I've learned some tricks and I will share one with you. If the pup is not having problems with vomiting (or, it has been controlled)

and it is too early to feed the pup solid food, I use Pedialyte (by Ross Labs) either with a feeding tube or in their water bowls. It may be purchased in any pharmacy over-the-counter. Normally, it is used for fluid and electrolyte replacement in young children with severe diarrhea, but it also works very well for young puppies (especially those who are still too sick to get up and drink but to whom you don't want to give the fluids intravenously or subcutaneously).

Spray a cookie sheet with Pam to cook golf ball-sized hamburger meatballs. When cool, place the cookie sheet and meatballs in the freezer. When they're frozen, remove the balls and store in a Ziploc bag in the freezer for those special hot-weather treats. They are extra special for teething puppies. You may also microwave the balls for a few seconds and hide pills in them when medication is necessary.

To temporarily distinguish very similar young puppies for whatever reason (medication, combining litters, etc.), simply color the tail tips with Magic Markers and make a note of which color belongs to the individual puppy or to each litter (if you need to distinguish which puppy is from which litter). You may need to recolor each tail tip every few days as the Magic marker colors do tend to wear away, but it is a good way to be sure you know which puppy is which.

Record Keeping

(See "RECORDS"—"Medical and Health")

Removing Dewclaws From Newborns

Sheltie Pacesetter printed an excellent article (including 12 photographs and two diagrams showing exactly how to remove dewclaws). This Charter issue has been sold out for many years, however you may purchase these three photocopied pages of this article for $4.50. Go to our secure website (www.sheltie.com under "Single Issues" and then under "Balance Due"...which is located near the bottom of the "Available Back Issues" page).

Before I ever whelped a litter of puppies, I was taught a method for taking off dewclaws that I still use today. It simply involves using one's thumbnail and index fingernail to remove the dewclaw. You can feel the base of the dewclaw and with a quick flick of the wrist, the dewclaw pops off. Of course, I am very, very careful to make sure that the two nail areas are clean and disinfected. There are several real advantages to this method. First, you can do this by yourself. You don't need any help from anyone else. Secondly, the dewclaws do not have to be removed immediately upon whelping. You may wait for a few hours until everyone is happily nursing or you may do it the next day or two. You can leave the removal until you are sure that the puppy is strong and healthy (adjusting the removal depending upon the strength of each puppy). Also, there is little or no bleeding when the removal takes place during the pup's first day.

If newly cut dewclaws should become infected, swab the scab off using cotton dipped in warm water. Dab a generous amount of Panolog Cream or Forte Topical into the open sore. The next morning it will be clean and dry.

I found a new way to cut dewclaws which is especially helpful if you do it alone. I sit on the floor, back against the wall, with my knees drawn up and put my equipment right beside me. I spread a towel on my lap and press it down between my thighs. Then I place the puppy between my thighs with his head facing downward. He feels very secure and barely struggles at all. His rear legs are free for me to work on. For the front, I cup him in my left hand (resting his rump on my lap) with his neck between my thumb and forefinger which would then hold the paw I was working on. Both positions seem to give the pup a feeling of security and I had the least "fight back" I have ever had with a dewclaw session.

If you have problems with your puppies' legs getting infected after you remove their dewclaws, try this: after removing the dewclaw, dab a Q-Tip that's been soaked in hydrogen peroxide in the wound and then apply your coagulant.

When removing dewclaws, I use a product called Xenodine. It greatly reduces bleeding and does not burn when applied. It promotes rapid healing without the big scabs which may form after a dewclaw has been removed. You may obtain Xenodine through your vet.

Sanitation

(Also see "ELIMINATING BAD BEHAVIORS"—"Housebreaking")

If your puppy has an accident, blot up as much moisture as possible. Then rub the spot with a solution of vinegar or lemon juice and warm sudsy water. Blot a few times, and then pour straight club soda over the spot and blot again. Place a dry towel over the stain and put a heavy object (like a book) on top of it. Replace the towel if it becomes soggy and repeat blotting. For cat accidents, follow the same steps but when the spot is dry, rub with a cloth dampened with ammonia. This will take the offensive odor away and it will prevent the cat from ever going in that spot again.

I keep a towel on a hook right outside my back door. I have taught my dog to sit and wait (when he comes inside) until I wipe all four feet. As dogs are creatures of habit, I must wipe his feet and even on the driest of days, he will wait and "paw the air" (until I wipe him). It really cuts down on the amount of water and mud that he tracks into the house. He stays cleaner between bathings and my carpet stays cleaner between vacuumings.

I leased a bitch who was used to being kept in the kennel. When she stayed in my home she would pee everywhere. This became very tiring so I went to the store and bought a package of the potty training pull-ups (the largest size they had). I carefully cut an approximate two-inch vertical slit for her tail to go through and it acts like a diaper. She never had an accident again. Amazing what it will hold. *You need to change the diaper as soon as it's soiled so bacteria doesn't build up and for the dog's comfort. Remember to take it off when the dog is crated.*

I was having some trouble housebreaking an older puppy. I found a most welcome solution. I bought disposable diapers for her. I cut an "X" approximately one third of the way down the diaper for her tail and taped it on. We have not had one accident since. She will hold it until she is outside and the diaper is taken off. *(Be sure you do not leave a dog alone with a diaper on as your dog could try to tear it off and choke on the plastic.)*

Make your own "Handi Wipes" for dog show trips or summer travels. Cut a roll of heavy paper toweling such as Bounty or Viva into pieces which will then fit into a Tupperware or Rubbermaid type of covered container. Whip the following liquid ingredients and pour over the paper towels. The liquid ingredients are: 2 capfuls of rubbing alcohol, 2 squirts of baby oil, 2 squirts of baby soap and 1/4 cup of water. Keep in covered container.

There was a discussion on the internet as to whether it was okay to bathe a bitch who is in whelp and due in about a week-and-a-half. When my bitches are pregnant and too big to pop in the tub, I spray Self Rinse Plus where the bitches are dirty and then wipe clean. It's very easy and less stressful on the mother-to-be.

To help prevent parvo, I keep a cat litter pan with a piece of carpet in it and a plastic milk container filled with a solution of bleach and water on my front porch and at the front door of our motor home. When anyone returns home or "doggy" friends come to visit, I pour in a bit of solution and walk them through before they enter. When you have tiny puppies at home, it is worth that little bit of extra effort. We also carry this setup with us to shows and use it before entering our motor home. Be sure to use a new solution each time (as the bleach evaporates into the air and only water will remain in the pan after a period of time).

We use Baby Wipes for a multitude of reasons-cleaning a "just-used" thermometer, any area that's been stitched or sutured, a quick ear cleaning before a show, on a messy puppy face and on babies just learning to eat from a pan. The least expensive ones are more moist, and you'll be surprised how many uses you'll find for them.

When a puppy begins spending the night in a crate but isn't old enough to last the night without wetting, I hook two wire crates together. If a puppy is small or the crate's large, I put bedding in one half of the crate and newspaper in the other half. (I put computer paper over the newspaper to keep the puppy from getting newsprint on himself.) When the puppy's old enough to last the night without having to wet, I take away the crate along with the newspaper.

With a parvovirus threats we take a special precaution before leaving shows. The dogs are pulled from their crates. The papers are changed and the inside is sprayed with Clorox solution. Then each foot is dipped into a jar of solution (a small wide-mouth peanut butter jar is good for this). The dog is then returned to his clean, dry crate without making contact with the floor or the ground at the show. Then, before entering the car, each person gets the bottoms of his shoes sprayed as well.

With the threat of so many viruses affecting our dogs and puppies, we are all finding it necessary to take extra precautions. Aside from dog classes and shows from which we potentially track home the unknown, we also have three children and all their friends generate quite a bit of foot traffic throughout our home. I keep a spray bottle of Clorox and old carpet pieces in our garage. The children spray the soles of their shoes or take them off before entering the house. They always wash their hands before playing with our puppies. I also solved the dilemma of visitors coming into our house through the front door. I purchased a rubber-backed doormat (the kind with some type of material in the middle). I spray this heavily with Clorox and ask people to please wipe their shoes on the mat.

Skin and Coat

A cure or to relieve the discomfort from a bee or a wasp sting is first remove the stinger. Then apply uncut ammonia water or a paste of baking soda and water.

Are you troubled by scars on a particularly nice show prospect? Try equal parts of lanolin, camphorated olive oil and peanut oil. Massage in twice to three times daily. It also helps the hair grow in faster after a skin infection or disease.

Corn oil prevents hairballs in pets. Add a few drops of corn oil to your pets' food to prevent hairballs from forming. The thick oil helps the fur pass through the animal's system much quicker and easily.

Does your dog get sore or raw spots under his tail? An almost magic cure for small puppies who get sore and raw under their tails (from too much licking by the mother or from diarrhea) is to apply Fuller's Earth. The difference may be seen in 24 hours.

Every summer my dog would chew holes in his coat. It would sometimes happen at the back of his tail (his anal glands were removed when he was very young so that wasn't the problem) and some places along his legs, etc. Our vet called it a seasonal skin allergy possibly due to fleas and/or grass allergies. The vet prescribed some flea medications which helped. Benadryl cream on the chewed places also helped. The yard was treated to kill fleas. But my dog still sometimes chewed. Then at a show, my mother talked to someone who recommended flax seed oil (100 mg. capsules are available at health food stores). At first, one per day was given and that helped. He stopped chewing his coat. Eventually, the one per day regimen proved an overdose. Now, we just give him one every other day. So far, he has quit chewing.

For hot spots use Upjohn's Mycitracin (a people product and used for impetigo). It helps clear blemishes and acts quickly on hot spots.

I boarded a dog for a few days who I had previously sold (I don't generally board those other than my own). I noticed something I'd not seen before. This four-year-old had a loss of hair on the sides of his nose and his muzzle. I spoke with the new "on call" vet and she suggested that it might be either mange or ringworm. I doubted either as, unfortunately, I've seen both. Mange is doubtful in a previously unaffected four-year-old dog. Ringworm has a look all it's own. Neither occur on the nose (generally). My thought after reading my own information was "collie nose" (nasal solar dermatitis). The vet agreed that this might be the cause, however upon researching further, I decided this would be located on the top of the nose. I alerted the owners to the hair loss and said that if any irritation, oozing or crusts occurred, they should take him to the vet. When my own experienced vet returned, he had a rather simple explanation. He suggested the dog was "nuzzling" and merely wearing his hair off. In questioning the owners, they said indeed the dog did this, on the couch, on the rug, etc. That was a simple explanation which I hadn't thought about. The longer we breed dogs, the more we encounter.

If your older dog develops a ridge on its nose, it can be removed quickly, painlessly and easily by simply gently rubbing the affected area with a file made for pedicures (available at any beauty supply store).

Living in a humid climate with my dogs who are friendly with cats, I occasionally find that my dogs (males especially) will get a fungal skin disorder, such as ringworm. I have used numerous vet care products for this, but none has been as successful as Desenex Antifungal Spray Foot Powder. It is an anti-fungal for athlete's foot but it does well on dogs. It is a powerful spray and gets through the hair to the skin...where it counts. Other dog breeders in the area swear by it and I have had success the few times I have used it.

Maalox in terrific for drying up hot spots before they become infected.

Olive oil makes your pet's coat shinier. Add a bit of olive oil to your pet's food to give them a healthier, shinier coat.

Remove burrs from your dog's fur by working oil into the tangle or by crushing the burrs with pliers. You may comb out the crushed burrs as they lose their holding power.

Vitamin E is great to use outside the body as well as inside. It works wonderfully for skin problems of many types. Just put a small hole in one of your Vitamin E gel capsules and squeeze the oil out directly on the sore, rash, raw skin or whatever. It soothes and helps to heal.

When our dog has an irritation on his skin (such as a rash, chafing or redness), we apply Mexsana Medicated Powder which may be bought from any drugstore. It really helps to relieve minor skin problems.

Teeth

All of us have probably experienced the show prospect who retains a puppy tooth too long (which then results in crooked canines). You can take the pup to the vet and have him pull the tooth but this is costly. I finally hit upon a solution which works for me. When I see the adult tooth coming down and the puppy tooth is loose but not coming out, I take a rag out and let the dogs play tug-of-war. Soon the puppy tooth is gone. The pup never notices and it surely saves on the vet bill.

All puppies will love this—take a small rag or old washcloth, soak it in water and wring most of the water out. Then freeze it. They will love the coldness on their sore gums and will choose chewing on this instead of furniture, etc.

A quick way to clean the last minute "yuckies" off your dog's teeth is to quickly wipe off your dog's teeth using squares of dry gauze. While it will not remove the tartar, it gets the between-meal snacks off his teeth.

A really fun toy for our dogs is their "tug rope." We buy a 6-foot piece of rope (natural fiber jute or hemp, not nylon) at the hardware store. Then tie a large double knot at each end, leaving about 6" of rope extending past the knots. Our dogs love playing tug-of-war with these. They are also useful in that tugging on them helps remove puppy teeth. (No more trips to the vet to remove any retained puppy canines.) With the older dogs, tugging at the frayed ends of the rope seems to help clean between those front teeth which are too close to each other.

Baby canine teeth which are too slow in falling out may cause his permanent canines to grow in crooked. Save a trip to the vet for the puppy, recycle your kids' old cotton socks and at the same time, give your pups a knotted old sock so they may play "tug-o-war." This way they can have lots of fun while they unknowingly play "dentist" by pulling out each other's loose baby teeth.

Cleaning teeth is quicker, easier, more complete and comfortable for the dog by using a dowel. Beginning at an early age of the dog, we insert a small dowel (about 4 1/2" long) behind both sets of molars such that it protrudes on either side. The dog's mouth must be fully open and under control for scraping and brushing. Believe it or not, they do get used to it.

For cleaning teeth, gin (that's right, your basic 80 or 100 proof martini stuff) works wonders in loosening plaque. Just dip a Q-Tip in the gin and rub the dog's teeth and gums well. In a few seconds, your scaler will take the gook off easily. After that, rub gin on your own teeth and gums and you won't remember what a chore it was.

For teething puppies, take an old (or new), thick, clean sock, knot it in the middle, wet it and then freeze it inside a Baggie. Take it out when frozen and give it to the puppies. This keeps the teething puppies occupied for several hours. The cold numbs their gums. I have not had any destructive chewing since I began using these frozen socks for my teething puppies.

Give your dog raw carrots and hard rubber toys to chew and this will help keep his teeth clean.

Gly-Oxide (a "people product") is very effective in cleaning up minor gum line irritations before they become major problems. This is available at most drugstores.

Having several dogs at home who are 10 years old and older, we have to pay special attention to their teeth. We have found that Anbesol (an antiseptic anesthetic liquid for people) reduces the twinges of pain the dogs might feel when the dental tool grazes the gums during tooth scraping, and it helps the sensitive dogs tolerate a full cleaning session without undue wiggling. It's available at most drugstores.

If you have trouble with tartar buildup on your dog's teeth, try brushing two times a week with an Oral B Sulcus toothbrush and Pearl Drops tooth polish. This does not foam as badly as toothpaste which may cause choking. Be sure to angle the brush to get under the gums.

If your dog has bad breath as mine did, I suggest that you take a washcloth or a rag and wrap it around your finger. Then dip it into Listerine (a mouthwash) and rub your finger around each tooth. You should notice a change in your dog's breath immediately. Repeat if needed.

I periodically give my dogs beef bones which I get from the butcher. A local meat shop sells beef bones for dogs in packages of one to two pounds. I always check for sharp ends or bones which might splinter easily. I remove any sharp pieces. The dogs get the rest of the bones and will chew on them long after any trace of meat is gone. Their teeth will be cleaner within a week and you will find that you will not have to clean teeth with the scraper nearly as frequently as before. It is also good exercise for the gums and may prevent gum infections and early loss of teeth.

I've had very good results keeping my dogs' mouths in good shape by using an anti-plaque rinse once a week or so. I dip gauze in the liquid, squeeze out the excess and scrub the teeth thoroughly. The dogs even seem to enjoy it.

I would like to pass around a hint to puppy owners who need a soft puppy toy. Take two socks and roll one up so it will fit inside the toe of the other sock. When this is accomplished, you should have a soft bulge at the end of the sock. Tie it onto a crate or table leg. This toy is also great when it's not tied onto an object. You may use it for a teething aid as well.

Spray a cookie sheet with Pam to cook golf ball-sized hamburger meatballs. When cool, place the cookie sheet and meatballs in the freezer. When they're frozen, remove the balls and store in a Ziploc bag in the freezer for those special hot-weather treats. They are extra special for teething puppies.

Teeth cleaning may be made easier with the use of hemostats. They chip tartar off quickly with less apparent bother to your dog.

To help with scaling of teeth, put straight gin or vodka on a piece of cotton. This liquid will soften the tooth plaque, thus making scaling easier. Soak the cotton ball well and apply it to the plaque for a few seconds (to allow the alcohol to penetrate the plaque). Scaling will then be easier. A small pair of blunt-nose pliers can be used successfully to put pressure on the soaked cotton

balls applied to the heavy buildup of plaque on your dog's back teeth. Finish up with a scaling and polishing. Polishing may be accomplished nicely with a cloth or a brush dipped in peroxide and then into baking soda.

When a pet has bad teeth, bacteria may circulate around the gums. The bacteria float around the bloodstream and eventually settle on the heart valve. To help keep your pet's teeth clean, brush or scrub his teeth daily.

When scaling my dogs' teeth, I take a clean old cloth such as a diaper, towel or flour-sack dish towel and twist one end up. I put that end in the mouth between the top and bottom rear teeth. Then I gently close the mouth and start scaling. The excess cloth can be used to wipe teeth dry before you start to work and to clean the scaler and teeth as you work. You will find this method faster than using a dowel, and you will have a lot less slips than ever before.

Vaccinations

If you give your own vaccinations, be sure to read the label for directions and follow them exactly. The label will tell you whether to give the injection in your dog's muscle or subcutaneously. The difference may not seem important but it is. For example, rabies vaccine given intramuscularly is 100 percent more effective and provides more resistance than the same vaccine given subcutaneously. The pharmaceutical companies have devoted time, money and research to determine how best to administer their products. Take advantage of their investment by reading each label.

I give my own puppy shots, so for each puppy I peel off the label from the vials and place those labels on a sheet of paper. I also include (for each puppy) the date, weight, height, worming (date and type of medication), vet's physical date and any other pertinent data or information on this sheet of paper or "data sheet." When a puppy goes to his new home, his "data sheet" goes with him. By keeping this type of record, there is no question about the type of vaccinations or times given when the new family takes him to their vet for a physical.

Veterinary Services

To save dollars when going to the veterinarian, ask your vet what he or she would charge to do several various procedures. Then inquire as to what would be the charge to do several of these procedures under one anesthetic. I routinely get all my show dogs debarked. Usually at the same time I get tattooing done, get nails trimmed, vWD testing and, occasionally, I combine my OFA x-rays with a good teeth cleaning. Some of these procedures cost $50+ each...if done separately. If you combine several of these elective procedures under one anesthetic, you usually pay for the initial procedure (often for the most costly procedure) and then much less for each additional procedure. Not only do you save money but think of the stress you spare the dog as well.

Weight Problems
(See "FEEDING"—"Weight Problems")

Worming
(See "PARASITE and OTHER PEST CONTROL"—
"Roundworms and Other Worms")

〉〉 〈〈

In The Home

Cleaning

A capful of liquid peppermint (Castile) soap in a quart of warm water should be kept handy to clean spots when your dog has an accident. Pour the mixture on a sponge and go over the entire spot. Then flush the sponge and repeat the process. No rinsing is necessary. This will not only neutralize the ammonia odor and remove the stain but will leave a fresh, natural smell in its place. Two or three capfuls in a bucket of water cleans linoleum, tile and other no-wax floors. A capful in the final rinse of washing dog blankets cleans and deodorizes them and helps repel fleas. Bathing your dog in it leaves the coat shiny and smelling nice longer than special dog shampoos. Liquid peppermint soap is sold at most health food stores.

A good neutralizer and freshener for urine on a carpet is blue Windex Glass Cleaner. Spray liberally and rub with a towel, to dry. It will totally eliminate the urine odor.

A slicker brush is a great tool to use in the house to get the dog hair from the carpet near the edges of the wall where the vacuum doesn't quite reach and on carpeted stairs particularly the risers (backs).

An inexpensive tool for cleaning up the kennel yard is a child's leaf rake (which you may purchase at Big Lots). Big Lots also has heavy-duty dust pans with the long handles (which means no bending over). They work just as good as the ones you buy in the pet catalogs or in the stores and what's better, you save money.

Drop half of a moth cake into the vacuum tank and it will kill flea eggs. You can also put the moth cake in a regular vacuum bag and it, too, will kill flea eggs and helps to deodorize.

For really stubborn carpet odors and before you rip up the carpet to start over, try a chemical called neutroleum alpha. It neutralizes almost all odors. You may buy it from pest control companies (usually in 1-gallon containers) although you will not need that much for one or two problem areas. Transfer the chemical to a spray bottle of some kind and dampen the carpet with chemical. Let dry and wait two days. If odor is still noticeable, repeat. Note: it is safe for most carpets, but test a small area for colorfastness first.

For those of you who love to hang framed photos of your dogs, as well as all of their ribbons, plaques and other accomplishments, I am sure you have found that they are incredible dust magnets. I keep a coffee can on my dryer and put used dryer softening sheets in the coffee can. I have found that they are the perfect dust rag for all those frames, ribbons and plaques. This material picks up the dust and the fabric softener oils the wood. Most importantly... the chemicals on them cut static electricity (which is what attracts all that dust and doggy hair). You may safely use them on anything you notice which attracts dust and hair.

Here's a great tip for getting out a grease stain from your show clothing. It's for silk but it should work on anything. Place the spotted area on a soft, clean white cloth. Now spread cornstarch on the grease stain and rub it carefully into the spot with a white paper towel folded into several layers. Place the paper towel over the cornstarch and put a heated iron on the paper towel (careful, don't touch the silk with the iron) so as to heat the cornstarch. Remove the paper towel and brush off the cornstarch. The stain should disappear.

I am not one to buy gadgets so when my sister-in-law gave me a DustBuster as a gift, I could only think "Oh great, another thing to collect dust—not in it, but on it." How wrong I was. This is going to sound like a commercial but I love this self-charging little tool as it gets into dog crates, under dog crates, picks up spilled dry dog food, hairy stairs and hairy corners for quick pick ups not to mention picking up spilled potted plants. It sure beats dragging out the vacuum cleaner and all those clumsy attachments that go along with it.

If you don't have a wet/dry shop vac, you should think seriously about investing in one. They're marvelous for vacuuming out crates and for catching those "fuzz puppies" which accumulate in the corners of your kennel building.

If your dog or puppy has a "messy" accident on your carpet, try using cat litter. Pour cat litter over the soiled area and let it sit until the cat litter absorbs all the moisture. Cleanup will then be much easier. In an emergency, dry sand or dirt works well, also.

If your puppy has an accident, blot up as much moisture as possible. Then rub the spot with a solution of vinegar or lemon juice and warm sudsy water. Blot a few times, and then pour straight club soda over the spot and blot again. Place a dry towel over the stain and put a heavy object (like a book) on top of it. Replace the towel if it becomes soggy and repeat blotting. For cat accidents, follow the same steps but when the spot is dry, rub with a cloth dampened with ammonia. This will take the offensive odor away and it will prevent the cat from ever going in that spot again.

I have a great solution for keeping that dog hair off your show clothing. All you have to do is spray some Static Cling on your show clothes. It sounds too simple, but it works. Make sure you bring a can to the show so right before going into the ring, you may spray yourself and be free of dog hair.

I have a tip for those owning an Electrolux vacuum cleaner. Mine is over 10 years old, however I assume this would apply to newer machines, also. The machine may be purchased with either a carpet/floor tool or with the tool and a power nozzle. After years of abuse, my carpet/floor tool broke. I contacted my salesman who supplied me with a tool from a machine older than mine (at no cost to me). The carpet side of this tool has a multi-grooved metal piece which the newer one did not have. It is superior to the new one for picking up dog hair. I'd say that it even picks up hair better than the power nozzle and has the added advantage of having no brushes to entangle the hair. If you own an Electrolux and don't have a tool of this type, it would be well worth your effort to contact a salesman or dealer. Perhaps he'll give you one or sell one at a reasonable price.

I have found that lightly misting my carpet with water before I vacuum aids in picking up all the dog hairs.

I have found the DustBuster Plus to be invaluable in my dog room. I use it daily to keep the crates clean and to swoop up loose dog hair. It is particularly useful during the flea season because it effectively picks up flea eggs and dirt and is so easy and quick to use. The vacuuming power is much greater than the original DustBuster.

I keep an extra old slicker brush in with my cleaning tools to clean carpets around baseboards and on stairways. It does a great job of removing dog hair.

I keep a towel on a hook right outside my back door. I have taught my dog to sit and wait (when he comes inside) until I wipe all four feet. As dogs are creatures of habit, I must wipe his feet and even on the driest of days, he will wait and "paw the air" (until

I wipe him). It really cuts down on the amount of water and mud that he tracks into the house. He stays cleaner between bathings and my carpet stays cleaner between vacuumings.

I learned a helpful, step-saving hint from a friend. Empty squeeze bottles (dishwashing detergent bottles are ideal) are filled with a 1-to-5 mixture of pine oil and warm water and placed in cabinets throughout the house along with rolls of paper towels. Place these spray bottles in the kitchen, the family room, the kennel room and wherever else puppies are let out for socialization. When accidents occur, cleanup is just an arm's reach away.

Instead of using expensive commercial stain removers on carpets for urine or fecal stains, try shaving cream. Squirt a little cream on the area, scrub in with a small scrub brush and let it dry. Vacuum when dry. It works quite well and there are many fragrances from which to choose. Be sure to test the carpet, however I have found no discoloration so far. Club soda will remove urine stains from your furniture.

My dogs are all house dogs and also are running on gravel when outside. After years of tracking gravel dust into my home, my rugs are permeated with the gravel dust. Even after trips to the cleaners for shampooing, these rugs are still permeated despite frequent use of a good vacuum. My rugs are Oriental area rugs. The small rugs may be turned over and vacuumed on one side and then the reverse repeatedly (which removes a lot of the dust), however this is impractical with a large rug. One day when brushing with an old slicker, I tried brushing the rug and was amazed at the amount of dust that it "brushed out." I can't say this preserves the nap of the rug but after many doses of deodorizer, the rug wasn't in the best shape anyway. I now keep my "rug brushes" on hand because they work.

My puppies' playpen is in our dining room and having a no-wax floor sure helps. I encountered a problem when the newspaper print (both color and black-and-white) stained the floor. To remove those stains, I found that WD-40 worked well. First, make sure all puppies are out of the area to be sprayed. Spray the WD-40 directly on the stains. Use a clean, dry paper towel to rub the spots out. Then clean those areas thoroughly with soap and water. It works like magic and is safe for no-wax floors.

Remove your pet's hair from your clothing by using masking tape. Roll tape out and attach the tape backwards on the roll so the sticky side is out. Roll the tape on your clothes and the hair will stick to the tape.

To get dog hair off furniture, I lightly mist the furniture with an anti-static spray, let it dry and then go over the furniture with a lint remover. It works great.

To remove excessive hair from clothing, dampen a sponge and briskly rub clothing. Hair should ball up and you'll then be able to pick off the hair balls.

To remove hair on your furniture and/or clothing, rub a rubber glove (like the ones used when washing dishes) over the surface and pet hair will roll up. Pick up pet hair and throw it away.

Vacuum floors and carpets often during flea season. Put salt or mothballs in the vacuum cleaner bag to kill hatching fleas.

We all fight dog hair continually. I suggest using a "miracle brush." It is available at your local Kmart or other similar stores. It is great for picking up hair from clothing. It is great for picking up hair from furniture, bedspreads and even rugs.

We all know how invaluable those folding exercise pens are for the dogs but don't hide them away between dog uses. They are good to use as a base for a cutting board while cutting out patterns, as a support while cutting out lumber or with a piece of plywood on the top to make a wonderful temporary table.

When a puppy wets the carpet, mop up what you can with a paper towel, cover the area with a little kitty litter and let it set, then vacuum. The kitty litter will soak up extra wetness and deodorize at the same time.

When a walk past the family dog gives your clothes a new mohair look, you may be certain the season is finally changing. Pets may lose hair throughout the year but when a thick, winter coat gives way to a sparser summer coat, the results may be hairy. You may help prevent your pet's hairs from sticking to your clothes, carpeting, draperies and furniture by spraying each pet with Static Guard (the odorless anti-static spray made by the Alberto Culver Company). Stray hairs may also be removed by spraying lightly with Static Guard, and then brushing or vacuuming pet hairs away. This Static Guard won't stain, discolor or build up and is safe for most colorfast fabrics. You may also use Static Guard as a grooming aid for your pet. If you've been tempted to wear a mask to protect your nose from airborne hairs as you brush your pet, try spraying your grooming tools and you'll find it easier to keep excess hair where you want it. You'll also be able to control your pet's hair and keep it from standing on end. Controlling loose animal hairs is just one handy way to use Static Guard. Since it neutralizes electricity, applying it to your clothing prevents static cling and lint build-up. In dry weather, spraying your carpets and the soles of your shoes eliminates static electric shocks when you touch metal or another person. And you may apply it to your own brush or comb to keep your hair from flying away as you groom.

When combing out dogs who are blowing coat, try using a clean, dry milk jug. This milk jug will hold a ton of hair. Just clean the hair off your brush, roll the hair in a ball and then poke it into the opening of the jug. This is much cleaner and less messy than putting the hair in a grocery bag. For easy access, hang the milk container from the handle on your grooming arm. When you are done, just toss out the jug.

With the threat of so many viruses affecting our dogs and puppies, we are all finding it necessary to take extra precautions. Aside from dog classes and shows from which we potentially track home the unknown, we also have three children and all their friends generate quite a bit of foot traffic throughout our home. I keep a spray bottle of Clorox and old carpet pieces in our garage. The children spray the soles of their shoes or take them off before entering the house. They always wash their hands before playing with our puppies. I also solved the dilemma of visitors coming into our house through the front door. I purchased a rubber-backed doormat (the kind with some type of material in the middle). I spray this heavily with Clorox and ask people to please wipe their shoes on the mat.

Furnishings, Flooring, Etc.

A plastic shower curtain may be used to protect a bedspread both at home or at motels for those "bed potatoes."

Because of the wear and tear on our screen door (caused by our dogs), we were replacing either the screen or the screen door every few months. Each time we made a replacement, we put on stronger guards. The new screen would last a little bit longer but then it would soon need replacing. Finally, we got smart and put in a screen door which was solid at its bottom. This door cost more and still saved us money since we haven't had to replace either the screen or the door in eight years.

Having a baby? Don't rush out and buy a changing table. If you won't be needing your grooming table for a while, use your grooming table as a changing table. Buy fabric (which appeals to you and your future baby) and elastic so you may make a skirt to wrap around the table. Then push the grooming table against the wall. Presto, you now have a changing table for the newest member of your family.

I buy Softex Bath Mats at Walmart. They are 17" x 36" and have tiny suction cups on the bottom of each mat. In the winter I keep my puppies in a dog room where the floor may get cold because the flooring is vinyl (on top of concrete). I put two of these mats together and the puppies may then lie on top of them which keeps the pups off the cold floor. Water will drain through these mats and, best of all, they are machine washable. Also, because of the tiny suction cups on the bottom, the mats don't scoot around. This eliminates the need for newspapers in the area of my home where the mats are positioned. The mats also work well as a floor in the #200 Vari Kennel. There is also a smaller mat (16" x 23") which fits perfectly in the crate. I found the smaller mats at Target.

I found the most marvelous thing in the baby department of Walmart. It is called a "soft gate" by Gerry. It's a collapsible gate that's approximately 26" high and expands from 27" to 42". The whole thing fits into a carry case that's about 3" in diameter. It's great when traveling.

If you find stepping over your puppy gates getting tougher as you grow older, try using a pair of shutters in the doorway.

If you have an older dog who is going blind or who is blind, make moving about your home easier for him by spraying a light air freshener scent on all the furniture and other obstacles which would be at nose or head height. Be sure it goes onto the furniture and not just into the air. Use a different scent for general air freshening.

If you have dogs who are playing and crashing into your newly cleaned glass sliding doors, make butterflies or flowers out of resin. You can get different size molds and make them in different decorative colors. These are very attractive glued on your glass doors and dogs and children will then know when the glass door is closed. If you're not energetic and don't want to make them, you may buy decorative decals made out of mylar at most glass and mirror stores.

If you have trouble with house-raised pups getting into your potted plants which sit on the floor, try covering the soil with pine cones which should keep your furry critters out and the soil in. Pine cones are not favorite chew toys for most pups.

In the house, I put carpet remnants between crates and walls to protect the walls.

I partition my kitchen off from the rest of the house when housebreaking a youngster by using indoor shutters and decorative wood trim. The trim pieces are cut, spaced and nailed along the outer edge of the doorway in such a way that one or more shutters may slide into the doorway (depending on the size of the puppy). They are easy for adults to step over but too high for a puppy to jump. The trim pieces and shutters may be stained or painted to match your decor.

I wouldn't wish this on my worst enemy but I fell and broke my hip. (Yes, I was out on the ice trying to get a dog). After surgery (and moving around the house on a "walker"), I was given something called a "grabber." This allowed me to pick up things without bending (which I wasn't supposed to do). Well, as things progressed and I could finally pick up pens, toys, dishes, etc., I found this "grabber" an invaluable tool. It has sort of "claws" on one end plus a handle that one may press in order to close its claws. This came from OT (occupational therapy) at the hospital.

Most people use exercise pens to keep dogs confined in a place. I do, too, but I also use my exercise pens to keep dogs out of certain places.

Our puppy has a new accomplishment which is both useful to us and also a bit of a nuisance. Her housebreaking has not been 100 percent (partly because she is like our other dogs and just stands by the door to ask to be let outside). If we don't happen to see her right away, she just finds a convenient spot on the floor. We located a little bell which was one of our Christmas ornaments and hung it from the doorknob so it is dangling about puppy-head height. It only took her a couple of days to learn that if she bumped that bell and made it ring, someone would come and open the door. Now she rings it when she has to go out.

Secure electrical cords to baseboards or make them inaccessible to your dogs. *If your dog chews on them, he may suffer electric shocks, burns and could possibly die.* To hide those cords (which can't be made inaccessible), you may place empty paper towel rolls or toilet tissue cardboard rolls over the cords. Place construction-type cardboard on the walls to cover over cords which can't be put into cardboard tubes.

The soft insulators which go around pipes are great for the tops of exercise pens. Just pop them on and the metal ex-pen will not mark or scratch your walls or anything they touch.

Thinking of redoing your kitchen or utility room floor and don't know which kind of linoleum will hold up best? With your next litter, ask a local flooring place for some tile samples (usually given free) and use them as a base underneath the newspapers in your puppy exercise pen. You will soon know which styles and brands will hold up best. If it can take the constant cleanup of puppy droppings, it can withstand anything. (I found that the deeper grooved designs, while being stylish, are far harder to clean.)

To help keep your puppy from chewing on the furniture, carpet, etc., be sure he has his own rubber toys. On furniture (table, chair legs, etc.) on which he is chewing, try putting a little oil of cloves on the wood. The odor should keep him away and if not, the bitter taste will.

To protect the outside of our wooden storm doors from our happy and bouncy dogs, my husband covered the panel below the window with a sheet of plexiglass. It allows the wood to be seen, and yet it protects it from scratches and is easily cleaned of muddy paw prints. Now the dogs who like to bounce against the door can't cause any damage to our wooden door.

To stop annoying bowl pushing on slippery floors, I spray Firm Grip on the bottom of the bowl. It prevents food or water bowls from getting pushed and then probably spilled. It also works great on the slippery bottoms of my shoes before going into the ring and/or on my sweaty palms.

We have only one living area in our home as we built it with only a den and no formal living room. When our older son moved out, we made his bedroom into a little study or sitting room which is now an ideal place to visit with people who come over to "talk dogs" and when my husband is glued to a football game on TV in the den. The new room has rattan furniture and the coffee table has a glass top. I taped photos of our dogs on the underside of the glass table top and the effect is really beautiful. Everyone loves it and it provides effortless access to photos of all the dogs we've had through the years. If you have a coffee table with a wooden top, you could have glass cut to fit over that wooden table top. Then you could tape photos under the new glass top. It's a wonderful way to display photos of your special dogs and brighten up the room at the same time.

When pups start teething around our place, we did practically everything possible to keep furniture, carpet, etc., from being destroyed. I tried commercial products, vinegar, etc. They didn't work. In desperation I was going to try quinine but it was pretty expensive. So I tried the next best thing which was tonic water. It cost me less than a dollar and there was no more chewing. I would suggest that before trying this, test the tonic water on an inconspicuous spot first as some fabric might discolor.

Yard sales and flea markets yield a variety of wall-hanging mug racks. These are great for hanging leashes, chokes, etc.

Grooming Tables In The Home
(See "GROOMING"—"Grooming Tables")

Indoor Enclosures
(See "ENCLOSURES"—"Indoor Enclosures")

Odors and Stains
(Also see "GROOMING"—"Removal of Skunk's Smell")

A capful of liquid peppermint (Castile) soap in a quart of warm water should be kept handy to clean spots when your dog has an accident. Pour the mixture on a sponge and go over the entire spot. Then flush the sponge and repeat the process. No rinsing is necessary. This will not only neutralize the ammonia odor and remove the stain but will leave a fresh, natural smell in its place. Two or three capfuls in a bucket of water cleans linoleum, tile and other no-wax floors. A capful in the final rinse of washing dog blankets cleans and deodorizes them and helps repel fleas. Bathing your dog in it leaves the coat shiny and smelling nice longer than special dog shampoos. Liquid peppermint soap is sold at most health food stores.

Again—black pepper: I always hated "rubbing a pup's nose" in his messes as I feel that is degrading. When your puppy makes a mess, scold him and rush him outside. While he is gone, clean up and liberally dump pepper on that previously-soiled spot. That is all except for cleaning up the pepper two hours later. Invariably, your pup will return to "the spot" to sniff and I have never had to use that method more than three times before the pup decides that outside is better than inside for that kind of business.

A good neutralizer and freshener for urine on a carpet is blue Windex Glass Cleaner. Spray liberally and rub with a towel, to dry. It will totally eliminate the urine odor.

Baking soda in the rinse water will leave your pet's coat odor free, plus softer and shinier.

Boil your show bait (liver) with a dash of vinegar in the water and watch your dog take your hand off in the ring trying to get at it. Is your food or your dog's food too salty? If so, try adding a spoonful each of vinegar and sugar. Rid your hands of onion odors by using vinegar. Putting a few drops of vinegar in the cooking water keeps cabbage smells from drifting. Hot vinegar takes paint stains off glass, softens stiff paintbrushes and dog coats after a show. For clean, fluffy and soap-film free hair, do a final rinse with vinegar.

Bothered by unwanted dogs around your property when a bitch is in season? Try vinegar. When the bitch puddles, pour white vinegar on the spot immediately. I have done this for years and I have never been bothered by unwanted male visitors.

For really stubborn carpet odors and before you rip up the carpet to start over, try a chemical called neutroleum alpha. It neutralizes almost all odors. You may buy it from pest control companies (usually in 1-gallon containers), although you will not need that much for one or two problem areas. Transfer the chemical to a spray bottle of some kind and dampen the carpet with chemical. Let dry and wait two days. If odor is still noticeable, repeat. Note: it is safe for most carpets, but test a small area for colorfastness first.

Ground coffee will mask almost any odor. I cut old panty hose into sections. Then tie one end shut, add coffee and tie the top end shut. Toss these under furniture, under crate grills, into garbage cans, vehicles, etc.

Gypsum is very cheap and when spread over ground will take all kinds of dog smells away.

I have several dogs in the house but abhor a house that smells like dogs. When vacuuming, I pour a little Nilodor on a Kleenex and stick it into the vacuum bag. I also add a bit to my mop water and any basin of water I use for cleaning. For shampooing rugs, add Nilodor, etc. I even put it in the dogs' laundry and a little bit in their bath water. Even my non-dog friends comment on the absence of dog odor which makes the extra effort worthwhile.

I keep a large shaker-type dispenser filled with Arm & Hammer carpet deodorizer handy in our home. Whenever we are expecting guests, a few sprinkles here and there will freshen up the whole house. Be sure and mark your shaker so it won't be confused with another product.

Need help getting rid of odors? I use Spic and Span Pine Cleaner (other brands are good, too). I use it in the area where the dogs go to the bathroom. It disinfects and deodorizes. For larger kennels, it may be mixed with water to make it go further.

Nilodor is a wonderful product to use on pet odors. I keep a mist spray bottle filled with it at all times. Not only is it an easy way to freshen up the inside of crates, but it is also an easy way to freshen up the carpets.

One quick, easy way to freshen your entire house is to run half of a lemon down the garbage disposal.

Since I raise my puppies inside my home, I always make a homemade potpourri to keep those doggy odors away. Buy some spices at any grocery store. I use: 1 or 2 cinnamon stick(s), 1 whole clove, 1/4 teaspoon orange peel, 1/4 teaspoon apple pie spice and 1/2 teaspoon whole allspice. Boil these ingredients in a small saucepan half full of water for 1 minute, then reduce to a simmer and enjoy the wonderful smell.

Those commercial rug deodorizers are expensive and I'm not altogether convinced that they are totally safe for animals. Instead, I use good old baking soda with an addition of baby powder. For every 8 ounces of baking soda, I add 2 ounces of baby powder. This mixture is put into a shaker bottle (a bottle which has a cap). The baking soda absorbs the "doggy" odors and the baby powder just plain smells great. It's also an odor my dogs are familiar with and nobody (including me) gets the "sneezes" from the residue.

To quickly rid your house of doggy odor, put a tablespoon of ground cloves and a squeeze of lemon juice in rapidly boiling water. Boil for a few minutes and your house will take on a pleasantly spicy aroma.

To wash away strong odors and cut soap film, add vinegar or

lemon juice to the rinse water.

Vinegar is wonderful as a deodorant for accidents on carpets. You may pour it directly onto any color carpet without worrying about staining, and it eliminates the odor (even to a sensitive doggy nose).

We accidentally learned that after vacuuming up cinnamon, our vacuum cleaner made the whole house smell heavenly after use (eliminating doggy odors).

We make a simmering potpourri for those "puppy odors." In a small saucepan combine: 3 cups water, 1 teaspoon whole spices (allspice, cloves and nutmeg), 1 cinnamon stick and 1/2 cup of fruit. We have orange trees so we use oranges but any fruit you have on hand (apples, berries and even raisins) will do. Boil this for five minutes on the stove, then turn down to low and let it simmer. Replace water level as needed and you may keep it going all day. Guaranteed to please even the fussiest nose.

When you can't get the odor out of your carpet, try using a hypodermic syringe and needle to inject your favorite deodorizer under the carpet. It really works.

When you have a bitch in for breeding, do your boys go out of their minds even when separated by as much distance as space will allow? Try burning scented candles in the room with the bitch. *Make sure each lit candle is beyond the reach of your pet.*

~~~~~~~~~~ ≫ ≪ ~~~~~~~~~~

Kennel Maintenance

"Doggy-Doo" Patrol

An inexpensive tool for cleaning up the kennel yard is a child's leaf rake (available at Big Lots). Big Lots also has heavy-duty dust pans with the long handles (no bending over). They work just as good as the ones you buy in the pet catalogs or in the stores and what's better, you save money.

As I am not a "glove person," I've had lots of years of cold hands while doing my outside chores. When I grabbed onto a frozen metal pooper scooper, my hands would be aching by the end of my cleaning. I just tried something that works very well and thought that I'd pass it on. I wrapped the handles of my "scooper" with Vet Wrap. It's very inexpensive (at the feed stores) and comes in beautiful colors—even hot pink. It makes a soft, warm pretty handle to grab for those morning chores.

Clean the pooper-scooper pan by soaking it in the toilet and then flushing several times. Dry and spray with Pam.

Clean your pooper-scooper pan by washing it thoroughly and then spraying it with Pam. It will stay cleaner longer, especially in the winter.

Do you need large wrapping paper for mailing packages or sturdy paper for crafts or patterns? You already have them. Most dog food bags are made of several layers of paper. Cut off the top and bottom stitching and these layers separate. The middle layer is usually a strong, brown paper. There are many uses for this paper and the bags. Opened out, the paper makes a great garbage can lining. It stays in place better than the slithery plastic bags you buy, and it is more absorbent. Left as a bag, you have a portable container for "doggy-doo," aluminum cans, lawn clippings and general yard cleanup.

During the cold winter, I train myself to use my oven timer on the stove. After letting somebody out for a potty break, I turn it on so that I don't forget my dog is still outside.

Ever own a determined digger? Ever wonder what to do with your daily collection of doggy dung? Simple—just deposit problem "number 2" into problem "number 1" and pack over with 2" to 4" of dirt.

Ever poop-scoop at night and your lighting doesn't seem to light the entire area of your runs, or you can't examine those stools for possible parasites (especially after worming)? Solution: go to your local drug or discount store and pick up a "pen light" (one that lets you read maps, menus, etc.). Tape the slender flashlight to your scooper stick, and voila...let there be light.

For those of you who live in northern climates cleaning your dog's run is difficult when the wind chill is minus 30 degrees and the "you-know-what" is stuck to the concrete and/or the snow. After breaking a new, much-loved pooper-scooper trying to dislodge some, I began using an old putter of my husband's. Don't know if my golf scores will improve but it sure does the trick.

If you are only cleaning poop up for a few dogs, a good way to "store" it is in an old baby diaper pail. Plastic liners fit easily. There is a good handle and lid (some even lock), and there is a place for a deodorizer. They may be bought cheaply at yard or garage sales.

If you are tired of papers covering the entire puppy area, try this: after my puppies get the idea what the papers are for, I take my metal tray from a puppy crate and line it with papers. Placing this in the puppy play area, I remove the rest of the papers and they quickly get the idea that this is their spot. The tray is a nice size, providing your puppies room for walking and still find their favorite spot but is small enough to provide the puppies room to play. Your puppies soon learn where to go, the tray is easily cleaned and the puppies can't slide into messes as they spend the rest of their time playing. The tray is also nice when you have carpeting (since papers leak but metal does not).

I have a small boarding business and with customer's dogs and my own dogs, I had a problem with disposing of their stools. Solution: the Hefty Steel Sak Trash Bags work quite well for the pooper-scooper. Put the stools in the sack and if you use crushed stones like I do in the runs, the stones may go in the sack, too. These sacks are strong enough to hold everything.

I use bathroom bowl deodorizers in the garbage cans in which I place the dog droppings. Some are called toilet bowl deodorant (perfumed). I use wire ties to hold onto the plastic or wire (since moisture in the can may cause them to drop off). Sometimes in the summer it takes two.

Make it easier on yourself while picking up after your dogs. For pottying your dogs on those dark nights at a motel or on the showgrounds, get yourself a Flexi-leash with a little flashlight attached. It makes finding your dog's poop in the dark much easier. You may find them at Petsmart, Dollar General, etc., and online. I save mine to use at the motels and now there's no more hunting around for after-dark poo (especially in rainy or cold weather).

My husband does a "poo-poo patrol" several times a week. Paper bags turned out to be an inefficient way of containing the stuff. We now use empty bread bags, the plastic bags our newspaper come in, dinner roll bags, hot dog and hamburger bun bags, dog food bags, all kinds of plastic bags you get things in from the grocery store (makes me feel a tad better about how much we spend there), etc. They are perfect for the job and they are free.

Place mothballs in the bottom of your trash cans to discourage flies *(be sure to keep mothballs away from the dogs as those mothballs may be toxic if eaten)*. Keep a tight lid on to keep the vapor inside.

To combat yellow grass (which occurs from urine on the grass), mix 1 cup of agricultural lime with 3 gallons of water. Mix constantly as the lime does settle out. Pour onto the yellow grass. *Keep pets of grass until the grass is completely dry.*

To help pick up loose stools of females after whelping, use potting soil. Leave some over the spot after pickup as it absorbs and helps keep the flies away.

To put a stop to that canine "poop-scooper" in the back yard, try sprinkling Accent on his food. This seems to discourage him from eating poop.

Want an easy way to clean a pooper-scooper in cold weather when the hose is put away for the winter? Just soak the pooper-scooper in the toilet for a few minutes. Cleanup is a snap (or... should I say a flush?).

Want a pooper-scooper that doesn't require precise maneuvers? Try a dust pan and a coal shovel.

We keep our poop-scoops in buckets with water with a proper amount of clorox added. *Be sure that your dogs cannot get to it.*

Dog Runs and Outdoor Enclosures

A board across the width of your dog run (around 12" high for a medium-size dog) encourages jumping back and forth for improving your dog's muscle tone and is also good preparation for later advanced Obedience.

After writing an article on gravel runs, I have continually been plagued by urine odor in the run which is covered by an overhang. I mentioned that "Trail" was generally effective but I then tried kitty litter and felt it worked better. The problem with covered gravel runs is that the elements (rain, snow, etc.) do not wash away the odors. I have also used Nilodor on that run. It didn't do much to help either. My latest ploy is to use vinegar. I started with a 25 percent solution of vinegar. The acid in the vinegar neutralizes the ammonia from the urine. My dogs then smelled like vinegar. I spoke with my vet who suggested a 10 percent solution of vinegar mixed with a dash of dish-washing detergent to make the vinegar adhere to the gravel.

As a breeder of dogs, at one time or another you have probably rushed to the aid of a yelping puppy *to find a pup who has managed to get his head wedged between the bars of the exercise pen.* In a panic you work to remove the puppy's head from between the bars (while he fights with all his might to resist your help). Newspaper and cardboard modifications to the exercise pen's bars are fine but these fixes make it impossible to fold up the exercise pen. I found that if you take a roll of weaving strips (used to repair lawn chairs) and weave those strips in and out of the bars of the exercise pen, it then becomes safe, escape proof and easy to fold up and to transport. This weaving material is usually the same height as the exercise pen's bars.

A way to keep puppies warm and busy outside in the late fall is to put the leaves you rake up in a 10' x 10' pen (size may vary) and put the puppies inside the pen. They'll have a ball because they love romping through the leaves. If there are some small twigs with the leaves, the pups may chew on them and play "keep-away." Once the pups tire out, the leaves will keep them warm.

A wise precaution to take (if you have small puppies exercising in a dog run which has the chain-link cyclone fence fabric) is to put 12" to 24" of 1-inch mesh or hardware wire all around the bottom and on its outside. *I had a seven-week-old puppy who put his head through the 2 1/2-inch diameter opening and got stuck.* While I held the puppy so he wouldn't struggle, a neighbor (who had heard the commotion) used pliers to unweave the fence (at its base) in order to free this puppy's head. If I had used the wire mesh, this could have been avoided. I was lucky because I hadn't left those pups unsupervised and I saw this dangerous incident as it was actually occurring.

Before letting your dogs out to run in the snow, generously apply Vaseline between the toes on each foot. This will prevent the formation of ice balls *(which cause a great deal of discomfort)* and will keep the snow from adhering.

Bothered by unwanted dogs around your property when a bitch is in season? Try vinegar. When the bitch puddles, pour white vinegar on the spot immediately. I have done this for years and I have never been bothered by unwanted male visitors.

Discarded platform skids (often found at local lumber yards, fence dealers or home centers) make fine sunning platforms (when covered with indoor/outdoor carpeting, linoleum or board) for puppies or older dogs when set out in your runs. In the heat of the day, the dogs like to dig down under them to the cool dirt below not to mention the neat chasing games that are encouraged—especially "King of the Mountain."

During the summer months, I always purchase two of the kiddie wading pools. One day, while in a pinch, I found that the combination of a kiddie pool and an eight-panel playpen makes a great corral for toddling puppies and even for older puppies. It's waterproof and may be lined with paper. The extra kiddie pool may quickly replace the other pool when you're cleaning it.

Fireplace tongs make great arm extensions for reaching over exercise pens to either place or to retrieve bowls.

For a cheap exercise pen, I buy compost bins (used for storing leaves after raking, etc.). I quite often find them on sale at hardware stores. They are approximately 4' by 4' square and two or three bins may be attached together to make a larger pen. They make a great pen for the mom and her puppies and also make excellent whelping boxes. You may put them around a cardboard box and deliver the puppies inside and still keep the bitch enclosed.

For a new litter of puppies or kittens, confine them in a mesh playpen. Tape screen around a wooden playpen with wooden slats so pups or kittens won't get out. Children's plastic pools are great for new puppies. The pool may be rinsed out to rid odors or messes.

For inexpensive shade, my son covered the run with leftover wire fence. Then he covered the top with a bed spread. By covering just the top, it did not create an eye sore. I had shade in summer and in winter I removed the bed spread to let in the warmth of the sun.

For those of you with gravel runs, if they begin to get smelly (particularly after a rain), add Kitty Litter containing chlorophyll. It will remove odors caused by urine.

For those who have wire handles on exercise pens, make it easier on your hands. Get an old piece of hose (a garden hose works well) and measure the amount of hose you'll need for the handle where your hand will grip it. Slice the hose on one side from one end to the other. Slip it onto the handle and tape hose shut with tape. (I find friction tape works well.) Wrap the tape around the length of the hose several times. It makes pens so much easier to carry.

Give your dogs extra shade during the hot summer afternoons and at the same time, give yourself the bonus of really fragrant runs by planting a sweet-smelling vine on the west side of your pen or run areas. We used honeysuckle because it grows extremely fast and the blossoms are so sweet. It blooms all summer, too. I was really concerned at first that bees might be a problem, but we've had the vines for four years now with no bee problem.

Gypsum is very cheap and when spread over ground will take all kinds of dog smells away.

Having trouble keeping those little puppies inside that wading pool? Try putting chicken wire around the pool. It's very flexible, comes in different heights and it's very easy to remove (so you may store it away for your next litter).

Here's a twist for the outdoor or indoor dog bed. I filled a durable cloth pillow case with one-half cedar shavings and one-half of those white packing pellets *(make sure dogs don't eat the pellets)*. The cedar shavings give the bed a nice fragrance, and the white packing pellets absorb the dog's body heat (providing him with a nice winter bed in his doghouse). I stitched in a zipper but a piece of Velcro with a flap would serve nicely, also. I have heard that cedar shavings repels fleas.

How do you stop the mud next to your fence? Try getting some room-sized rug pieces which are being discarded. Place them in the area and watch the muddy feet disappear. When they become too worn, throw them away.

I buy old couch cushions at second-hand stores. These work great to put in my indoor and outdoor runs in the winter to keep my dogs off the cement. If they chew the cushion, I just get more cushions. I was surprised one morning to discover pieces of paper money torn up all over. Someone had hidden $17 in a cushion and my dogs had discovered it. Needless to say I washed, ironed and taped the bills back together and traded them in at the bank. The bank tellers had a good laugh, too.

If you can spare it, an old exercise pen is great to provide temporary protection for a small section of a garden or lawn where plants are emerging and are still in that tender stage.

If you have unwanted grass or weeds around your dog's run or exercise area, be careful what you use to kill the unwanted plant growth. *Some poisons are retained in plants (even after those plants are dead from being sprayed by weed killer). If a puppy or adult chews on the exposed grass or weeds, dogs could become seriously ill.* Instead...use salt to kill unwanted grass or weeds. If your dog eats it, the salt will not seriously hurt him but it will kill the weeds

If you're tired of having those aluminum clip-on water dishes knocked over by active puppies, find some smooth, round or oval palm-sized rocks and put them in the dishes before adding water. They clean easily in soapy water with a potato scrubbing brush and fit in the cutlery section of most dishwashers. The rocks I've been using weigh approximately 1/2 pound to 3/4 pound and are about 1" thick and 3" oval/round. You'll get used to the strange looks and remarks from visitors after awhile, but it really does help.

If you use an All-Weather Blanket (or Space Blanket with one reflective side) or any other kind of cover with grommets to cover

your exercise pen, use "S" hooks for attaching the cover to your exercise pen. Put one end of the "S" hook into the grommet and tighten with a pair of pliers. The open end may be attached to the wire of the exercise pen and works very well to keep the cover from blowing off (clothespins seem to get blown off easily.) My cover only has four grommets and at a show one weekend where it was very windy, it never blew off.

I had a puppy with a habit of digging into my chicken cage and stealing the chickens. As this could become hazardous to his health, I devised something that keeps dogs from either digging out of or into another kennel. I had tried burying large cement blocks under the edge, but they always just dug under the blocks so I cut chicken wire into 12-inch-wide strips and carefully secured it to the bottom pole of the kennel with baling wire all the way around. Then I buried it in about 10" of dirt. When the dogs dug and hit the chicken wire, they can go no farther and usually give up after a few tries. Be sure to lay a strip inside and outside of the kennel to prevent digging in or out.

I have a couple of large pens where several dogs run together. When they're excited, they all jump against the gate making it almost impossible to open without an "escape." One day when coming home to the excited group, I noticed a throw-can of pennies that I'd left by the pen when silencing a barking episode a few days earlier. A simple shake sent the dogs scurrying. I now keep such a can by each gate and may easily enter even when the dogs are excited.

I have found a fine pair of shoes for kennel work. They are waterproof moccasins that keep my feet dry as I hose down the runs. They may be ordered from the Sears Winter Catalog and are not expensive. They are comfortable, lightweight and warm. I often use them for shopping on a rainy or snowy day. My husband has a pair from the "Bean" catalog. These, however, are more expensive. Also, they come in handy for wet show grounds.

I have found that hanging an animal-drinking bottle (the kind used for rabbits and other small animals) on the pen when puppies are just beginning to move around allows them to quickly learn to drink from the stainless steel tube. This helps keep the puppies more content when they're thirsty and also keeps them drier (since they can't spill pans of water).

I have started a lot of people using chicken or rabbit cages for their new puppies *(be sure wire does not allow pups' feet to fall through openings which might hurt their tender paws)*. These wire cages have pullout trays so unmentionables will fall through and keep the puppy high and dry. Also, be sure to clean out whatever does not fall through the wire. What's more, these cages are half the price or less than the same type of cage designed and sold specifically for dogs. I buy mine at a nearby animal feed store. They may be cleaned even while the puppy sleeps. After lining the trays with newspaper or brown sacks, I pour a little cat litter on the tray which absorbs all odors.

In the East, a good base for dog runs is 1 1/2-inch rock. Rocks here are glacial and so smooth. Rocks this large will not be moved around much by the dogs and may be sprayed easily with a hose for cleaning. We use 12" to 18" of rock in the dog yard and find it easy to clean or disinfect and extremely attractive to look at. It drains beautifully, too.

It used to be difficult to keep hair webs from collecting and looking unsightly in my professional dog runs. I tried the hose on them including the expensive power hose kind that you rent for a lot of money. This looked great until everything dried and the hair webs came right back. I tried picking them out by hand and brushing them out with all kinds of brushes. One person told me I should burn them out with a torch. I have a lot of covered professional runs that are 6' high and did not want to go the burning route if I could avoid that. Finally, one day after dusting down the cobwebs from my house, I thought of a bright idea. I took my fluffy little wool cobweb duster out to the kennels. There I began dusting my very webby runs. Now I always keep a duster (little wool pom-poms on a stick) in the dog runs. I have the cleanest runs in town. Try it, you'll like it. I buy my Dustbusters at a supermarket. They come in all kinds of bright colors, too.

I wouldn't wish this on my worst enemy, but I fell and broke my hip. (Yes, I was out on the ice trying to get a dog). After surgery (and moving around the house on a "walker"), I was given something called a "grabber." This allowed me to pick up things without bending (which I wasn't supposed to do). Well, as things progressed and I could finally pick up pens, toys, dishes, etc., I found this "grabber" an invaluable tool. It has sort of "claws" on one end plus a handle that one may press in order to close its claws. This came from OT (occupational therapy) at the hospital.

Lack of shade may cause really "icky" sunburned coats. (I am speaking from experience.) We have finally found a solution by lacing shade cloth over the pen areas until our trees get to a decent size.

Light rain may intensify all those kennel odors. Use 1/2 cup of bleach to 1 gallon of water. Pour it onto the concrete and spread it around with an old broom. Be sure to wear old clothes and shoes in case of splashes. Don't rinse. The next day the cement will smell fresh and clean. *Keep your dogs off the wet cement until there is no chance they could come in contact with any bleach.*

Make a fun "fort" for your dogs. We use bales of love grass (a fine stemmed prairie hay) to build forts for the dogs. They love playing "King of the Mountain," "Hide and Seek" and all sorts of games on, around and under these bales. They create a terrific windbreak, too. We surround the big shade tables in the pens every fall with fresh bales. Our dogs go wild as they love playing on these bales. In the spring, the same hay is used to mulch the trees, garden, etc. *You do have to continually check for loosening wire or rope so the dogs do not get injured*...but with common sense, it is a terrific form of exercise and enjoyment for our dogs.

Many clip-on food/water dishes do not fit snugly on wire crates and play pens. Decide where you want to put the dishes (in puppy pens, put the dishes toward the back to keep the little darlings' feet out of them as they stand and jump to greet you). With masking or adhesive tape, circle the wire a few times until the clips fit tightly. The tape is easily removed (especially masking tape), and then the tape and dishes may be raised up as the puppies grow in height.

Most people use exercise pens to keep dogs confined in a place. I do, too, but I also use my exercise pens to keep dogs out of certain places.

Need a cheap exercise pen for puppies? Try a compost rack, located in the garden section of Walmart. It is a lightweight, 4' x 4' x 3' plastic-coated metal cage.

Protect your garbage bags from outdoor pests by spraying the outside of the garbage bags with Pine Sol. This will repel animals intent on tearing the bags open.

Provide a cool and moist outdoor environment for your dogs

on the hottest days by attaching one of the flat tube sprinkler hoses to the top edge of your fencing aiming the tiny holes toward the pen. You may provide a very fine mist or a light rain shower by adjusting the water pressure and the dogs love it. It's especially great for puppies and for dogs you are trying to keep in decent coat condition. Naturally, it works best if there is shade provided as well.

Shower curtain rings are very handy to a dog owner. These shower curtain rings hold water buckets on the fences (we use the relatively light two-quart stainless steel type). Some are attached to the Space Blankets we use to cover the exercise pens at outdoor shows. They are light, easily opened, not prone to rust and are inexpensive.

Simple and inexpensive pen tops for the 4' x 4' pens may easily be made from one single section of the type of pens that are "built" by individual sections. Our pen tops overlapped the 4' x 4's by about a foot, and I finally discovered that it was easy to bend that one foot over by standing on the pen section and pulling up. Then simply strap the top on with those elastic straps (bungee cords) which we use to tie down pens, etc., to our station wagon racks.

Since I cannot pass up a usable item which is left out in the trash to be picked up, I usually toss it in the back of my station wagon. I saw some discarded oak wood pallets, with the planks close together and (with the help of a friend) we loaded a couple of them in the car. I took them home, disinfected them and had them placed in my dogs fenced yard. My dogs love to stretch out on them to get a good sunning. A unexpected benefit is that my dogs' coats are staying cleaner and these pallets cost me nothing. There is no problem of wood splinters due to gnawing since oak is a hard, tight grain wood.

Since I have room for only a few dogs and can't build a good kennel set-up, I make do with two 6' by 12' cyclone runs in my back yard. To discourage diggers and to provide a solid base for the kennels to sit on, my husband sunk railroad ties about two thirds into the ground and sat the cyclone kennel runs on those railroad ties. The inside area may be either poured-in concrete, filled with gravel or shavings. All work well.

Spread Borax (1 pound per 100 square feet and watered down) to kill all worm larvae in your runs. Caution: it will also kill all the grass. *Keep your dog away until the mixture is dry.*

The best thing to use in the dog runs and on all the slippery spots in the kennel yard (when those icy days arrive) is Kitty Litter. It is very effective, cannot burn the dogs' feet and if they lick their feet, it is harmless if ingested. It is also the most effective to use (at a dog show or during any other travel) if your car is stuck in a slippery spot as it will provide instant traction.

The home improvement center in our neighborhood sets its broken pallets out for anyone to take away—for free. Often these pallets are only cracked or slightly broken but they can no longer be used to hold heavy loads. Taken home, they make wonderful sleeping or playing platforms for your dog runs. I usually cover mine with artificial turf and I put molding around the edges so that puppies can't get at the edges to chew. *Check the pallets carefully before you use them to make sure there are no nails sticking out.*

The large 32-ounce plastic water bottles used in rabbit cages work great for medium-size dogs. Just hang them on the outside of your exercise pen or kennel run. I do not use them as a sole source of water for adults as I also provide a bucket. But for puppies and supplemental water for the adults they work great. *They are not to be used in sunshine.* Follow the directions on the bottle to prevent excessive dripping. They keep puppies from getting wet, from playing in their water buckets, along with having hair, dust and shavings not falling into the water. Puppies and adults both seem to catch on right away regarding how to use them, and they enjoy the noise the roller makes as they lick the bottle. To teach your dog how to drink from them, first make sure your dog is thirsty. Put your finger where the bottle is dripping very slightly. Your dog will lick your finger with water on it and then start licking the spout. A bit of peanut butter on the tip of the spout could be used for very slow learners. Puppies seem to catch on all by themselves about four weeks of age. I have tried Farnam, Lixit and Oasis brands and they all seem to work equally well. They are available in most pet shops. I use a large, #500 crate for whelping so I also fasten one of these water bottles to the outside of the crate door so the bitch has unlimited water always available to her.

The Ortho Dial 'N Spray Hose-End Sprayer is a great accessory for cleaning or disinfecting kennels and runs. Fill it with your cleaning solution or disinfectant and attach it to the end of your hose. Set the dial for the dilution factor that works best for you (anything from less than an ounce to 8 ounces per gallon of water). Turn on the hose and spray your perfectly-mixed solution.

To combat yellow grass (which occurs from urine on the grass), mix 1 cup of agricultural lime with 3 gallons of water. Mix constantly as the lime does settle out. Pour onto the yellow grass. *Keep pets of grass until the grass is completely dry.*

To discourage dogs from jumping out of an exercise pen, I attach about a 4-inch piece of fine chain to his web collar. At the end of the chain a tennis ball is attached *(make sure the chain is no longer than 4" because you don't want your dog to be able to chew the tennis ball)*. When my dog jumps, the ball bounces against him and he is quickly discouraged from this practice.

To keep stray dogs or other animals from attacking your garbage, sprinkle full strength ammonia over the garbage bags before placing them in the cans.

To make our portable runs truly portable, we leveled the ground where we wanted to set up the runs, smoothed it with sand and laid it with concrete stepping stones. They are wonderful. You don't have to be a professional to install them. They give you all the advantages of concrete and if you have to move you can just pack them up, tell the prospective buyers it's a "garden patch" and off you go.

To provide water while in a kennel or in a exercise pen, we use large rabbit bottles. Just hook the bottle to the outside with the spout pointing into the enclosed area.

To save multiple trips into a dog run, I hang a two-quart stainless steel bucket on a light chain to hold water. By doing this, I just need to go up to the fence, raise the pail, rinse and fill it up with clean water and then lower it back into it original position. I keep the chain's length just long enough to let the pail rest on the ground. It then cannot be tipped over. I have another pail set up in the same manner which I fill with dry kibble when my dogs are on a self-feeding plan.

Troubled by ants and don't want to use a poison in your dogs' yard or run? Try sprinkling the area with ants with cucumber peelings (instead of using insecticides which may be dangerous to your dogs).

Usually my puppies are confined during the day in their puppy yard. To expand their experiences, I sometimes let them explore the main yard and patio, but first I puppy proof it. I place an exercise pen around an ornamental pond to prevent them from falling in and another pen around tender plants that they might destroy.

We have two exercise pens sitting under our covered patio which we use to keep our two dogs in during the night. They don't bark whenever they're kept inside these outside exercise pens, plus they are protected from the rain. I have two large wooden boxes in which they sleep. During the summer being outdoors is fine; however in cold weather, I wanted something to protect them from the drafts and wind so I made a cover which is easily removed but which can't be knocked off. The 1/4" panelling I've used surrounds the exercise pen. Remember to leave an opening for entering and exiting.

When building an outdoor run, lay wire fencing on the ground before the gravel is put down. Dogs will not be able to dig any further down than to the level of the wire.

When my puppies are very young, I put a bunch of cardboard boxes of varying sizes in their play area. They love to climb on top of them and play "King of the Mountain." This seems to help with training them to be on a grooming table since they are already accustomed to being off the ground.

Which exercise pen is yours? Ever wonder about that when traveling with several others to a show or when taking down a community setup in the dark? I mark my pens by attaching one of those little metal pet-collar tags which are personalized with dog's name, owner's name and address. I substitute my kennel name for the "dog's name" part. The metal collar loop attaches the tag to the pen permanently. My tags come from Milk Bones (via box tops) but they are also usually available in your vet's office and in pet stores.

Would you like some inexpensive kennel items? Take advantage of your local swap meet, flea market and garage sales. You would be surprised how many people have goodies (like old fencing) for sale. They are more than willing to sell them for very reasonable prices.

You may use the plastic tubs that peanut butter or butter come in as feeders and water pails which may then be attached to your exercise pen or wire crate. Also, they store grooming powder safely.

Outdoor Housing

Do you have an early and noisy riser in your kennel? I do. He wakes everyone up. So I put a sheet over his enclosure (just as is done with a bird). Now he stays quiet until I remove the sheet and it's time to get up.

Even though our puppies and visiting bitches are kept in air-conditioned areas, we often direct a fan toward them for extra cooling during those hot summer months. Since they are kept on newspapers, it used to be a big problem to keep the papers from blowing all over the place. I learned that by overlapping the newspapers (similar to shingles on a roof) and by starting at the farthest point away from the fan and putting each new section about halfway over the last, each paper holds the other in place. The last section (which is closest to the fan) is weighted with nice, fat complete sections of newspaper (for the extra weight needed to hold down the paper completely).

For the people who need to leave their dogs in a kennel or

in the house alone when they are at work during the day, I have found that it's a good idea to always turn on a radio whenever I am away. By turning on music, my dogs always have something consistent and soothing to listen to rather than hearing outside noises which may then cause them to bark. It works very well in an apartment, too.

Here's a twist for the outdoor or indoor dog bed. I filled a durable cloth pillow case with one-half cedar shavings and one-half of those white packing pellets *(make sure dogs don't eat the pellets)*. The cedar shavings give the bed a nice fragrance, and the white packing pellets absorb the dog's body heat (providing him with a nice winter bed in his doghouse). I stitched in a zipper but a piece of Velcro with a flap would serve nicely, also. I have heard that cedar shavings repels fleas.

I buy old couch cushions at second-hand stores. These work great to put in my kennel building and in the indoor-outdoor runs in the winter to keep my dogs off the cement. If they chew the cushion, I just get more cushions.

If you don't have a wet/dry shop vac, you should think seriously about investing in one. They're marvelous for vacuuming out crates and for catching those "fuzz puppies" which accumulate in the corners of your kennel building.

If your dog stays outside in a doghouse, make a flap for the doghouse's entrance to keep the wind and rain out. A rubber floor mat or carpeting cut to size and slit up the middle makes a nice flap.

I have found that hanging an animal-drinking bottle (the kind used for rabbits and other small animals) on the pen when puppies are just beginning to move around allows them to quickly learn to drink from the stainless steel tube. This helps keep the puppies more content when they're thirsty and also keeps them drier (since they can't spill pans of water).

I have started a lot of people using chicken or rabbit cages for their new puppies *(be sure wire does not allow pups' feet to fall through openings which might hurt their tender paws)*. These wire cages have pullout trays so unmentionables will fall through and keep the puppy high and dry. Also, be sure to clean out whatever does not fall through the wire. What's more, these cages are half the price or less than the same type of cage designed and sold specifically for dogs. I buy mine at a nearby animal feed store. They may be cleaned even while the puppy sleeps. After lining the trays with newspaper or brown sacks, I pour a little cat litter on the tray which absorbs all odors.

In my kennel building, I put carpet remnants between the crates and the walls to protect the walls.

Instead of using sawdust shavings for dogs, I use the cedar shavings which you may purchase at Walmart. It's inexpensive and your dogs will smell so good.

Rather than spend a lot on commercial vinyl tiles for cages and pens, I suggest you go to a good carpet or linoleum store. I picked up an end of linoleum which was also coated with plastic on the reverse side. It made great pads for my outdoor doghouses. They are sturdy and easily washable.

The large 32-ounce plastic water bottles used in rabbit cages work great for medium-size dogs. Just hang them on the outside of your exercise pen or kennel run. I do not use them as a sole source of water for adults as I also provide a bucket. But for puppies and supplemental water for the adults they work great. *They are not to be used in sunshine.* Follow the directions on the bottle

to prevent excessive dripping. They keep puppies from getting wet, from playing in their water buckets, along with having hair, dust and shavings not falling into the water. Puppies and adults both seem to catch on right away regarding how to use them, and they enjoy the noise the roller makes as they lick the bottle. To teach your dog how to drink from them, first make sure your dog is thirsty. Put your finger where the bottle is dripping very slightly. Your dog will lick your finger with water on it and then start licking the spout. A bit of peanut butter on the tip of the spout could be used for very slow learners. Puppies seem to catch on all by themselves about four weeks of age. I have tried Farnam, Lixit and Oasis brands and they all seem to work equally well. They are available in most pet shops. I use a large, #500 crate for whelping so I also fasten one of these water bottles to the outside of the crate door so the bitch has unlimited water always available to her.

The Ortho Dial n' Spray hose-end sprayer is a great accessory for cleaning or disinfecting kennels and runs. Fill it with your cleaning solution or disinfectant and attach it to the end of your hose. Set the dial for the dilution factor that works best for you (anything from less than an ounce to 8 ounces per gallon of water). Turn on the hose and spray your perfectly-mixed solution.

Those washable and reusable air-conditioning filters make nice beds. When my crate's dog floors finally gave out, I used these filters. They may be put into the washing machine (gentle cycle only) and washed. You may also sprinkle flea repellent (such as Sevin dust) underneath each filter.

⋯⋯ ≫ ≪ ⋯⋯

Naming Your Dog

Have you ever been in a quandary trying to name your puppies? I know it was always a problem for me until I discovered *Names Not Currently Available in the American Stud Book*, published by The Jockey Club, 40 East 52nd Street, New York, NY 10022, (212) 371-5970. There are about a half-million names in each edition and I have shared mine with many friends in several different breeds. I consider it one of the most welcome additions to my library. One copy would last a lifetime.

Having a problem coming up with names for your young hopefuls? Start keeping a notebook now. Whenever you see or hear a phrase you like, write it down. Next litter you'll have several names from which to choose.

Having trouble thinking of registered names for your dogs? Pick up scratch sheets or a racing form at a race track or a race book. There are about 200 names of thoroughbred horses per sheet.

I have found many great names for bitches by reading the names of various beauty products. I keep a notebook filled with these and other great dog names.

Specialty shops and stores have fabulous names for your future puppies. Whenever you see a clever and possible name for that special future pup, write it in a notebook (which you should carry in your car). By writing down these unique names, when your litter has arrived, all those many names will be quickly available.

⋯⋯ ≫ ≪ ⋯⋯

Obedience and Performance

Clothing

If you wear dark pants and white shoes in Obedience work, your dog will have a visual advantage since the white contrasting shoes serve as excellent guides in both the "heel" and the "recall."

Equipment

A board across the width of your dog run (around 12" high for a medium-size dog) encourages jumping back and forth for improving your dog's muscle tone and is also good preparation for later advanced Obedience.

To keep the ends white on your show dumbbell, try using the white nontoxic shoe polish (as used on children's shoes).
It's easy to apply and it dries quickly for that "just-painted" look at every show.

Judging

(See "RECORDS"—"Judges and Judging")

Training

(Also see "TRAINING"—"Performance Training")

Accustom your future Obedience champion to jump the painted bar jump by starting him out as a puppy jumping a 4-foot-long, 1/2-inch wooden dowel. We paint ours black and white like the bar jump and start our puppies jumping...just for fun. By the time your dog is ready for advanced Obedience, the black-and-white bar is a familiar signal (for fun and not something to be feared).

If you have a dog who absolutely refuses to carry a hard, wooden dumbbell in his soft little mouth, try using an old play sock or rag and wrap the center bar until it is soft and chewable. As the dog becomes more and more relaxed with carrying it, cut away layers bit by bit until you are finally back down to the naked bar.

If you have ever trained a dog in Obedience, I'm sure you'll agree that one of the exercises which demands accuracy in the footwork of both dog and handler is the Figure 8 exercise. In trying to simulate two posts, I have used a variety of objects, animate as well as inanimate, but I had difficulty in regulating the size of the circle. A friend of mine gave me the idea to use two Hula Hoops. They approximate the area that a human post would occupy and they're easy to store, brightly colored and inexpensive.

Occasionally that excellent Novice dog rebels when he moves on to Open Obedience because he hesitates to work away from his owner. We solved that problem by beginning "go-outs" with puppies. Start with an upside-down margarine container. Put a lead on the puppy (he doesn't have to be lead-trained, just willing to accept a little control). Place a tiny bite of liver, bologna, etc., on the bowl. Take the puppy back a couple of steps and tell him, "go out" or whatever command you choose to say. He'll gobble up the tidbit and you must immediately call him back to you. Then feed him another tiny mouthful when he arrives. You can increase the distance gradually until your three- or four-month-old puppy can do a "go-out" from 20 feet. I started this with a seven-week-old puppy and he was a pro at four months. This is also a good way to increase trainability with Conformation pups. It is a high-enthusiasm, no-punishment exercise which reinforces the bonds between you and your pup.

We all know not to call dogs to us for punishment (otherwise they'll never come), but sometimes we don't realize what, to a dog, is considered as punishment. I noticed my usually friendly and obedient dogs were refusing to come when I called them. I then realized that every time I called them to me it was because I intended to kennel them and they knew it. Now when I call them to me, I pet them and let them go their way before kenneling them (usually with food waiting for them...inside their crates).

When show-training young dogs, I have found an easy solution to instill self-confidence. I work the young dog on a brace with an older, seasoned show dog. It helps the youngster to relax. Soon he starts to imitate and compete with the older dog and begins to enjoy every minute of it.

———— ≫ ≪ ————

Older Dogs

An increased or decreased appetite, unexplained weight gain or weight loss may be linked to many different conditions especially in an older dog. These include internal organ disease (kidney, liver or heart), diabetes, oral problems (periodontitis, abscessed teeth, mouth tumors), hormonal imbalances, abdominal tumors and/or parasitic disease. An accurate diagnosis is critical for effective treatment.

Before putting an older or ill dog to bed, fluff a towel in the dryer and place it in the bed to make a cozy sleeping area.

If you have an older dog who is going blind or who is blind, make moving about your home easier for him by spraying a light air freshener scent on all the furniture and other obstacles which would be at nose or head height. Be sure it goes onto the furniture and not just into the air. Use a different scent for general air freshening.

If your older dog is limping or exhibiting lameness, the most common cause is arthritis (also called DJD or degenerative joint disease). Besides limping, dogs with DJD may be stiff or reluctant to exercise and may have trouble getting up or climbing stairs. Treatments include anti-inflammatory pain medication, joint and nutritional supplements, exercise therapy and, most importantly, weight control. Other causes of lameness include injury, various diseases and cancer.

Pedialyte is an oral electrolyte solution (which you may keep on hand) for both newborns and for older dogs. Give a weak newborn puppy a dropperful every hour. Pedialyte is found in the canned milk section of the baby department. It comes in several strengths so *check with you vet for the best strength to use for your pup or older dog.*

Reuse old crib bumpers as liners for dog beds and crates. They are especially useful for the older dog so he may lean against something soft.

Small, benign fatty tumors are common in older dogs. After being diagnosed, they are often left in place unless they become larger, interfere with movement or there is a change in appearance and firmness, however other more aggressive tumors should always be treated. Surgical removal is necessary treatment for most skin tumors and radiation therapy or chemotherapy may also be advised.

Teaching your dog hand signals prior to old age and loss of hearing seemed to help our older dogs cope with their handicap when their hearing was no longer keen. It also helps us to cope. I also taught them to come to the back door when the porch light is flashed on and off at night. It surely beats trying to find them in the dark (during those cold nights) to let them back in the house when they can't hear you call them.

Your older dog might have a dental disorder, sinus disease or mouth tumor if he is dropping food from his mouth, has difficulty chewing, is chewing only on one side, rubbing his face or has bad breath. Sometimes lack of appetite, weight loss, sneezing or nasal discharge are also occurring. Teeth cleaning, removal of diseased teeth and antibiotic treatment should be investigated.

Other Pets

Birds

If you have an indoor bird as a pet and he gets loose in the house, try this method of catching him: close the drapes and turn off the lights. Birds will usually stay motionless in the dark and you'll be able to catch him easier. Try letting the bird out of his cage and train him to step on your finger. This will encourage a better relationship and a happier bird.

If you're a bird lover, make nesting easier by providing building material. Collect bits of string, yarn, hair from your brush and lint from your dryer. Fasten them together lightly and attach them to a tree branch.

In winter, treat birds to a pine treat by covering pine cones with hardened bacon grease (or other fat) and roll in bread crumbs or bird seeds. Pine cones may also be coated with peanut butter and rolled in sunflower seeds.

To attract birds to an outdoor birdbath, drop a few colored marbles into their water.

When your dog is tired of playing with his Frisbee, fill it with water and place it in an area where the birds may drink and bathe in that Frisbee.

Cats

A cardboard box will make a great toy for your cat. Cut holes in these small boxes. Make those openings just a little larger than your cat's paw. Tape the flaps down (so they're closed). Place some small toys inside (like a ping pong ball or a cat's toy filled with catnip). You could even include dry cat food or cat treats.

Acetaminophen (which is found in Tylenol) and other medications, *may cause liver damage in dogs. Cats are even more sensitive to Acetaminophen. Ingestion of a single 325 mg. tablet by a 10-pound cat may cause anemia and even be fatal.*

Always keep the toilet lid down if you use toilet bowl cleaners as *these cleaners are often strongly alkaline and tempting for pets to drink.*

Antifreeze may be fatal to a cat (even in small amounts). They will need immediate emergency care. Symptoms of antifreeze poisoning include drunk-like behavior, vomiting, excessive urination, drinking and depression. Pets may appear to recover within a few hours, but the antifreeze continues to poison their systems and is often fatal.

A ping pong ball inside an empty tissue box makes a great toy for your cat. Use a rectangular-shaped tissue box and not a square box so your cat will have more room to bat the ball around.

A spray bottle of water will quickly train a cat not to do something.

As safe as air shipping is, there was an unfortunate situation where a cat in a Sky Kennel was injured. The crate was accidentally tipped over and *the poor kitty's leg was trapped.* Tape down your pegboard floors.

Attach a string to a ping-pong ball and hang it on a chair or shelf to entertain your pet.

Batteries may be toxic to both dogs and cats which may lead to ulcers in the mouth, esophagus or stomach.

Be certain automotive antifreeze is kept out of reach and any antifreeze drippings are totally removed. Pets are attracted to its scent. *Antifreeze is highly toxic.*

Cats and other pets are vulnerable to hypothermia and frostbite. Immediately take your pet to a vet if he is shivering, disoriented and lethargic or if his hair is puffed out and standing on end. Frostbite may turn skin bright red, pale or black. Skin at tips of ears and on extremities (including reproductive organs) are particularly at risk.

Cats hate plastic so...keep your cat off your chairs by covering the chair with plastic until he learns it's "off limits."

Cats love to hide in empty boxes or paper sacks.

Chocolate may cause seizures and death in cats and dogs. Darker chocolate (such as unsweetened baker's chocolate) is more toxic than milk or white chocolate. Even cocoa bean mulch, when eaten in large quantities, may be a problem.

Corn oil prevents hairballs in cats. Add a few drops of corn oil to your pets' food to prevent hairballs from forming. The thick oil helps the fur pass through the animal's system much quicker and easily.

Detergents and fabric softener sheets may cause ulcers in the mouth, esophagus and stomach in cats and dogs.

Ethylene glycol is found in antifreeze, windshield de-icing agents and motor oils. Cats and dogs are attracted to the sweet taste of Ethylene glycol but as little as a teaspoon in a cat or a tablespoon in a dog may cause kidney failure.

Fertilizers may contain poisonous amounts of nitrogen, phosphorus, potassium, iron, zinc, herbicides and pesticides. Keep cats and dogs away from treated lawns until they are dry. Follow the product's instructions before permitting pets to walk on the lawn.

For a new litter of kittens, confine them in a mesh playpen. Tape screen around a wooden playpen with wooden slats so kittens won't get out.

Garbage bag twist ties and the plastic rings from the neck of plastic gallon milk containers are hours of entertainment for cats.

Household cleaners, such as bleach, drain cleaners, ammonia and toilet bowl cleaners may cause gastrointestinal ulcers and other problems in cats and dogs.

If you have a large box, cut the bottom out and make a play tunnel for your cat. If you have several boxes, put them together and make a little adventure land for your cat. Hide toys or treats in the corners of the boxes.

If you play a guitar and have a guitar string available, you can make a fishing pole-type toy for your cat. Secure a small toy to one end (such as a fuzzy mouse, a feather or whatever other small, lightweight toy you may have). Then make a handle by duct-taping a popsicle stick to its opposite end.

If your cat eats just one of your acetaminophen cold or flu pills, it could be fatal.

If your cat has an accident, blot up as much moisture as possible. Rub the spot with a solution of vinegar or lemon juice and warm sudsy water. Blot a few times, and then pour straight club soda over the spot and blot again. Place a dry towel over the stain and put a heavy object (like a book) on top of it. Replace the towel if it becomes soggy and repeat blotting. When the spot is dry, rub with a cloth dampened with ammonia. This will take the offensive odor away and it will prevent the cat from ever going in that spot again.

If your cat has an encounter with a skunk, wash your cat in tomato juice while you're both in a well-ventilated area. Then wash with shampoo and water. Rinse with a gallon of water to which a few tablespoons of ammonia have been added. Thoroughly rinse your cat with clear water.

Insecticides in flea and tick products may cause problems if not used according to labels. *Insecticides which are meant for dogs may cause severe toxicity in cats, leading to signs such as vomiting, seizures and difficulty in breathing. Products intended for treating the yard or house should not be used on pets.*

Jimson weed, also known as devil's trumpet, may cause restlessness, drunken walking and respiratory failure in cats and in dogs.

Kerosene, gasoline and tiki torch fluids may cause drooling, drunken walking and difficulty breathing in both cats and dogs. If these products contain antifreeze, they are even more problematic (potentially life-threatening).

Lilies (Easter, day, tiger, Japanese and Asiatic varieties) may cause kidney failure in cats. Lilies of the valley may cause heart rhythm problems and death in cats and dogs.

Make your own catnip-filled toy by filling a small, clean sock with dried catnip. Then stitch the opening closed...so the catnip can't escape.

Mothballs (especially if they contain naphthalene) may be toxic to dogs and cats (resulting in vomiting, increased drinking and urination, diarrhea and seizures) and could be potentially life-threatening.

Nonprescription medication, such as ibuprofen, may lead to severe ulcers and anemia as well as liver and kidney failure in pets (which could be potentially life threatening).

Onions, garlic, leeks and chives may be toxic to both cats and dogs. When chewed or swallowed, these ingredients may cause anemia and gastrointestinal upset.

Outdoor cats and wildlife often will sleep under hoods of cars when it's cold. *Bang on the hood before starting the car to give the animal a chance to escape.*

Paper bags can be an endless source of fun for your cat. Make tunnels by cutting the bottoms of the bags and then taping the paper bags together.

Prescription medications (such as antidepressants and ADHD and cardiac drugs) are commonly ingested by pets when pills are dropped on the floor or left on counters. Even a small dose may cause problems.

Rodenticides (such as mouse and rat poisons) may contain a number of different toxins which have different effects on cats and dogs. Several common ingredients, like warfarin and coumarin, may cause blood clotting problems and hemorrhaging.

Sago palms are one of a number of toxic plants to both dogs

and cats. *Ingestion may lead to vomiting, diarrhea and seizures as well as liver failure in dogs.*

Secure electrical cords to baseboards or make them inaccessible to your dogs. *If your dog chews on them, he may suffer electric shocks, burns and could possibly die.* To hide those cords (which can't be made inaccessible), you may place empty paper towel rolls or toilet tissue cardboard rolls over the cords. Place construction-type cardboard on the walls to cover over cords which can't be put into cardboard tubes.

To check your cat's pulse, feel on the inside of his back thigh where his leg joins his body. Normal for cats is 110-170 beats a minute. Normal for dogs is 70-150 beats a minute.

To keep cats off of tables, put strips of double-faced tape on the table. Cats will not like the feel of the sticky substance on their paws.

Tulip bulbs may lead to mouth irritation, drooling, vomiting and diarrhea.

Unbaked bread dough may expand in a cat's stomach. If the stomach twists (cutting off the blood supply), emergency surgery is needed. The yeast in the dough may also produce alcohol which could lead to seizures and respiratory failure.

Use pet-friendly versions of products which melt ice on steps, driveways and sidewalks. Products such as Safe-T-Pet Ice Melt *avoid chemicals that irritate cats' paws and their stomachs, if they lick their paws.* These pet-friendly products are usually colored so you can also see where you've sprinkled them.

Use plastic food and water bowls instead of metal *because your cat's tongue may stick and freeze to metal when it's below freezing and you're feeding your cat outdoors.*

When washing your cat, a cream rinse is helpful for cats who have fur which tangles.

When your cat refuses to take liquid medicine, spill the medicine on his fur. He will lick himself clean and take medicine at the same time.

Windshield wiper fluid may contain methanol or ethylene glycol. Ingestion of methanol may cause low blood sugar and drunken walking in cats and dogs.

Xylitol is a sugar-free sweetener commonly found in chewing gum, breath mints and toothpaste. In dogs, it may lead to dangerous drops in blood sugar and liver failure and it's toxic to cats.

Yard products (including snail and slug bait, herbicides and fertilizers) are dangerous for pets.

Zinc toxicity may happen when cats and dogs eat metal or coins. Ingestion of even a single zinc penny may be fatal. Zinc may cause anemia as well as liver, kidney or heart failure.

Ferrets

A little peanut butter spread on a ferret's tummy (or, possibly, other pets' tummies) may distract him long enough for you to clip his nails. You can use a nail file to file down the sharp ends on a frisky animal's nails—the metal ones, on nail clippers, for bigger animal's and emery boards for smaller animals.

High carbohydrate candy may cause major problems for ferrets, rabbits and prairie dogs with insulinomas.

Holiday Hazards and Warnings

(Also see "WARNINGS"—"Halloween and Holiday Warnings")

All but the most social dogs should be kept in a separate room during trick-or-treat visiting hours as too many strangers dressed in strange Halloween outfits may be frightening to your dog.

Be careful of dogs and cats moving around a lit pumpkin and candles because pets may knock them over and cause a fire. Curious kittens especially run the risk of getting burned.

Be very careful that your dog or cat doesn't dash out an open door during trick-or-treat time.

Do not leave your dog or cat outside in the yard near or on Halloween. There are plenty of stories of vicious pranksters who have teased, injured, stolen and even killed pets during this time.

Don't dress your dog or cat in costume (unless you know he loves it) because it may put a lot of stress on your dog or cat. If you do dress up your pet, make sure the costume doesn't hinder his vision, movement or air intake and that his costume isn't constricting, annoying or unsafe. Be careful never to obstruct your dog's or cat's vision since even the sweetest pet may become snappy when they can't see what's going on around them. If the costume has metallic beads, snaps or other small pieces, be aware that some metals (especially zinc and lead) may result in serious poisoning if ingested.

Doors are made to both open and close and both may cause trouble for a pet. Opening a door is dangerous because your pet could escape to the outdoors, and closing the door is dangerous if your pet gets caught in the door and is crushed. Trick-or-treaters and party-goers create opportunities for danger if a small pet is on the loose. On Halloween or during a party, small animals do best if they're safely tucked away in an enclosure or in a safe room away from all the activity.

During Halloween, cats who have punctured and chewed glow sticks and glow jewelry may be in trouble. *While not usually life-threatening, chewing these objects may cause mouth pain and irritation as well as profuse drooling and foaming.*

High carbohydrate candy may cause major problems for rabbits, prairie dogs and ferrets with insulinomas.

If you think your dog may have ingested any chocolate, call a vet or the Animal Poison Control (800-213-6680) right away for medical assistance. Untreated, chocolate poisoning in dogs may result in vomiting, diarrhea, lethargy, agitation, increased thirst, an elevated heart rate or seizures.

Instead of candy, some people hand out mini-boxes of raisins during Halloween. Even very small amounts of raisins, grapes and currants are poisonous to dogs and may cause kidney failure.

Keep your dogs and cats inside during the days before and the day of Halloween because many pets are stolen, tortured and killed during these days. Be especially careful if you own a black cat.

Large consumption of sugary, high-fat candy by pets may lead to pancreatitis which is potentially fatal. Signs include: decreased appetite, vomiting, diarrhea, lethargy, abdominal pain and possibly kidney failure or organ damage.

Some Halloween food-related hazards for pets are candy wrappers, raisins and general candy overindulgence.

The use of candles increases dramatically around the Halloween and other holidays. Whether inside pumpkins or adding pumpkin, cinnamon or other holiday scents to the air, candles pop up all over. A curious pet on the loose might get burned by the flame or knock over a lit candle and cause a fire. Placing a candle on a counter or table doesn't mean it's safe from a pet because some pets are able to climb or glide (flying pets) which makes it possible for them to reach unexpected places.

Thinking of using a fog machine for a spooky effect during Halloween? Keep your pet well away from this machine and its fog. Also, check with your veterinarian to determine whether it's safe for your pet to breathe the fog. If you create fog by using dry ice, be absolutely sure your pet can't touch it or get to it by any means.

Trick-or-treat candies are not for dogs or cats as chocolate is poisonous to many animals. Also, tin foil and cellophane candy wrappers may be hazardous if swallowed by your pet.

Watch out for holiday decorations which have feathers or rubber (and even styrofoam may have a lot of decorations) since they may be deadly. Also, the rubber sticky decorations that go on the window or on a glass door may be hazardous.

When pets eat candy, sometimes they also eat the wrappers. Ingestion of foil and cellophane wrappers may cause a life-threatening bowel obstruction which may then require surgery. Watch for vomiting, decreased appetite, not defecating, straining to defecate or lethargy. X-rays may be required in order to diagnose this problem.

While Halloween sound effects (like spooky sounds and loud music) aren't an obvious danger to pets, they might cause stress to rabbits, guinea pigs, chinchillas or other critters. If the stress is severe, it might then cause illness.

Parasites, Pests and Invading Varmint Control

Crawling (On The Ground) Pests, Etc.

Having trouble with crawling bugs? Try putting out boric acid (in powdered form). Most hardware stores carry it. It's much cheaper than those products with fancy labels and it does the same thing. Sprinkle it liberally in out-of-the-way places (like behind furniture and cabinets, inside kitchen cabinets, etc.). By putting it in these out-of-the-way places, *your kids and animals can't get to it,* and the bugs will still crawl through the boric acid and carry it back home to kill their family.

If you have slugs and snails and do not want to put out poison bait because your puppies or dogs might eat it, place beer in shallow saucers around the garden. Slugs and snails love beer, get drunk and die, but your dogs are not harmed.

Many breeders in the Midwest have problems with ants in or near the dog pens. You need only to follow their trail to find their mound. I have the perfect solution for those who are bothered by plain old ants or even fire ants. Recently I learned of a safe, effective way to eliminate them without dangerous insecticides. You just cook 'em. Pour a large pan of boiling water directly into the mound. All it takes to stop a thriving ant community is for the boiling water to reach the queen ant. If at first you don't succeed at reaching the queen, try again. To date, I have found that only one dousing is necessary. By getting the queen, you not only stop reproduction, you stop the other ants as well. Any late-arriving worker ants won't hang around long without their queen.

Not wanting to use pesticides on our land, we were interested in hearing that ducks are great bug eaters. They eat bugs and, in addition, they are amusing pets. They supply us with fresh eggs for the dogs. Egg yolks add gloss to the coat and these yolks got my picky eater gobbling his food again.

Stings and bites from insects such as scorpions, spiders, bees, wasps, etc., are dangerous to your dog.

Spread Borax (1 pound per 100 square feet and watered down) to kill all worm larvae in your runs. Caution: it will also kill all the grass. *Keep your dog away until the mixture is dry.*

To keep ants out of your pets' dishes, place the food dish inside a pie pan of water.

To keep ticks and mosquitoes away from your dog, sprinkle cinnamon into his dog food.

Troubled by ants and don't want to use a poison in your dogs' yard or run? Try sprinkling the area with ants with cucumber peelings (instead of using insecticides which may be dangerous to your dogs).

Ear Mites

Save those plastic squeeze-type containers. They are great for dispensing ear powder, pumice (just squeeze onto the ears), kennel dust (squeeze into the corners of the crates) and other powders.

When dipping my dogs for mites, fleas, etc., I use Paramite which, though effective, is quite hard on the dog's skin and coat. To alleviate this harshness, I add 2 tablespoons of Derma-oil (inexpensive and available through your vet) to each gallon of dip solution. Not only does it help the skin and coat but it also slightly reduces the odor of the dip.

Fleas

A capful of liquid peppermint (Castile) soap in a quart of warm water should be kept handy for fighting fleas A capful in the final rinse of washing dog blankets cleans and deodorizes them and helps repel fleas. Bathing your dog in it leaves the coat shiny and smelling nice longer than special dog shampoos. Liquid peppermint soap is sold at most health food stores.

A good way to keep your dogs clean and smelling good is to use cedar chips for bedding. When the chips lose their scent, you can just spread them out on your lawn. These cedar chips also help repel fleas.

A groomer shared this neat trick with me. Palmolive Liquid Dish Soap is an excellent flea shampoo. I tried it and it works. It will soften coats a bit but it's fine for those dogs not being shown. It's cheap and it's great not to use chemicals.

As the weather begins to get warmer, more and more fleas, flies and ticks will be out. This is a good time to start putting vinegar into your dogs' drinking water as this helps repel flies, ticks, fleas, etc., which bother our dogs in warm weather. The vinegar also encourages their appetites.

Brewer's yeast rubbed on your dog's coat prevents fleas.

Cedar is supposed to help repel fleas and make your dog smell nice, but cedar-filled dog beds are very expensive. Make your own by buying cedar in bulk at the local feed or farm store. Fill inexpensive zippered pillow covers with the cedar. Then slip an inexpensive muslin pillowcase over the filled cover. The pillowcase may be washed whenever you wish while the cover remains clean. Change the cedar inside regularly. Pillowcase-sized beds fit nicely

in airline crates so you could use crate bottoms to make a comfortable open bed at home.

Does your dog have fleas? Here's a way to check: put your dog on a white or very light-colored surface (such as a bathtub). Run your hands through the dog's fur (giving the fur a good ruffling for at least 10 seconds or so). Remove the dog from the surface and spray the residue left from his coat with a light misting of either water or a household cleaner. If the little flecks that landed on the bathtub or table turn red, you have fleas. The flecks are dried flea feces. They cling to the dog's coat until they are rubbed or brushed off.

Drop half of a moth cake into the vacuum tank and it will kill flea eggs. You can also put the moth cake in a regular vacuum bag and it, too, will kill flea eggs and helps to deodorize.

During flea season, my dogs get dipped about every 80 days and are then drip-dried. There is nothing like being sprayed when they shake off this excess dip. This solution has worked very well for me: as soon as they are dipped, I put on one of my husband's old T-shirts. They may shake all they want and I don't get wet.

For extra flea control, save those ends of flea collars (did you ever visualize the size of the dog they would actually fit?). Put a piece of that flea collar inside your vacuum bag. This should kill those fleas you hope you're vacuuming into the vacuum bag.

For fleas in your carpets, mix together one-half 22 Mule Team Borax powder and one-half table salt and sprinkle in carpets. Vacuum up a day or two later. For use on dogs (even newborn pups and nursing mothers), try a spray called Organic Formula 365 (which is an Aloe product). You may purchase it in a health-food store.

Here's a twist for the outdoor or indoor dog bed. I filled a durable cloth pillow case with one-half cedar shavings and one-half of those white packing pellets *(make sure dogs don't eat the pellets)*. The cedar shavings give the bed a nice fragrance, and the white packing pellets absorb the dog's body heat (providing him with a nice winter bed in his doghouse). I stitched in a zipper but a piece of Velcro with a flap would serve nicely, also. I have heard that cedar shavings repels fleas.

How do you get rid of fleas in the house? Rosemary (an herb which may be bought in most health-food stores) repels fleas. Put one to two tablespoons of rosemary in a pan of boiling water. Let it boil with the lid off for several minutes. Then let it simmer with the lid off for 10 to 15 minutes until the whole house smells like rosemary (this smell reminds me of Thanksgiving turkey). Cool and strain water and sprinkle lightly on carpets starting at the corner farthest from the outside door and working toward the door. Then sprinkle the outside steps with the remaining water. Fleas will leave in a hurry. Repeat one to two times per week until there are no fleas.

I came across this recipe for flea shampoo in the newspaper: 3 ounces glycerine, 3 ounces Joy, 1 1/2 ounces of white vinegar and 24 1/2 ounces water (makes a full quart or 32 ounces total). It works.

If either you or your dogs are bothered by bites from mosquitoes or fleas, hydrocortisone cream or spray may be purchased in the pharmacy sections of stores without a prescription. If the bite is no more than an hour old, one application will take away the itching and swelling in a few minutes. Older bites require several applications. This cream is also great for any contact allergy like poison oak or poison ivy. Buy several tubes and keep one in your tack box, one with camping gear and another at home.

If, unfortunately, a bitch "in whelp" picks up fleas or you find yourself with small infested puppies, use Johnson's Baby Oil on the inside of legs, tummy, on the head and under the tail and throat. The fleas will vacate immediately and the bitch will not object. The same treatment may be used on the mother without side effects. Although they look greasy the first day or so, the oil will be totally absorbed. For chasing down a lone flea, put the baby oil in an old nose spray bottle or an eyedropper, release a drop of oil on the flea and he will immediately expire.

If you don't have a wet/dry shop vac, you should think seriously about investing in one. They're marvelous for vacuuming out crates and for catching those "fuzz puppies" which accumulate in the corners of your kennel building.

If you're going to use a flea collar on your pet, be sure to put it on before flea season starts.

I use flea shampoo when washing kennel blankets and puppy towels and, also, when cleaning crates. This helps to control fleas in the crates and keeps the fleas off young puppies and the bitch while they're in the puppy pen.

Johnson's Baby Oil is good for cleaning inside the ears. It may also be applied to small puppies who may have picked up fleas. It will be totally absorbed by the coat in a day or so and may be used on the head and face.

Kitchen dish soap is a flea-killing dog shampoo. Kitchen dish soap (not dish detergent) can double as dog shampoo for its flea-killing abilities.

Looking back through an old *Sheltie Pacesetter* magazine (can't remember which issue, forgive me), I ran across a "Trade Secrets" on flea control that uses a mixture of one-half 22 Mule Team Borax powder and one-half table salt. I've tried this and, believe me, it works like a charm. However after careful thought, I've adapted it in the following ways: instead of using table salt, use non-iodized salt, mix the ingredients in a non-metallic container and store in something like a Tupperware or Rubbermaid canister. I apply the mix using a cheap plastic saltshaker. There are no chemical reactions with metals with this procedure. I've had kittens on the floor and have walked through it barefoot without a problem.

Put mothballs in your vacuum bag. They will kill any eggs or fleas that might have made it into your vacuum bag.

Save those plastic squeeze-type containers. They are great for dispensing flea powders, kennel dust (squeeze into the corners of the crates) or other powders.

To aid in the control of fleas, sprinkle your flea powder or Sevin dust on the bottom of the crate and then replace the Masonite fiber board floor. By doing this, fleas cannot hide under the raised floor area without coming in contact with the insecticide. Also, your dog is not in direct contact with the flea powder. I have had good success with this method.

To keep fleas, ticks, mosquitoes and flies away from your dog, sprinkle cinnamon into his dog food.

To kill fleas, we wash our dogs and spray our runs with Shaklee's Basic H. This product is 100 percent nontoxic. It is biodegradable and really works. This product does not use poisons to kill insects but emulsifies the oils on the insect's body and smothers it. We wash crates with it, spray garbage cans with it (as it repels flying insects including mosquitoes) and we never have a flea problem.

To rid your pet's house of fleas, place pine needles in the house or under his bedding. Salt crevices of doghouses to keep fleas out.

Vacuum floors and carpets often during flea season. Put salt or mothballs in the vacuum cleaner bag to kill hatching fleas.

Wash your pet in salt water to kill the fleas on them, *but be sure to rinse thoroughly since salt water may irritate your dog's skin.*

When dipping my dogs for fleas, mites, etc., I use Paramite which, though effective, is quite hard on the dog's skin and coat. To alleviate this harshness, I add 2 tablespoons of Derma-oil (inexpensive and available through your vet) to each gallon of dip solution. Not only does it help the skin and coat but it also slightly reduces the odor of the dip.

When we find that one of our dogs has chewed his coat and fleas are the reason for his chewing, we apply Vitamin E oil to the area. The fleas stay away, the chewing stops and this Vitamin E oil stimulates hair growth.

When we purchase flea collars for our dogs (and cat), we use a Carter's Sharpie felt laundry marker (it writes and stays on practically everything) to write the animal's name, our name, address and phone number on the flea collar. There is enough room for all the info and it does not wear off. This is a very helpful way to identify a beloved pet if it is lost.

Flies

As the weather begins to get warmer, more and more fleas, flies and ticks will be out. This is a good time to start putting vinegar into your dogs' drinking water as this helps repel flies, ticks, fleas, etc., which bother our dogs in warm weather. The vinegar also encourages their appetites.

For very effective fly control, occasionally leave the tops off your poop cans for a couple of hours and promptly sprinkle granulated fly bait over the top of the fresh contents. We use tall garbage cans, so there is no chance of the dogs getting to it. It's most effective to bait the can just after scooping the runs on a sunny day. Leave the tops off for a couple of hours and you will be amazed at how many little fly bodies are left in the can. Fly bait may be purchased at feed stores and many garden supply stores.

If you have dogs kenneled outdoors during the hot fly season and your dogs are plagued with annoying fly bites on their ears, I purchase green netting (sold at War Surplus supply stores) and cover the entire kennel (including all the sides and the top). This netting provides a nice shaded kennel area which still permits breezes to blow through and keeps all the flies out. It is used on tents as window screening and comes in large rolls. It's reasonably priced.

I hate flies and have used Golden Malrin Fly Bait for years to kill the varmints. I've found that you may use it safely (inside the pen with puppies or with grown dogs) by sprinkling it on an old cookie sheet and then putting that inside a locked wire crate. The flies may get to the bait easily but the dogs can't. You'll also attract more flies by adding something sweet to the cookie sheet. Fresh watermelon rind is a favorite or you may use sugar water.

Place mothballs in the bottom of your trash cans to discourage flies. *Be sure to keep mothballs away from the dogs as those mothballs may be toxic if eaten.* Keep a tight lid on to keep the vapor in.

Save those plastic squeeze-type containers as they are great for dispensing kennel dust which may be squeezed into the corners of the crates or inside the kennel.

To aid in the disposal of the ever-present poop, I use a plastic pail with a lid lined with a garbage bag. I found that my lid was not tight-fitting and no matter how hard I tried, I always had a fly problem. Now I hang a No-Pest Strip inside the pail and have had no flies since I started using this strip.

To control flies, put two or three pieces of red, raw meat in a jar, punch holes in the lid, cover the meat with water and set or fasten onto a table, doghouse, fence post, in your kennel runs or pens. These jars do attract flies and keep them from bothering dogs. They don't contain chemicals or poisons.

To keep flies off your dog's ears, rub in 6-12 fly repellent daily. The tube type works the best.

To keep flies, ticks, mosquitoes and fleas away from your dog, sprinkle cinnamon into his dog food.

To protect your dogs from those miserable black flies that play havoc with their ears so relentlessly, try applying Avon's Skin-So-Soft bath oil to the ears each morning. I put it in a little Windex or Glass Plus spray bottle for easy application (after that spray bottle has been completely cleaned). It works.

Invading Animals and Varmints

Protect your garbage bags from outdoor animals and pests by spraying the outside of the garbage bags with Pine Sol. This will also repel animals intent on tearing those bags open.

To keep stray dogs or other animals from attacking your garbage, sprinkle full strength ammonia over the garbage bags before placing them in the cans.

Mosquitoes and Heartworm

Because mosquitoes carry heartworm disease, your dog must be on heartworm preventive if you live in an area where mosquitoes are present.

For those who have dogs on Caracide to prevent heartworms, put the liquid Caracide in a clean, empty bottle of Linatone coat conditioner with the pump on top. One pump is exactly 1 cc which is the average dose for a 20-pound dog. It makes feeding much faster as you just put one squirt in his feed dish, or for fussy eaters put one squirt in his mouth.

If either you or your dogs are bothered by bites from mosquitoes or fleas, hydrocortisone cream or spray may be purchased in the pharmacy sections of stores without a prescription. If the bite is no more than an hour old, one application will take away the itching and swelling in a few minutes. Older bites require several applications. This cream is also great for any contact allergy like poison oak or poison ivy. Buy several tubes and keep one in your tack box, one with camping gear and another at home.

To keep mosquitoes and ticks away from your dog, sprinkle cinnamon into his dog food.

To kill mosquitoes, we use Shaklee's Basic H. This product is 100 percent nontoxic. It is biodegradable and really works. This product does not use poisons to kill insects, but emulsifies the oils on the insect's body and smothers it. We wash crates with it and spray garbage cans with it as this product repels flying insects (including mosquitoes).

We use liquid heartworm medication and place it right on the dogs' food. To be sure it is consumed, squirt the liquid onto a small piece of bread. The preventative soaks right in and the bread is readily consumed.

Other Flying Pests

A cure or to relieve the discomfort from a bee or a wasp sting is first remove the stinger. Then apply uncut ammonia water or a paste of baking soda and water.

Stings and bites from insects such as bees, wasps, scorpions and spiders are dangerous to your dog.

To keep mosquitoes and ticks away from your dog, sprinkle cinnamon into his dog food.

To kill flying insects, we use Shaklee's Basic H. This product is 100 percent nontoxic. It is biodegradable and really works. This product does not use poisons to kill insects but emulsifies the oils on the insect's body and smothers it. We wash crates with it and spray garbage cans with it as this product repels flying insects.

Poisons

(Also see "WARNINGS"—"Poisons and Poisonings")

Available for free is the "Antidote and First Aid for Poisoning" chart at most drugstores. Ask your pharmacist for one. Mine is taped inside my kitchen cabinet door with my vet's phone number written on it.

D-Con has changed its mouse and rat poison formulas. *If your dog ingests the product, have your veterinarian call D-Con immediately! The treatment is not the same. If left untreated, ingesting either product may kill your dog.*

If you need to make your pet vomit for some reason, put 1/2 to 1 teaspoon of salt on the back of his tongue and hold his mouth closed for a few seconds.

Roundworms and Other Worms

A little grated (not shredded) carrot in your dog's daily diet is said to help prevent roundworm infestation.

On worming kenneled dogs: if you kept two dogs together and need a fresh stool sample from each dog, try adding red food coloring to one dog's food and put blue food coloring in the other dog's food. It won't affect a "worm" feeding.

Spread Borax (1 pound per 100 square feet and watered down) to kill all worm larvae in your runs. Caution: it will also kill all the grass. *Keep your dog away until the mixture is dry.*

The horse wormer Strongid T is a very concentrated form of the canine wormer Nemex. Use 1/2 cc per 10 pounds of body weight. It comes with 60 cc to a bottle. This is a safe wormer and I start worming my puppies at two to three weeks. It only takes a few drops. We have found these early wormings, repeated in two weeks, have eliminated worm problems in our pups. Worm their dam, too.

When de-worming puppies, it's easy to lose track of which pups have been wormed. To prevent an accidental overdose, simply cut each puppy's toenails as you de-worm. Then by the time you need to de-worm again, the nails need to be cut again. Pups who have been wormed are identified by their short toenails.

Ticks

Always check your dog for ticks after he's spent time outdoors.

As the weather begins to get warmer, more and more fleas, flies and ticks will be out. This is a good time to start putting vinegar into your dogs' drinking water as this helps repel flies, ticks, fleas, etc., which bother our dogs in warm weather. The vinegar also encourages their appetites.

To keep ticks and mosquitoes away from your dog, sprinkle cinnamon into his dog food.

Photos and Photography

Organizing, Displaying and Utilizing Photos

(Also see "RECORDS"—"Photos and Photography")

A friend of mine sent photos of a litter she had. Behind each pup was a card with a number on it. I had a litter of (sigh...) six males who were all similarly marked, therefore it was difficult to tell one pup from another. I used her idea and when I photographed the pups, I had their handler also hold a 3" x 5" card behind each pup when their pictures were being taken. I then recorded the exact markings of each pup on his card. In the case of two almost identically marked puppies, I put nail polish on one pup (to distinguish that puppy from the other) and I also recorded that nail polish marking on his card. It ended up as a sort of joke as we kept referring to #1, #2, etc. It did, however, work well. Four of the six went as show breeding prospects. It would have been difficult to identify them without this aid.

A fun way to show off your dogs is to create a Photo Purse. I made one years ago and have thoroughly enjoyed it. Simply buy a purse box at a hobby store (or build one if you are handier than I am) and glue your photos to it in a collage. Let the photos dry and coat the photos with a decoupage solution (from a hobby store). Add a handle (also available at a hobby store), and presto...you have an instant "family album." I also made one for my mom with pictures of all her grandchildren and she loves it.

Ever receive dog photos which you would like to keep but must return to the owner? I photocopy the pictures on a good copy machine and file them away for future reference.

If you accidentally get your glossy color print wet, use your hair dryer on high and blow the hot air on the wet areas until it's completely dry. The defrost on your car will do the trick, too. I've only had to use this on glossy prints but when they dried, you couldn't tell that they had gotten wet.

If you are wondering how that picture will reproduce in an ad, just photocopy it. The photocopy will show you if you have enough contrast, shadows in funny places, etc. It helps distinguish between the quality of the dog and the quality of the picture.

It's hard to find photo albums which will hold all the different size photos in a store-bought photo album so I have made my own using an ordinary vinyl binder and the clear sheet protectors (which may be purchased in any office-supply store). Photos which are 8" x 10" fit right inside the pages and 5" x 7" or any other size may be mounted on photocopy or typewriter paper (or colored paper, if you prefer) by using clear mounting corners. I further customize my album by buying the binders with the plastic sleeve over the front and back which allows you to create your own cover. This idea not only displays your favorite shots of your special dogs together in one album, but it has the added bonus

of taking extra care of those show photos. The PVC in most photo-album pages will break down the surface of your photos over a period of time. These pages contain no PVC and come in several styles and thicknesses of plastic from which to choose. Some are backed with black paper as a background.

I've found that a neat way to store photographs is to purchase little boxes (the kind used for business cards) from your local print shop. They are just the right size for most prints, very sturdy and cheap. Each box contains the photos for a particular dog (clearly marked with a Magic Marker). All the boxes may be stored in a drawer or in a large cardboard box. I particularly like the cardboard file boxes which are available at office supply stores. This way, it's easy to find that particular photo you want. Valuable negatives are also placed, along with one print of that photo, in a photo album so that reprints may be made later.

To keep from losing negatives of your favorite photos, have a special album in which you place one reprint of the photo along with its negative in a small envelope. You can store several per page, and it's easy to glance through the album to locate exactly which print you need when the time comes to make reprints or enlargements.

We have only one living area in our home as we built it with only a den and no formal living room. When our older son moved out, we made his bedroom into a little study or sitting room which is now an ideal place to visit with people who come over to "talk dogs" and when my husband is glued to a football game on TV in the den. The new room has rattan furniture and the coffee table has a glass top. I taped photos of our dogs on the underside of the glass table top and the effect is really beautiful. Everyone loves it and it provides effortless access to photos of all the dogs we've had through the years. If you have a coffee table with a wooden top, you could have glass cut to fit over that wooden table top. Then you could tape photos under the new glass top. It's a wonderful way to display photos of your special dogs and brighten up the room at the same time.

When advertising with a black-and-white photo of a dog, state under the photo or somewhere in your ad the color of the dog. Sometimes even the blues look like sables and tri-factored sables are often hard to distinguish from tris. It would also help with stud dogs to tell whether they are tri-factored, white-factored or pure-for-sable, etc.

Taking Photos

A great non-slip surface for placing your dog on (when taking pictures) is a Rubbermaid bath mat. The suction cups on the back of the mat hold firmly to any slippery surface.

Encourage your puppies to use their ears without constant human contact. An inexpensive child's pinwheel toy, with the wooden handle shortened, taped and tied to the fencing of their outdoor play area attracts their attention as the wind spins it. Be sure to fix it securely and above their reach (when standing on their hind legs) and reposition it higher as your puppies grow taller. Wind chimes will also attract their attention. In addition to using their ears, when cocking their heads from side to side while trying to figure it all out, they'll assume adorable poses so you may capture those special candid shots in pictures.

For table training my young puppies for future grooming, I use a little one-step stool with a rubber vinyl top. They work great for stacking puppies and for getting puppies used to being on a table. The rubbery top feels like a real table. You may even sit down on the floor or in the yard while stacking the pups. I have even stacked puppies on the stool in order to take their pictures, shoot videos and to measure them.

For taking photos of my dogs and puppies, I purchased a Therm-a-Rest at a sporting goods store. It is approximately four feet long and inflates slightly when you roll it out. It is perfect to lie on while taking photos of your dogs. If the ground is wet, it protects you from getting wet. We have even laid it when snow was on the ground and took photos. It may also be used to lay your sleeping bag on while camping. The Therm-a-Rest provides a little padding (like an air mattress), but it self-inflates. The material is very durable and doesn't puncture like an air mattress.

I always keep a mini-calendar (free at Hallmark stores) attached to my camera strap. Every time I take a picture, it's information is recorded on the calendar. This takes all the guesswork out of dating puppy pictures along with keeping any other pertinent information regarding each photo I take.

If you are taking pictures by yourself and are having trouble getting the dog to bait, try making a recording with lots of different sounds before you plan to take photos. Then put the tape player in the location where you would like the dog to look and turn it on.

I have always wanted a videotape of my dog romping around with me, but I don't own a video camera. The cost to rent one is quite reasonable so I rented one for the weekend and had a friend of mine capture some special moments that we had together. When my dog's time comes to leave this good earth, I am sure I will treasure that tape even more.

In order to get a really good look at head quality and expression of a young puppy, tuck the pup up against your shoulder and look into a mirror. From this secure position, the pup will not wiggle as much and will frequently follow his own reflection. You may get a long look, straight on, without having to dangle the pup at arm's length. This works especially well if you hold two, three or even four pups up in a line for comparison. Somehow, too, evaluating through the mirror seems to increase your objectivity (similar to seeing photos or videos of your own dogs). Try taking their photos from this position.

I would like to suggest some things to those who are trying to take their own pictures of dogs or puppies for future advertising. Hopefully, you are using a 35 mm camera. If not, beg, borrow or buy one. The main thing I would like to suggest is to keep the trees in the distant background. You may be using a black-and-white print for advertising and the trees will appear too similar to the same shade as the dog. You do not want the dog to blend in with the background. You want contrast. I strongly recommend blurring your background for any black-and-white (color may be another issue). Your dog should be in focus anyway, but this will make him appear even sharper and give the photo a standout quality. The wide open spaces are best for outside shots but if they are not available, try getting a sheet or two of paneling from your local building supply store. You may prop them up against the house, car, anything. They make great backgrounds, are inexpensive, easily stored and come in a variety of shades. Remember to get one that contrasts with your dog (for color, gray looks surprisingly good behind sables). I like to take pictures in the early morning (especially for taking photos of black dogs) because there are no shadows (just nice, even light) and a black dog will appear more as a blue-black rather than a reddish-black. It is also cooler in the morning (both you and your dog will

have more patience with each other). An added plus would be that the birds are wildly chirping along with a dozen other odd sounds which accompany morning time and thereby keeping any normal dog almost constantly alert. Late afternoons are better for sable or brown dogs because they will appear more red in a color photo. Head shots are best taken on the same level as the dog's head. For full-body shots, raise the height of the camera some as I think full-body shots taken at eye level make the dog look high in the rear.

My local photo shop, "Photo Pro" (who processes photos in-house rather than sending them out) gives away small plastic film holders for free. Sometimes they will give away a whole sackful of black and clear plastic holders. These have any number of uses. You may write on them with waterproof, small-tipped marking pens to indicate their contents. Put about three small pebbles in one and put it in your pocket when taking dog photos. When the dog is in place (if all else fails to get him to use those ears), take it out, shake it once and throw it far in front of him so it rolls and bounces.

When you have been trying to get some good head photos of your dog and he refuses to look anything except bored, there is one last trick that might work. Blow in his face. You will almost certainly get his immediate attention since his ears will go up and he will pull his head back into his ruff and will look particularly alert (instead of just hungry.). This is especially useful if you are trying to take the pictures by yourself.

Puppies

Cleaning

A very effective item I have found (for cleaning puppies before prospective buyers arrive at your home and for cleaning your show dog's ears before going into the ring) is Diaparene Baby Washcloths. They are safe to use on your young puppies and when used on ears, these washcloths are fast drying because of their alcohol base. They are easy to use, easy to take to a show and easy to trash.

We use Baby Wipes for a multitude of reasons-cleaning a "just-used" thermometer, any area that's been stitched or sutured, a quick ear cleaning before a show, on a messy puppy face and on babies just learning to eat from a pan. The least expensive ones are more moist, and you'll be surprised how many uses you'll find for them.

Newborns

(Also see "BITCHES," "ELIMINATING BAD BEHAVIORS," "ENCLOSURES," "FEEDING," "HEALTH," "GROOMING," "PARASITES," "PHOTOS and PHOTOGRAPHY," "RECORDS," "TRAVELING and SHIPPING," and "WARNINGS" and "WHELPING")

A new device (designed by a veterinarian to save lives of baby pigs) may help save puppies, too. Called a Pig Resuscitator, this device pumps air into the lungs of non-breathing newborns. If the animal is not breathing, first clean out his mouth and then tilt his head back in order to open his air passage. Slip the mask over his nose. Then compress the bellows to force air into his lungs. Next, pull off the mask (to allow fresh air to enter). Repeat until the animal breathes on his own. It's available from Joseph Magrath, D.V.M., Box 148, McCook, NE 69001.

Extra tiny newborn puppies dehydrate very easily especially when subjected to the artificial heat sources (which are sometimes vital to keep them from becoming too chilled and subsequently dying). I have found that keeping a very close watch on them for the first several days is vital and checking several times daily for any signs of dehydration (like pinching up the skin on the back). *If a pup's skin stays up at all, dehydration is beginning.* I keep a bottle of Ringers Solution (purchased from my vet) at home at all times. At the very first sign of dehydration, I give subcutaneous (under the skin) injections of the Ringers using an allergy syringe and needle. You may purchase allergy syringes at many pharmacies (without a prescription), or you can simply get a prescription from your vet or physician. Remove the Ringers from the bottle with one of your regular-size needles, then replace the regular-size needle with the very fine allergy needle (which will be used for the actual injection). I also heat the solution in the syringe by holding it under hot water for a bit or putting it in the microwave oven for a split-second *(without the needle). Test the heat on the inside of your wrist as you would a baby's bottle.* Body-temperature Ringers eliminates the shock to the body that cold solution would cause and it saves puppies.

From the time my puppies are about a week old until they are about three weeks of age (while Mom is still cleaning up after them), I do the following while cleaning out the whelping area. I hold the pup for Mom, placing her pup upside down on my lap and let Mom clean this puppy. Of course, I am seated on the floor. Mom seems to appreciate this and does a thorough job (since she has no squirming puppy to contend with). It is also a good way to get puppies familiar with being handled at an early age (which we should be doing anyway). Puppies don't mind it a bit as Mom is tending to them. It seems to form a bond between all of us. This is, also, how I begin cutting each puppy's toenails.

I use a Fisher-Price nursery monitor in my back bedroom where I keep mothers with their very young babies or my "in-whelp" bitches. I can go about my daily household chores and hear constant feedback as to what's happening in there. The monitor is so sensitive that you may even hear the mother's breathing. It's no substitute for constant supervision but it helps relieve my anxiety as to what's going on in there at all times. It has been very helpful and its cost is moderate.

The fastest and safest way to warm a puppy (if he is small, weak or cold) is to carry that pup in the front of your blouse or shirt (making very sure that he can't slip out while your carrying him). I had to prove it to myself with two small premature puppies weighing only 3 1/2 ounces. They wouldn't nurse so I carried them around all afternoon in the front of my blouse and, presto ,they are now three weeks old, fine and healthy. «»Editor's note: based upon reading and research, handling puppies in this manner will also help their temperaments when it comes to bonding with humans and wanting to be cuddled.«»

When my bitch has only one puppy in a litter, I buy small stuffed animals to put inside the whelping box. During the summer I go to yard sales and purchase those stuffed animals at a very low price. You can even stock up if you know your bitch will be having a litter in the future. When the puppy is little, he likes to snuggle up with his "foster" littermates and when he gets a little bigger, *I take the eyes and nose off of those stuffed animals so my*

single puppy won't swallow them. Soon these stuffed animals will become the puppy's toys and his best pals since he's a single pup.

Play Toys
(Also see "WARNINGS")

A good substitute for chew sticks are unpeeled carrots. Cut each carrot into 4-inch to 6-inch lengths. My pups love them and usually end up eating the raw carrots.

A great toy for puppies is the buffing attachment which is made for an electric drill. Mine is made from lamb skin and wool fleece. So far, this toy has proven indestructible and hasn't even shed.

A great toy (that puppies love) is the cardboard tube from a roll of toilet paper or from paper towels.

All puppies will love this—take a small rag or old washcloth, soak it in water and wring most of the water out. Then freeze it. They will love the coldness on their sore gums and will choose chewing on this instead of furniture, etc.

A lot of the fast food restaurants were giving stuffed toys as premiums along with their happy meals for children. These were small puppy-size toys which had no parts that could be chewed off (as everything was embroidered on instead of glued). Of particular interest was the "Babe" promotion that McDonald's was offering. This collection included a sheep, Border Collie, cat, cow, etc. The sheep is adorable. We buy them at local yard sales, auctions, flea markets, etc. If they get dirty, they wash really well. We have accumulated quite a collection and have started the practice of sending them along with the puppies we place into their "forever" homes. The new owners now have a start on their own toy collection and the puppies love them because it's a familiar toy (which smells like home and their littermates). Even our older dogs love them. There's also a wildlife collection with tigers, lions, monkeys, etc.

A nerf ball is great to take on the road for your canine ball player. It may be bounced off floors and walls with no noise or damage, and it's a great way to exercise your dog while in a motel room.

Annoyed with dog toys which don't stand up to the working over a puppy gives them? Try Cressite rings. They're sweet-smelling and stay in one piece.

A piece of rope tied to a table leg or a doorknob makes a great teething aid for puppies and your pups are not as likely to gnaw on furniture, etc.

A really fun toy for our dogs is their "tug rope." We buy a 6-foot piece of rope (natural fiber jute or hemp, not nylon) at the hardware store. Then tie a large double knot at each end, leaving about 6" of rope extending past the knots. Our dogs love playing tug-of-war with these. They are also useful in that tugging on them helps remove puppy teeth. (No more trips to the vet to remove any retained puppy canines.) With the older dogs, tugging at the frayed ends of the rope seems to help clean between those front teeth which are too close to each other.

A really great turn-on for puppies is real sheepskin. We keep large swatches for play toys in the house and I often take a small piece into the ring...especially in the Puppy Classes. This really makes the babies feel at home (as it's like their security blanket). Sheepskin may be purchased in various forms. I've used the lining from an old sheepskin coat for years and am currently working on taking it from a pair of old slippers. It may be purchased from most places that make leather goods (saddles, etc.) or for the city folks, you may find it in the form of polishing mitts or pads for floor polishers or automobiles.

Are your puppies and adults bored? Try going to the carpet center and asking for one of their unneeded used cardboard rolls. Cut it into 2-inch-wide to 4-inch-wide pieces and watch the fun. They last ten times longer than other cardboard rolls.

Are you tired of pups chewing on everything but the rawhide chews that you provide? Soak them in some bouillon or broth for a few minutes (the rawhide chews, not the pups) and watch the renewed interest.

Children's small stuffed toys may be used as puppy toys. *(Be sure to remove any eyes or other small parts which could be chewed off and swallowed.)* I buy them at garage sales. My puppies play with them as they grow. When it's time for a puppy to go to his new home, I send a small, furry, lumpy, familiar-smelling toy with him (to keep him company in his strange, new environment).

Don't let your dogs play with tennis balls. A number of newsletters have reported on the futile efforts to save a Scottie in Oregon *who suffered fatal liver damage from chewing on and biting into a new tennis ball. Apparently there were some toxic dyes used in the balls as well as chemicals used in ball inflation.*

Dry some orange peelings and then let your puppies or older dogs chew them. They like chewing on these orange peelings and it is a good source of Vitamin C. The peelings work well as a pacifier as well as a good breath and room deodorant.

For an inexpensive, easy to obtain toy for small pups, save empty rolls from toilet paper, plastic wrap, paper towels, etc. They are lightweight and our pups love carrying them around.

For a puppy toy, I use an empty plastic gallon milk container. I remove the cap and make an indentation in one side so the puppies can grip onto it and, also, onto the handle of the carton. When soiled, just throw it away and replace with another milk container.

For our young puppies, we buy baby toys (the terry-cloth kind). *Make sure no pieces can be pulled off, no squeaker inside the toy and that it contains only a fiber stuffing.* Best of all, they're washable. It gives each puppy a friend and it's something that doesn't cost a lot. We also bought a cloth dumbbell and our puppies think it's the greatest.

I find that two or three old nylon panty hose tied together in several knots make for a lot of fun with puppies who are, at least, five weeks of age. They love tug-of-war or it may be tied overhead for a single player.

If you are having problems with puppies chewing everything in sight, take a shoelace and tie it around the leg of a chair. I guarantee it will keep their attention to the point that they will ignore all the other goodies including your shoes, feet, toes, etc. If you want to go first class, use a leather shoelace.

If you want your puppies to get more exercise and to play more with each other, don't put too many toys in with them. One old sock with two or three puppies can make for a wonderful game of tag.

I have a great toy for my dogs. It's a tetherball game for children but the dogs love it, too. My dogs spend at least three hours a day batting the ball around the pole. It's such good exercise for them and they never seem to get bored. It's also fun to watch them play.

I have found a way to clean your children's old stuffed animals and toys. This also makes your two-, three- or four-year-old child very contented when he or she wants to "help Mama" groom the dogs. Spray the stuffed animal with doggy waterless shampoo, then rub them briskly with a turkish towel. They look almost brand-new when you are done. All you add is a new red bow.

Inexpensive (actually...free) and much-loved puppy toys are the lids that come on household sprays like Pam, etc. We swear they prefer the red ones.

I tried handwashing a multitude of puppy toys and one day I tossed them all (even the plastic ones) into the washer along with the daily supply of puppy towels, blankets and heating pad covers. After going through the wash, I removed the plastic toys and put everything else in the dryer. Now we always have a generous supply of fresh toys which are squeaky clean.

I used to throw away my pizza crusts (which I didn't want to eat) but I discovered a way to recycle them. I use them as "bones" for puppies who are too young to eat them (around five to eight weeks of age). The puppies love to play with the crusts and after they've had fun for a while, I throw the crusts away.

I would like to pass around a hint to puppy owners who need a soft puppy toy. Take two socks and roll one up so it will fit inside the toe of the other sock. When this is accomplished, you should have a soft bulge at the end of the sock. Tie it onto a crate or table leg. This toy is also great when it's not tied onto an object. You may use it for a teething aid as well.

My dogs are avid ball players and trying to keep balls handy, yet not underfoot, was a problem. I purchased a Pet Net and it works fine. Pet Net is a net which hangs in a corner of a room and it's used to hold children's stuffed animals.

Old sheets may be torn into small strips which then may be knotted at each of their ends. These will make tug-of-war toys for both puppies and adults. The close weave will prevent the snagging of teeth. They are easy to wash or just throw them away when they become soiled.

Renew the flavor in old rawhide chew bones by letting them soak for a few minutes in boiling, heavily-salted water. I then add about 1/2 teaspoon of Liquid Smoke (available in the bar-be-que sauce section of your grocery store). Drain but do not rinse. Serve when dry or, at least, when it's cool.

Tape your L'eggs' egg together (as a single unit) and give it to your young puppies (under three months of age) as a toy. Puppies love to roll them around. The eggs are big enough that they will not break and cause injury to the pups. This egg is lightweight and easy to carry. For added attraction, put a chew-bone inside as a rattle.

The cardboard cylinders from toilet paper rolls or paper towel rolls make wonderful and cheap dog toys. They are easily replaceable and there is an endless supply.

The cheapest and best place to get puppy toys is the baby department of your local discount store. You may be sure that there will be no small, easily swallowed parts in or attached to these baby toys. They also cost less than regular dog toys. Check out garage sales, too, for real toy bargains.

The first toys my puppies are given are the plastic adding machine toll cores or anything similar. They are light enough for puppies to carry around and to play with but not so small that they might get swallowed.

There is a toy I have found very good for puppies. Take about four rawhide bones and then tie each one together with strips of rawhide strings. The strings may be bought at any local saddle shop or in the section of your store where they sell shoestrings. These toys will keep your puppies from playing tug-of-war with your drapes and will keep them occupied for hours.

To help keep your puppy from chewing on the furniture, carpet, etc., be sure he has his own rubber toys. On furniture (table, chair legs, etc.) on which he is chewing, try putting a little oil of cloves on the wood. The odor should keep him away and if not, the bitter taste will.

To make an inexpensive puppy toy, take an empty Pringles' Potato Chip can and put some pieces of dry food or biscuits inside. Put the lid on and place the can inside a man's tube-sock. Then tie a knot in the end of the sock. To make a smaller version, use an empty bottle (vitamin, Nuprin, etc.) and use a smaller tube-sock.

We find that a clean, half-gallon plastic milk jug (with or without a short rope tied to the handle) is a safe and fun toy for a litter of puppies six or more weeks old. We only use a rope (knotted in many places) if they show little tendency to concentrate on just chewing the rope. If they get a hole gnawed in the milk container, we throw it away and give them a new one. *Most toys have dangerous possibilities and should be used only while you are supervising these small ones.*

When my bitch has only one puppy in a litter, I buy small stuffed animals to put inside the whelping box. During the summer I go to yard sales and purchase those stuffed animals at a very low price. You can even stock up if you know your bitch will be having a litter in the future. When the puppy is little, he likes to snuggle up with his "foster" littermates and when he gets a little bigger, *I take the eyes and nose off of those stuffed animals so my single puppy won't swallow them.* Soon these stuffed animals will become the puppy's toys and his best pals since he's a single pup.

When my puppies are very young, I put a bunch of cardboard boxes of varying sizes in their play area. They love to climb on top of them and play "King of the Mountain." This seems to help with training them to be on a grooming table since they are already accustomed to being off the ground.

When our children finally outgrew their sandbox, we considered briefly converting it into a flower bed. We decided against this because it soon became our dogs and puppies favorite place to play. Most races end with a tumble in the sand box. The puppies love to jump and stalk each other in it, and it's also a great place for them to dig without being scolded. A new pile of sand inspires games like "King of the Mountain" before happily tackling, climbing and tumbling levels this new sand pile.

Would you like some inexpensive puppy toys? Take advantage of your local swap meet or flea market. Also, you would be surprised how many people have puppy toys available for sale at their garage sale. They are more than willing to sell them for very reasonable prices. Other swap-meet finds are rubber baby dolls, stuffed animals (very inexpensive and they make great dog toys), old fencing, old wool blankets, etc.

You can make your own chew toys at home. Take an old soccer ball and let out some of its air (just enough to enable your dog to grip it with his mouth). Or, fill a rubber Kong toy with cheese or peanut butter. This will keep your dog licking and chewing for hours. Milk cartons, juice boxes and all different shapes and sizes of cardboard containers also make good and inexpensive chew toys. *Just be sure to remove any staples before your dog is given them...as these could be harmful.*

Young Puppies

(Also see "BITCHES," "EARS," "ELIMINATING BAD BEHAVIORS," "ENCLOSURES," "FEEDING," "GROOMING," "HEALTH," "IN THE HOME," "KENNEL MAINTENANCE," "PARASITES," "PHOTOS and PHOTOGRAPHY," "RECORDS," "SELLING DOGS," "TRAINING," "TRAVELING and SHIPPING" and "WARNINGS")

A non-slip surface on which to place your puppy is a Rubbermaid bath mat. I use mine on the dining room table and on the slippery linoleum kitchen floor. The suction cups on the back of the mat hold firmly to any slippery surface.

A tip for feeling testicles is to sit the puppy on your lap. Those questionable or disappearing lumps are much more easily palpated in this position than when the pup is standing. If the testicles are not down by four months, the pup should not be kept for breeding.

Before putting a puppy or an ill or aged dog to bed, fluff a towel in the dryer and place it in the bed to make a cozy sleeping area.

To temporarily distinguish very similar young puppies for whatever reason (medication, combining litters, etc.), simply color the tail tips with Magic Markers and make a note of which color belongs to the individual puppy or to each litter (if you need to distinguish which puppy is from which litter). You may need to recolor each tail tip every few days as the Magic marker colors do tend to wear away, but it is a good way to be sure you know which puppy is which.

When my bitch has only one puppy in a litter, I buy small stuffed animals to put inside the whelping box. During the summer I go to yard sales and purchase those stuffed animals at a very low price. You can even stock up if you know your bitch will be having a litter in the future. When the puppy is little, he likes to snuggle up with his "foster" littermates and when he gets a little bigger, *I take the eyes and nose off of those stuffed animals so my single puppy won't swallow them.* Soon these stuffed animals will become the puppy's toys and his best pals since he's a single pup.

Records

Identification

A friend of mine sent photos of a litter she had. Behind each pup was a card with a number on it. I had a litter of (sigh...) six males who were all similarly marked, therefore it was difficult to tell one pup from another. I used her idea and when I photographed the pups, I had their handler also hold a 3" x 5" card behind each pup when their pictures were being taken. I then recorded the exact markings of each pup on his card. In the case of two almost identically marked puppies, I put nail polish on one pup (to distinguish that puppy from the other) and I also recorded that nail polish marking on his card. It ended up as a sort of joke as we kept referring to #1, #2, etc. It did, however, work well. Four of the six went as show breeding prospects. It would have been difficult to identify them without this aid.

All of my dogs are tattooed and the tattoo is registered with the National Dog Registry. Their travel collars have a tag on them that says: "I am tattooed, please call 1-800-NDR-DOGS." Someone is always at the National Dog Registry, whereas who knows where I may be when I'm traveling.

Attach a pet tag (including your phone numbers) when you travel with your dog. Make sure your home, cell and your destination's phone numbers are all included on your pet's tag. Stores such as Petsmart, Petco and Walmart make it easy to print a quick pet tag using their equipment.

Be sure to have identification on your pet while traveling. Also include the area code with your telephone number. Two collars are better (just in case one collar falls off).

Include photos of your dog in your wallet so you have handy photos just in case you ever need to print flyers with photos of your lost dog.

Keep your dog leashed when walking in the snow, and make sure he is wearing an ID tag *since dogs may lose scents in snow and then become lost.*

To be prepared for a trip with your dog, pack the following: dog tags (identification with your phone numbers), your dog's photos, leash and an extra collar, a blanket or cushion from your dog's home bedding, prepared containers of your pet's meals, water dish, dog treats (keep to a minimum), dog toys, baby wipes (for cleaning purposes), trash bags and waste pickup bags along with a first ad kit.

To temporarily distinguish very similar young puppies for whatever reason (medication, combining litters, etc.), simply color the tail tips with Magic Markers and make a note of which color belongs to the individual puppy or to each litter (if you need to distinguish which puppy is from which litter). You may need to recolor each tail tip every few days as the Magic marker colors do tend to wear away, but it is a good way to be sure you know which puppy is which.

We have a large assortment of different collars our dogs wear and we hated the search required in order to find and change the tags to identify each dog. We solved this problem by purchasing several small clips and small key rings to which we attached each dog's license, tables tag and ID tags. Now when we go out, all we have to do is pick any collar and just snap that particular dog's tags onto his collar.

Judges and Judging

A hint for Obedience judging: to keep from having soggy score sheets during rainy outdoor matches or shows, buy plastic page protectors and insert the appropriate score sheet for each class you're judging. Make sure you get the kind which is closed on three of its sides. For each dog, write his score down using a wax pencil or crayon onto the protected sheet. Then (under a cover so the paper doesn't get wet) transfer the dog's scores and comments to a paper sheet at the table. Wipe the marks off the plastic and you're ready to go again.

I have kept a card file on individual judges, but I found I really needed more information than just information about the judge. I have started what I call a "Dog Show Diary." In a small spiral notebook (which doesn't take up much room in my grooming box), I make note of each show, date, city, where we stayed, address of motel, motel's phone number, how far from show site, available restaurants, room price, directions to the motel and the show site. Then I add which dog or dogs I showed, class or classes entered, place, points, judge and any comments I might have on the judge.

You would be surprised how helpful this may be from year to year.

I use a yellow Hi-Lite pen to highlight the judges' names in my breed magazine. When a show is coming up, I can glance through that breed magazine quickly to see which judges have placed what dogs.

Measuring Heights

A really simple and neat way to have a growth chart would be to use the one in *Sheltie Talk.* This book contains an excellent height chart for Shetland Sheepdogs. You could photocopy it or use tracing paper to make a rough overlay. At weekly intervals, you would measure and mark each puppy's height with a different color pen. Then you would connect the dots and you could then see at a glance how your little puppies are maturing (as compared with the chart's standard). Also, you will have the entire litter at a glance for future reference. If you have a dog of a different breed, you may use this same method over your own breed's growth chart.

A strip of masking tape on the dishwasher (with the measurements carefully transferred from a yardstick) would make a very convenient permanent measuring place for puppies. It's surely better than getting the stick out each time and taping it to the wall.

For measuring puppies, I use my husband's combination square. It is extremely accurate since it has a piece which attaches to the measurer. This piece slides up and down on the measurer. As soon as it is resting on the puppy's shoulder, it may be tightened into place. You can then remove the puppy and read the exact measurement.

For measuring your dogs, a wicket may be made in minutes with a coat hanger and pliers. Simply unwind the hanger and reshape. Measure 16" (or the maximum allowed height for your breed of dog) from each end and bend to a 90-degree angle. The crosspiece is about 10" and goes over the dog's withers. Hopefully, the ends will touch the ground.

If your puppy's feet keep slipping when you are trying to measure him, stand the pup on a sheet of sandpaper and there will be no more slipping and frightening a tiny pup.

Rubbermaid Sure Grip (for drawer lining) provides a great footing for measuring a puppy's height. It's also great for lining pens, tubs, tops of counters and any surface which you may use for grooming, etc. It's inexpensive, comes in great colors and you just throw it in the washer when it needs cleaning.

To make the measuring of puppies handy and convenient, I place a strip of masking tape on the wall of the puppy room and mark it off in inches. It makes weekly measuring less of a job.

When advertising with a black-and-white photo of your stud dog, state his color and his height under the photo or somewhere in your ad.

Medical and Health
(Also see "HEALTH" and "RECORDS")

An easy way to keep from forgetting to give medications is to keep each medication in a little crate watering cup. I use the cups designed for birds (plastic with wire holders) as the wires may be bent to accommodate any crate or pen. Attach the cup to the outside of the crate or pen. This way the pills are always handy and you can't forget them since they're right under your nose. Naturally, this is for indoor use only. It's perfect for visiting bitches' heartworm medication, vitamins, etc., and for keeping vitamins handy in the maternity ward.

Any client is entitled to a copy of any or all medical lab tests done on his or her dog. Generally, though, vets do not make copies of these tests for their clients unless specifically requested to do so. Not only do I want all medical test reports copied for my files, but I want them as soon as possible. The medical results may be faxed immediately to my home or, if they're ready, I'll take the copies with me.

During the excitement of selling a puppy or a dog, important dates may be forgotten (indicating when and what vaccinations and wormings the puppy was given and when they will be needed in the future). I use doggy note cards (which attractively represent our breed on the front) to record name and litter number of the puppy, name and number of the sire and dam, feeding schedule, complete record of dates and types of vaccinations, wormings, etc., along with a vaccination and worming schedule for the puppy owner's future use. Puppy buyers seem to appreciate having this information conveniently at their fingertips. The note cards also work well for listing show records.

How nice it would be if all our dogs were due for inoculations at the same time, but this is not the way it ever works. I eliminated the time-consuming chore of constantly sifting through records by making a chart of 12 squares (one for each month) and filling in each dog's name in the appropriate square. I hang this handy chart on the inside of my dog-supply cabinet and can tell, at a glance, who is due when.

If you feed at night and need to give medications also in the morning, put the bottle on the kitchen table (or other conspicuous place) after the evening dose has been given. Place the bottle back with your feeding supplies after the morning dose. This not only helps you remember to give the dose but also indicates whether you already have given it that day.

I give my own puppy shots, so for each puppy I peel off the label from the vials and place those labels on a sheet of paper. I also include (for each puppy) the date, weight, height, worming (date and type of medication), vet's physical date and any other pertinent data or information on this sheet of paper or "data sheet." When a puppy goes to his new home, his "data sheet" goes with him. By keeping this type of record, there is no question about the type of vaccinations or times given when the new family takes him to their vet for a physical.

I keep a calendar which has very large boxes for each day and hang it in a conspicuous place. As I do any work on any dog, I make a notation regarding that dog in the box for that day. It is then very easy to transfer breeding information, worming schedules, etc., to each dog's permanent files at the end of each month. Also, I am able to tell prospective buyers everything that has been done to their dog and when the next vaccination or worming should take place. I have tried keeping records using other methods and I've found that this is the easiest method and, therefore, it is the least likely to be forgotten.

I use a puppy calendar for all my dog notices and health activities (such as wormings, vaccinations, breeding, due dates, trips, etc.). At the end of each year, pertinent information is transferred to individual dog records. All calendars are kept in a file cabinet for easy access.

To check your pet's pulse, feel on the inside of his back thigh where the leg joins the body. Normal for dogs is 70-150 beats a minute. Normal for cats is 110-170 beats a minute. Remember to record each temperature so you may see your pet's progress.

Use thumbtacks or pushpins to hang a large, desk-type calendar on the wall in the room where you keep your kennel records. Write in show dates, breedings, whelping dates, shots and other useful information for easy record keeping and reference. When the month is over, simply remove, fold and file the page away with your permanent records.

When de-worming puppies, it's easy to lose track of which pups have been wormed. To prevent an accidental overdose, simply cut each puppy's toenails as you de-worm. Then by the time you need to de-worm again, the nails need to be cut again. Pups who have been wormed are identified by their short toenails.

When keeping records on my dogs, we use 3" x 5" cards for each dog. It makes it really handy to record shots, wormings and breeding information. These are a lot better than my old method of using calendars, which are so difficult to use after each New Year's day has passed and you need to bring out a new calendar.

Official Records and Registrations

When a buyer of two of my bitches said she was ready to sell them, I immediately offered to buy them back. While this lady received the two bitches' OFA certificates (when she purchased the dogs), this paperwork was not included when I bought them home (just photocopies of their OFA certificates). I requested copies directly from the OFA. For anyone needing something like this, all you have to do is send the OFA a copy of the AKC papers which prove that you are the current owner and OFA will send you the certificate at no charge. This is a very nice service of the OFA.

When sending out pedigrees of stud dogs, photocopy the dog's OFA and CERF certificates right on the back of each pedigree. If sending out pedigrees of puppies, you could include the dam's certifications or sire and dam if you reduce the certificate's size. By doing that, no one has to research the accuracy of the statement "normal eyes and hips."

Pedigrees

A lot of breeders use black-and-white copy machines to reproduce pedigrees. This is fast and easy but it looks cheap. I miss the beautiful red of the champions. I feel that a quality dog should have a quality-looking pedigree. Sometimes I make out one puppy pedigree leaving the champion places blank. After I make copies of this one, I fill in the champions in red. This saves some time and the results look impressive.

We use a pink highlighter pen to mark all titled dogs on our pedigrees and include a code or key explaining titles at the bottom of each pedigree. Pet puppy buyers really like this as many of them don't understand what the various titles mean.

When sending out pedigrees of stud dogs, photocopy the dog's OFA and CERF certificates right on the back of each pedigree. If sending out pedigrees of puppies, you could include the dam's certifications or sire and dam if you reduce the certificate's size. By doing that, no one has to research the accuracy of the statement "normal eyes and hips."

When typing up a pedigree for one of my stud dogs, I select a good photo of a head study and a full-body view of him. With a copy machine, I add both photos to the reverse side of the pedigree. This makes a great handout for anyone interested in your male photo and pedigree all in one.

Photos and Photography

A friend of mine sent photos of a litter she had. Behind each pup was a card with a number on it. I had a litter of (sigh...) six males who were all similarly marked, therefore it was difficult to tell one pup from another. I used her idea and when I photographed the pups, I had their handler also hold a 3" x 5" card behind each pup when their pictures were being taken. I then recorded the exact markings of each pup on his card. In the case of two almost identically marked puppies, I put nail polish on one pup (to distinguish that puppy from the other) and I also recorded that nail polish marking on his card. It ended up as a sort of joke as we kept referring to #1, #2, etc. It did, however, work well. Four of the six went as show breeding prospects. It would have been difficult to identify them without this aid.

Ever receive dog photos which you would like to keep but must return to the owner? I photocopy the pictures on a good copy machine and file them away for future reference.

I always keep a mini-calendar (free at Hallmark stores) attached to my camera strap. Every time I take a picture, it's information is recorded on the calendar. This takes all the guesswork out of dating puppy pictures along with keeping any other pertinent information regarding each photo I take.

In order to get a really good look at head quality and expression of a young puppy, tuck the pup up against your shoulder and look into a mirror. From this secure position, the pup will not wiggle as much and will frequently follow his own reflection. You may get a long look, straight on, without having to dangle the pup at arm's length. This works especially well if you hold two, three or even four pups up in a line for comparison. Somehow, too, evaluating through the mirror seems to increase your objectivity (similar to seeing photos or videos of your own dogs). Try taking their photos from this position.

I've found that a neat way to store photographs is to purchase little boxes (the kind used for business cards) from your local print shop. They are just the right size for most prints, very sturdy and cheap. Each box contains the photos for a particular dog (clearly marked with a Magic Marker). All the boxes may be stored in a drawer or in a large cardboard box. I particularly like the cardboard file boxes which are available at office supply stores. This way, it's easy to find that particular photo you want. Valuable negatives are also placed, along with one print of that photo, in a photo album so that reprints may be made later.

To keep from losing negatives of your favorite photos, have a special album in which you place one reprint of the photo along with its negative in a small envelope. You can store several per page. It's easy to glance through the album to locate exactly which print you need when the time comes to make reprints or enlargements.

Protecting Your Breed Magazines

Breed magazines stored standing on their spines age before their time due to the stress put on a magazine's binding each time it's pulled out from between two other magazines. This pulling breaks down its edge and the overall quality of the magazine. I use a stackable, acrylic, smoky-colored desk tray. This gives the magazines a break and keeps them at your fingertips where they do you the most good. Very minimal space is needed.

Since I have all my *Sheltie Pacesetter* magazines starting with the Charter issue (in 1977), I have many issues to go through when looking for an article, picture or a pedigree. I photocopied the "Article Index" and the "Photograph Index" which both appear in the first issue of each year. These copies are much easier to check through than going through each magazine individually. The magazines themselves are stored in calendar order so locating what I want is no longer a real chore. The photocopies are stored in a paper folder for ease of handling.

Since I store my breed magazines flat on a shelf, with the bottom of the page facing outward, I take a felt-tip pen and mark the month, year and issue number for that year along the bottom side of the magazine for easy identification (thus one reads "Jul. 84 No. 4"). I also add my initials. Then if I lend out an issue, I am identified as its owner and, hopefully, it will be returned to me.

To help preserve my precious issues of our breed magazine, I slip each one into its own plastic slipcover (the kind that are sold to protect comic books). I slip a note inside this bag to indicate any articles or ads to which I may want to research at a later date.

To protect my breed magazines from the hazards of heavy handling, I buy the clear plastic book covers (available at any college bookstore). While they may be expensive, they protect each cover from dirt, tears and dog-ears. I consider them very worthwhile since my magazines are read through several times and referred back to often.

To protect my breed magazines from wear and tear, I coat them with a polyurethane spray available at hardware stores. Simply open the magazine at the center and lay it face up. Place newspaper under each cover to protect the inside pages and spray the outside covers lightly. Allow to dry completely and you have a clear plastic finish.

To store your breed magazines, use heavy-duty three-ring binders and order plastic holders from J. H. Smith Co., 330 Chapman Street, Greenfield, MA 01301. Insert the pages of the magazine through the long opening in the plastic holder being sure that the "hole" side is out. Then snap the magazine into the binder. One binder or notebook will hold six magazines and may be placed on a bookshelf. I have marked the year on the side of the binder. The magazines stay clean and neatly arranged.

We store our breed magazines in jumbo letter files made either of plastic or metal. It keeps them from getting worn out. You may purchase these at most discount stores.

Records and Record Keeping
(Also see "SELLING")

During the excitement of selling a puppy or a dog, important dates may be forgotten (indicating when and what vaccinations and wormings the puppy was given and when they will be needed in the future). I use doggy note cards (which attractively represent our breed on the front) to record name and litter number of the puppy, name and number of the sire and dam, feeding schedule, complete record of dates and types of vaccinations, wormings, etc., along with a vaccination and worming schedule for the puppy owner's future use. Puppy buyers seem to appreciate having this information conveniently at their fingertips. The note cards also work well for listing show records.

I have begun organizing my dog information in a more orderly fashion with the use of three-ring binders and sheet protectors. One of the binders which receives the most comments and use is a large, three-inch binder in which I have compiled loads of information. I simply slide sheets of any information into the standard sheet protectors and insert them into the three-ring binder. What has evolved is a wonderful "fingertip" file of subscription blanks for our favorite dog magazine, information on different dog foods, club information, wholesale catalogs, special doggy novelties (such as knit sweaters, portraits, etc.), in addition to the more routine things such as growth and whelping charts. This binder is used daily and is wonderful to keep for those phone calls and e-mails from people who need an address for something doggy. I save much time by not having to search for these things, and it has totally eliminated the clutter of odds and ends around the area where my dog records and magazines are kept.

I keep a calendar which has very large boxes for each day and hang it in a conspicuous place. As I do any work on any dog, I make a notation regarding that dog in the box for that day. It is then very easy to transfer breeding information, worming schedules, etc., to each dog's permanent files at the end of each month. Also, I am able to tell prospective buyers everything that has been done to their dog and when the next vaccination or worming should take place. I have tried keeping records using other methods and I've found that this is the easiest method and, therefore, it is the least likely to be forgotten.

I use a puppy calendar for all my dog notices and health activities (such as wormings, vaccinations, breeding, due dates, trips, etc.). At the end of each year, pertinent information is transferred to individual dog records. All calendars are kept in a file cabinet for easy access.

Tear out catalog sheets of your wins or losses and attach them to your mileage charts and/or expense accounts. The IRS wants proof of your shows and catalogs tend to take up a lot of space.

Ribbons and Trophies

A good use for those red, yellow and white class ribbons (which many of us do not keep) has been found. Keep a few of them with your breed magazines and with your printed books. Use them as bookmarks. They are colorful and will be reminders of fun times as well as serve a useful purpose.

All those flat ribbons that you win at matches, etc., make excellent bookmarks for paperbacks and show catalogs.

Being still enough of a novice to treasure each and every ribbon and lucky enough to collect quite a few, I like to label them so they don't become a meaningless pile of color. By cutting a file card the width of the ribbon, you have room to print the dog's name, date (if not on the ribbon), judge's name, class, score (if Obedience or Performance), along with any other pertinent information, such as class size or placement. I then fold the top of the ribbon just over the card and staple it in place. They may then be placed in a clear plastic box and stored in a conspicuous place for admiration.

For those who can't find a place in which to keep their ribbons and certificates flat and neat, here's what I did: I got a three-ring notebook-type photo album with the magnetic pages. I placed a picture of the dog, a three-generation pedigree and all ribbons and certificates on the succeeding pages. Under each ribbon, I put the judge's name at that show and the number of points won, if any.

I stick a peel-off address label on the back of those flat ribbons with no tag. Then I write the date of the show, the name of the dog I entered, the placing, points and where the show took place. This way, when I look back, I can see which dog won a particular ribbon.

Not needing or wanting several old trophies that were given to me, I decided that the brass Sheltie statues on top of the trophies would make a nice statue. With the careful help of a hacksaw, I now have several beautiful Sheltie statues.

To display your flat ribbons, arrange them underneath a sheet of glass on an end table or a coffee table.

Selling Dogs and Puppies
(Also see "SELLING")

During the excitement of selling a puppy or a dog, important dates may be forgotten (indicating when and what vaccinations and wormings the puppy was given and when they will be needed in the future). I use doggy note cards (which attractively represent our breed on the front) to record name and litter number of the puppy, name and number of the sire and dam, feeding schedule, complete record of dates and types of vaccinations, wormings, etc., along with a vaccination and worming schedule for the puppy owner's future use. Puppy buyers seem to appreciate having this information conveniently at their fingertips. The note cards also work well for listing show records.

Having trouble keeping all the dog records separate but yet together? I bought a different color folder with pockets inside for each dog and also each puppy I sold or am going to sell. They were very inexpensive and were available at office supply stores. I put all the shot records, pedigrees, pictures, breeding information, etc., for each dog in a folder with the dog's name and AKC number on the front for easy identification. Then I never have to worry where all my information is located.

I give my own puppy shots, so for each puppy I peel off the label from the vials and place those labels on a sheet of paper. I also include (for each puppy) the date, weight, height, worming (date and type of medication), vet's physical date and any other pertinent data or information on this sheet of paper or "data sheet." When a puppy goes to his new home, his "data sheet" goes with him. By keeping this type of record, there is no question about the type of vaccinations or times given when the new family takes him to their vet for a physical.

Our puppy care packages include an ID (identity document) and we strongly encourage that they be printed with the words, "REWARD IF FOUND" along with the owner's area code and phone number. It's hoped that the dog will never be lost, but accidents do happen and we feel the knowledge of a reward will enhance the chance that someone will return your dog.

To keep the pet population down in your geographical area, sell every pet with no registration papers. Papers may be given to the new owners when you receive proof of spaying or neutering of that dog. Be sure (at the time of sale) that the buyer signs an agreement which states that they are buying a registered dog without papers. By doing this, that dog won't be bred to the pet down the road and produce more pets.

When a buyer of two of my bitches said she was ready to sell them, I immediately offered to buy them back. While this lady received the two bitches' OFA certificates (when she purchased the dogs), this paperwork was not included when I bought them home (just photocopies of their OFA certificates). I requested copies directly from the OFA. For anyone needing something like this, all you have to do is send the OFA a copy of the AKC papers which prove that you are the current owner and OFA will send you the certificate at no charge. This is a very nice service of the OFA.

When sending out pedigrees of stud dogs, photocopy the dog's OFA and CERF certificates right on the back of each pedigree. If sending out pedigrees of puppies, you could include the dam's certifications or sire and dam if you reduce the certificate's size. By doing that, no one has to research the accuracy of the statement "normal eyes and hips."

When shipping a bitch, we enclose all necessary papers (pedigree, test results, etc.) in an empty candy or cookie tin and put this tin inside the crate. This way papers can't be torn off the outside of the crate. They remain dry and safe inside. We can also include vitamins, raspberry leaves, etc., for bitches who are to be bred.

Shows and Show Entries

Before throwing out those premium lists, tear out the extra application blanks in the back. Cover the show name and address with blank peel-and-stick labels. I have a supply of these and they are great for when you don't get a premium list in time, early entry or for sending to a show superintendent whose mailing list you don't receive.

Envelopes may be easily addressed for mailing show entries by using a typewriter with a memory. Make up several at a time for quick use later.

Filling out show entries is no longer tedious work for me. I use a blank official American Kennel Club entry form, type in any information required and then I photocopy as many as I want. For each show, I only need to fill in the show name, date, entry fee and then sign it.

I have kept a card file on individual judges, but I found I really needed more information than just information about the judge. I have started what I call a "Dog Show Diary." In a small spiral notebook (which doesn't take up much room in my grooming box), I make note of each show, date, city, where we stayed, address of motel, motel's phone number, how far from show site, available restaurants, room price, directions to the motel and the show site. Then I add which dog or dogs I showed, class or classes entered, place, points, judge and any comments I might have on the judge. You would be surprised how helpful this may be from year to year.

I use a yellow Hi-Lite pen to highlight the judges' names in my breed magazine. When a show is coming up, I can glance through that breed magazine quickly to see which judges have placed what dogs.

Tear out catalog sheets of your wins or losses and attach them to your mileage charts and/or expense accounts. The IRS wants proof of your shows and catalogs tend to take up a lot of space.

Telephone

One of the breeders' most important tools is the telephone. With the arrival of the new long-distance companies, accurate record-keeping has become a necessity. Unfortunately, most calendars do not have the space available for our needs, therefore what I do is mark my calendar with the long-distance area code and the kennel name of the person I called. Since we all have the shortest possible kennel name, there is room on each calendar square for many more calls than is good for your checkbook.

Wondering what to do with all those business cards you receive? They are great to keep for addresses and phone numbers but what do you do with them? I mount them on paper, using

clear mounting corners which are found in any business-supply store. Then I slide them into the covers of vinyl binders which I use for holding information on my dogs. They are always right within view and make an attractive "create-your-own" cover (using the binders which have plastic sleeves on their front and back covers). I also mount some business cards on the larger-size index file card and put directions to those people's kennels in the remaining space. This is especially useful for those of us who do our fair share of kennel-hopping. It also saves phone time for future visits in case you forget directions (as easily as I do) as I just slide the needed card into my purse and I then have all the information I need at my fingertips.

Misc.

A light dusting of snow on a sidewalk or roadside makes it easy to see if your dog's paw prints are re-converging (to touch the center line) as should occur when a dog is trotting.

Selling Dogs

(Also see "RECORDS"—"Selling Dogs and Puppies")

Add the cost of your breed's magazine to the cost of your puppies and send in a one-year subscription for your puppy's breed magazine to each new dog owner. The additional expense is negligible and you will provide considerable pleasure to the newcomer as well as ensure a more educated and knowledgeable home for the puppies you sell.

A lot of the fast food restaurants were giving stuffed toys as premiums along with their happy meals for children. These were small puppy-size toys which had no parts that could be chewed off (as everything was embroidered on instead of glued). Of particular interest was the "Babe" promotion that McDonald's was offering. This collection included a sheep, Border Collie, cat, cow, etc. The sheep is adorable. We buy them at local yard sales, auctions, flea markets, etc. If they get dirty, they wash really well. We have accumulated quite a collection and have started the practice of sending them along with the puppies we place into their "forever" homes. The new owners now have a start on their own toy collection and the puppies love them because it's a familiar toy (which smells like home and their littermates). Even our older dogs love them. There's also a wildlife collection with tigers, lions, monkeys, etc.

A puppy will often whine (after going to his new home) because he misses his mother. To help your new puppy to adjust, wrap a towel around a warm hot-water bottle and place it in his bed. A ticking clock or a radio playing softly will also help.

A very effective item I have found for cleaning puppies (before prospective buyers come out and for cleaning your show dog's ears before going into the ring) is Diaparene Baby Washcloths. They are safe to use on your young puppies and on ears. They are fast drying because of the alcohol base. They are easy to use, easy to take to a show and easy to trash.

During the excitement of selling a puppy or a dog, important dates may be forgotten (indicating when and what vaccinations and wormings the puppy was given and when they will be needed in the future). I use doggy note cards (which attractively represent our breed on the front) to record name and litter number of the puppy, name and number of the sire and dam, feeding schedule, complete record of dates and types of vaccinations, wormings, etc., along with a vaccination and worming schedule for the puppy owner's future use. Puppy buyers seem to appreciate having this information conveniently at their fingertips. The note cards also work well for listing show records.

Have the editor of your breed club newsletter type a copy of your dog's *Standard* (or...do it for him or her) and ask that it be included in the next issue of the newsletter so that recipients of the newsletter may make copies (for free distribution to the newcomers who purchase pups from them). This is an inexpensive way to educate the nonspecialist pet owner about what is (or is not) a good specimen from the strictly professional point of view. Such a practice might help discourage the breeding of pet-quality animals and certainly makes a breeder more credible when he or she explains why the pet owner's bitch should not be bred.

I can't bear to throw away old breed calendar pictures or any pictures left if I'm dissecting paper-type books for filing stories and desired photos. I place these photos in a small, paperboard type, three-ring binder. A gorgeous dog "face" is glued onto the cover. Your dog's name goes on the cover, with brochures, immunizations, feeding schedule, spay/neuter contract agreements, crate usage brochures, a catalog from an area wholesale veterinary supply house (puppies can be more assured of top-of-the-line products when you help lead the new owners), lead-breaking tips and housebreaking suggestions, your national breed club's puppy brochure, a copy of the dog's pedigree, a breed magazine brochure and subscription blank and whatever else might help the new owner. Presto...a pretty and informational "puppy packet" has been created. These kinds of things aren't hard to do and they will add so much to the pet buyer's appreciation of his new purchase. I believe that these are the "homey" touches which set a breeder apart among so many pet store and pet mill breeders.

I give my own puppy shots so for each puppy, I peel off the label from the vials and place those labels on a sheet of paper. I also include (for each puppy) the date, weight, height, worming (date and type of medication), vet's physical date and any other pertinent data or information on this sheet of paper or "data sheet." When a puppy goes to his new home, his "data sheet" goes with him. By keeping this type of record, there is no question about the type of vaccinations or times given when the new family takes him to their vet for a physical.

I like to keep in touch with the owners of the puppies I have sold. I have found that sending a birthday or Christmas card and/or gift elicits a reply and usually a photo (in return). The card and/or gift of a soft toy along with a photo of the puppies' dam means a lot to pet owners, and the information they return to me more than makes up for the cost and time involved.

I've loaned crates to puppy buyers to help them during the first few weeks with their new puppy. I found a marvelous pamphlet to send along with our usual six-page instruction and care sheets for the puppy. It is "A Pet Owner's Guide to the Dog Crate" and I cannot recommend it highly enough. These pamphlets may be ordered from Nicki Meyer Educational Effort, Inc., 31 Davis Hill Road, Weston, CT 06883. «»Editor's note: you may also be interested in reading an article by Nicki Meyer entitled "Dog Crates as Aids to Pet Owners" in the September/October 1981 issue of the *Sheltie Pacesetter* magazine on page 140. A photocopy of this ten-page article may be purchased for $7.90. Contact Nancy Lee Cathcart at s.pacesetter@sheltie.com for details.«»

Our puppy care packages include an ID (identity document) and we strongly encourage that they be printed with the words, "REWARD IF FOUND" along with the owner's area code and phone number. It's hoped that the dog will never be lost, but accidents do happen and we feel the knowledge of a reward will enhance the chance that someone will return your dog.

Placing "for sale" cards at pet supply businesses and area vet clinics increases effectiveness when a photograph is attached. Besides, the puppies grow so much between four to eight weeks that a recent photo really is a must. Those old breed calendar pictures or breed magazine ad photos may be used for this purpose, also. A picture really is worth a thousand words and those "eyes" get them every time.

Tired of losing expensive leads? Make your own leashes using thin parachute cord cut to any length you desire. You may send one with each puppy you sell. Buy inexpensive hooks to knot on one end and sew down the loose end of the knot. Make a loop at the other end and sew off the dangling end also. The resulting leads are cheap, strong and durable. If you prefer leather leads, substitute boot shoelaces picked up at any shoe store for the nylon cord. A 50-foot package of nylon cord will make about eight leashes.

To keep the pet population down in your geographical area, sell every pet with no registration papers. Papers may be given to the new owners when you receive proof of spaying or neutering of that dog. Be sure (at the time of sale) that the buyer signs an agreement which states that they are buying a registered dog without papers. By doing this, that dog won't be bred to the pet down the road and produce more pets.

We get quite a few of the doggy supply catalogs in the mail. Instead of throwing them out, we save them and pass them on to new puppy buyers. Our "puppy people" love it since they may stock up on new puppy supplies at great prices.

When a buyer of two of my bitches said she was ready to sell them, I immediately offered to buy them back. While this lady received the two bitches' OFA certificates (when she purchased the dogs), this paperwork was not included when I bought them home (just photocopies of their OFA certificates). I requested copies directly from the OFA. For anyone needing something like this, all you have to do is send the OFA a copy of the AKC papers which prove that you are the current owner and OFA will send you the certificate at no charge. This is a very nice service of the OFA.

When advertising with a black-and-white photo of your stud dog, state his height and color under the photo or somewhere in your ad. Sometimes even blue dogs look like sables and tri-factored sables are often hard to distinguish from tris. It would also help with stud dogs to tell whether they are tri-factored, white-factored or pure-for-sable, etc., (depending on his breed).

When placing a puppy or dog in a new home, send a blanket or small rug along, preferably one that he has slept on previously. It gives him a sense of security.

When sending out pedigrees of stud dogs, photocopy the dog's OFA and CERF certificates right on the back of each pedigree. If sending out pedigrees of puppies, you could include the dam's certifications or sire and dam if you reduce the certificate's size. By doing that, no one has to research the accuracy of the statement "normal eyes and hips."

When shipping a bitch, we enclose all necessary papers (pedigree, test results, etc.) in an empty candy or cookie tin and put this tin inside the crate. This way papers can't be torn off the outside of the crate. They remain dry and safe inside. We can also include vitamins, raspberry leaves, etc., for bitches who are to be bred.

When typing pedigrees for my pet puppies, I add the name, address and price of the breed magazine on the back of the pup's pedigree. I have my most recent breed magazine sitting on the table while talking with each prospective buyer. The pictures in the magazine help show just how beautiful the dog can be.

With my litters, a week before they are to leave, I have their dam sleep on some hand towels. I give out these hand towels to the people acquiring a puppy. I have found that the puppies settle in great the first night (without the usual crying) because they each have a familiar scent nearby.

Shows

At The Showgrounds

After the horrible theft of a dog at a show, we started locking our crates at shows. We bought a dozen or so very small locks from Sears. We lucked out in that they were all identical and the same key fits all the locks we purchased. Every crate in our house has a lock hanging on the door and no matter which crate gets taken to a show, there is a lock just waiting to be used. They are not heavy-duty locks but they do the job. It is doubtful that someone thinking about stealing a dog will bother one who is locked up. Even if the lock could be picked or broken, they will look for an easier target. I keep a key pinned to the inside of my bait pouch for quick access in case of an emergency.

Any time you stay in a motel which offers free shower caps, be sure to save them. They take practically no space in your purse, glove compartment or grooming box and may come in very handy during those unexpected rain showers (when you're at dog shows and you must be out in the rain to exercise, groom or even to show your dog...if you're braver than I am).

Carry a trash bag in your car or grooming box so it could become an emergency raincoat. You may even cover your dog with it.

For better organization when going to the dog shows, I use a plastic laundry basket which has a hard plastic lid. This works well to hold everything that your tack box doesn't hold (like towels, newspaper, dog food, shoes, show clothes, picture albums, etc.). The plastic lid keeps everything in the basket so its contents don't get crushed.

Cleaning At Shows

(See "GROOMING"—"Cleaning"
and "SHIPPING and TRAVELING"—
"Cleaning While Traveling")

Equipment To Use At The Shows

(Also see "GROOMING"—"Equipment, Products and Supplies")

A 30-foot long line (used for exercising horses in a large circle) made of one-inch nylon webbing makes a great lead for exercising dogs (while at shows or places where safety is a concern). They may be purchased through wholesale catalogs or tack shops.

After attending a dog show where my dog was violently ill in the hotel room and I had no real clean-up supplies, I now travel

prepared. For dog-show trips, I now carry a container with cleaning items which contains moist towelettes, carpet cleaner (like Simple Solution), a roll of paper towels, hand sanitizer, some folded newspapers, spray disinfectant, a can of air freshener and/or Febreeze, a lint roller and some trash sacks. You may use off-brand and small or trial sizes of many of these items so they won't take up so much room.

A nifty towel rack may be made from a dry cleaner's wire hanger which has a cardboard tube attached. Remove one end of the tube and insert your roll of paper towels. Presto...you have a towel rack that travels to shows and which you may hang on a grooming table.

Any time you stay in a motel which offers free shower caps, be sure to save them. They take practically no space in your purse, glove compartment or grooming box and may come in very handy during those unexpected rain showers (when you're at dog shows and you must be out in the rain to exercise, groom or even to show your dog...if you're braver than I am).

Carry a trash bag in your car or grooming box so it could become an emergency raincoat. You may even cover your dog with it.

Fireplace tongs make great arm extensions for reaching over exercise pens to either place or to retrieve bowls.

For inexpensive shade, cover the top of your exercise pen with a bed spread.

For those who have wire handles on crates or exercise pens, make it easier on your hands. Get an old piece of hose (a garden hose works well) and measure the amount of hose you'll need for the handle where your hand will grip it. Slice the hose on one side from one end to the other end. Slip it over the handle and tape the hose shut with tape. (I find friction tape works well.) Wrap the tape around the length of the hose several times. It makes crates and pens so much easier to carry.

If you use an All-Weather Blanket (or Space Blanket with one reflective side) or any other kind of cover with grommets to cover your exercise pen, use "S" hooks for attaching the cover to your exercise pen. Put one end of the "S" hook into the grommet and tighten with a pair of pliers. The open end may be attached to the wire of the exercise pen and works very well to keep the cover from blowing off (clothespins seem to get blown off easily.) My cover only has four grommets and at a show one weekend where it was very windy, it never blew off.

Instead of purchasing a roller base for hauling all your equipment and dogs to your grooming area, a dolly or hand truck combination is available for less money. Use it horizontally and attach a rope or lead to pull it easily. It has wheels large enough to go over curbs and bumps. The front wheels swivel for turning with ease. It will stand up (out of your way), or it may be used for hanging your outfit (to keep your clothes wrinkle-free before ring time).

I wouldn't wish this on my worst enemy, but I fell and broke my hip. (Yes, I was out on the ice trying to get a dog). After surgery (and moving around the house on a "walker"), I was given something called a "grabber." This allowed me to pick up things without bending (which I wasn't supposed to do). Well, as things progressed and I could finally pick up pens, toys, dishes, etc., I found this "grabber" an invaluable tool. It has sort of "claws" on one end plus a handle that one may press in order to close its claws. This came from OT (occupational therapy) at the hospital.

Make it easier on yourself while picking up after your dogs. For pottying your dogs on those dark nights at a motel or on the showgrounds, get yourself a Flexi-leash with a little flashlight attached. It makes finding your dog's poop in the dark much easier. You may find them at Petsmart, Dollar General, etc., and online. I save mine to use at the motels and now there's no more hunting around for after-dark poo (especially in rainy or cold weather).

Shower curtain rings are very handy to a dog owner. These shower curtain rings hold water buckets on the fences (we use the relatively light two-quart stainless steel type). Some are attached to the Space Blankets we use to cover the exercise pens at outdoor shows. They are light, easily opened, not prone to rust and are inexpensive.

There are a lot of handy uses for your spray bottle besides misting when line-brushing. With the bottle always full of water and water only, set the nozzle on "stream." It will squirt across a room. My aim is not that good but I can generally get a barking dog's face and/or mouth very wet from across the room. Even if you just hit the body or dampen an ear, you do get their attention. If you don't think it shuts them up, try it. Also, my dogs are not afraid of the spray bottle, they merely respect it because they drink from it at shows. At hot outdoor shows, you may not have a bowl of water handy but you probably have a spray bottle within reach. My dogs love to have this water sprayed into their mouths, however you need to *make sure the nozzle is reset to "spray" (so it's not too strong) and that they do not receive too much, too rapidly because they might then vomit.* If you have sloppy drinkers and you are ready to go into the ring, but "Superdog" looks like he could use a drink, a squirt in the mouth is a lot neater than water slurped all over his ruff. I also use the spray bottle to rinse chalk off my hands when I'm in a hurry or off my shoes, clothes, etc. Believe it or not, I have been known to squirt the thing in my own mouth or at my nervous husband.

Which exercise pen is yours? Ever wonder about that when traveling with several others to a show or when taking down a community setup in the dark? I mark my pens by attaching one of those little metal pet-collar tags which are personalized with dog's name, owner's name and address. I substitute my kennel name for the "dog's name" part. The metal collar loop attaches the tag to the pen permanently. My tags come from Milk Bones (via box tops) but they are also usually available in your vet's office and in pet stores.

Feeding At Shows
(See "FEEDING"—"Travel and Feeding" and "Water")

Grooming At Shows
(See "GROOMING"—"Show Grooming and Preparation," "Grooming Boxes," "Grooming Tables" and "Equipment")

Health Problems At Shows
(Also see "HEALTH"—"Medications and Shots")

Identification
(See "RECORDS"—"Identification")

In The Ring
If, on a cold day, you are showing a dog whose ears tend to fly up in cold weather, try wringing out cotton or a cloth that's been dipped in hot water (it may be carried in a wide thermos) and holding it to the ears before going into the ring. *Be sure it's not too hot because you wouldn't want to burn your dog's ears.* Or...you may cup the ears in your hands and blow your warm breath on them.

If you eat a banana shortly before going into the ring, it will calm a case of show nerves. The potassium in bananas helps maintain a healthy nervous system and stable blood pressure.

If you have a dog who is a little apprehensive when a judge comes up to go over him, just take hold of a few hairs along the side of his head and below his ears. Hold him gently, but firmly, with your right hand and take a short hold on the lead with your left hand. You will find this will steady your dog and he will not pull away from the judge.

If you have a problem with dog hair sticking to your show clothing, wet a wash rag, wring it out until it is just damp and wipe over the area covered with dog hair. The hair will just roll off in clumps.

If your stud dog is more interested in an "in season" bitch than he is in showing, put a couple drops of a strong perfume on his nose just before going into the ring. This works wonders for me. Also, if it is your bitch who is "in season," you can work some of the perfume into her skirts so that she won't distract everyone else's male, too.

I spray Firm Grip on the slippery bottoms of my shoes before I enter the show ring and/or onto my sweaty palms.

I've found a product to use on slick shoe soles that is even better than rubber cement. It's called Shoe Goo II and I purchased it at a store that sells athletic shoes. It's very reasonable in price and easy to use (converting dangerous slick-soled shoes into safe shoes for show ring wear). It's made by Eclectic Products, Inc., 729 Basin Street, San Pedro, CA 90731. It's a tube of clear "goo" that you apply to shoe soles and it dries to a tough, rubbery coating.

Make new shoes (which have slick soles) slip-proof for safer footing in the show ring by applying a coating of rubber cement to soles and heels. Allow the rubber cement to dry overnight.

Remove your pet's hair from your clothing by using masking tape. Roll the tape out and attach the tape backwards on the roll so the sticky side is out. Roll the tape on your clothes and the hair will stick to the tape.

The Four Way Anglers Worm Pouch (which may be found at a sporting goods store) is perfect for carrying scissors, chalk and other small doggy items to shows and matches. The pouch is easy to carry and durable. The zippered compartments are transparent and roomy.

To prevent my dog from picking up bait from the floor while in the show ring, I place several pieces of liver on the floor (while still outside the ring). Then I gait my dog over and around the liver. If he tries to grab the bait, I use some good obedience corrections. It will take about three minutes of work before going into the ring...just to refresh his memory.

In The Vehicle
(See "SHIPPING and TRAVELING"—"While Traveling")

Lodging (Motels, Hotels, Etc.)
(See "TRAVELING and SHIPPING"—"Motels, Hotels, Etc." and "SHOWS"—"Lodging")

Raffles
Here's a great raffle promotion and incentive to get people to clean up after their dogs: for every bag of poop a person drops in a special trash can, they get one free raffle ticket.

Ribbons and Trophies

(See "RECORDS"—"Ribbons and Trophies")

Show Bait

(See "FEEDING"—"Show Bait")

Show Clothing

Any time you stay in a motel which offers free shower caps, be sure to save them. They take practically no space in your purse, glove compartment or grooming box and may come in very handy during those unexpected rain showers (when you're at dog shows and you must be out in the rain to exercise, groom or even to show your dog...if you're braver than I am).

Be sure to include Speed Sew on your list of necessities to take to shows. Beside using it for your dog's ears which need to be tipped, it's great for stopping a run in your panty hose...as well as mending a tear in your outfit. It also works well to fix a broken shoelace, however a lot must be used and it does take longer to dry. It's handy when you're in a hurry or when you don't have a needle and thread available. Just follow the directions on the Speed Sew tube.

Carry a trash bag in your car or grooming box so it could become an emergency raincoat. You may even cover your dog with it.

Hair-So-New cream rinse is a nice product to keep at home and in your grooming box at the shows. Not only is it a great coat spray for your dog but it is also perfect for touch-up misting on your own hair before entering the ring.

Here's a great tip for getting out a grease stain from your show clothing. It's for silk but it should work on anything. Place the spotted area on a soft, clean white cloth. Now spread cornstarch on the grease stain and rub it carefully into the spot with a white paper towel folded into several layers. Place the paper towel over the cornstarch and put a heated iron on the paper towel (careful, don't touch the silk with the iron) so as to heat the cornstarch. Remove the paper towel and brush off the cornstarch. The stain should disappear.

If you have a problem with dog hair sticking to your show clothes, wet a wash rag, wring it out until it is just damp and wipe over the area covered with dog hair. The hair will just roll off in clumps.

If you have trouble finding tops to wear at a show which have pockets for your dog's brush and his bait, I highly recommend checking out the uniform shops. They have a large variety of darling tops which are easily laundered, pack well, have super pockets and do not cost any more than a dull, everyday blouse.

If you want to keep your dog's hair from sticking to your show outfit, just before leaving for the show, spray your clothes well with Static Guard and the hairs will not cling. This product may be purchased at most grocery stores.

If you wear dark pants and white shoes in Obedience work, your dog will have a visual advantage, as the white contrasting shoes serve as excellent guides in both the "heel" and the "recall."

I have a great solution for keeping that dog hair off your show clothing. All you have to do is spray some Static Cling on your show clothes. It sounds too simple, but it works. Make sure you bring a can to the show so right before going into the ring, you may spray yourself and be free of dog hair.

I keep an extra old slicker brush in my grooming box so I may clean dog hair off of my show outfit. It does a great job of removing stray dog hair.

I spray Firm Grip on the slippery bottoms of my shoes before I enter the show ring and/or onto my sweaty palms.

I've found a product to use on slick shoe soles that is even better than rubber cement. It's called Shoe Goo II and I purchased it at a store that sells athletic shoes. It's very reasonable in price and easy to use (converting dangerous slick-soled shoes into safe shoes for show ring wear). It's made by Eclectic Products, Inc., 729 Basin Street, San Pedro, CA 90731. It's a tube of clear "goo" that you apply to shoe soles and it dries to a tough, rubbery coating.

Make new shoes (which have slick soles) slip-proof for safer footing in the show ring by applying a coating of rubber cement to soles and heels. Allow the rubber cement to dry overnight.

Remove your pet's hair from your clothing by using masking tape. Roll the tape out and attach the tape backwards on the roll so the sticky side is out. Roll the tape on your clothes and the hair will stick to the tape.

The Four Way Anglers Worm Pouch (which may be found at a sporting goods store) is perfect for carrying scissors, chalk and other small doggy items to shows and matches. The pouch is easy to carry and durable. The zippered compartments are transparent and roomy.

To remove excessive hair from clothing, dampen a sponge and briskly rub clothing. Hair should ball up and you'll then be able to pick off the hair balls.

To remove hair from your clothing, rub a rubber glove (like the ones used when washing dishes) over the surface and pet hair will roll up. Pick up pet hair and throw it away.

Use Static Guard as a grooming aid for your pet. If dog hair is flying as you brush your pet, try spraying your grooming tools. You'll also be able to control your pet's hair and keep it from standing on end. And...you may apply it to your own brush or comb to keep your hair from flying away as you groom.

We all fight dog hair continually. I suggest using a "miracle brush." It is available at your local Kmart or other similar stores. It is great for picking up hair from clothing.

When you get home from a show with your clothes hairy and chalky but not really in need of washing or dry cleaning, put them in the dryer on "fluff" (no heat) along with a sheet of Bounce or a washcloth which has been dipped in fabric softener and squeezed out. About 20 minutes in the dryer makes them fresh, hairless and chalk free. This may be done even with 100 percent wool (just be sure the dryer is on "no heat").

When your show clothes are covered with dog hair, spray each pet with Static Guard (the odorless antistatic spray made by the Alberto Culver Company). Stray hairs may also be removed by spraying lightly with Static Guard then brushing or vacuuming those pet hairs away. Static Guard won't stain, discolor or build up and is safe for most colorfast fabrics.

Show Entries

(See "RECORDS"—"Show Entries")

Show Grooming

(See "GROOMING"—"Show Grooming and Preparation")

Show Leads

For your dirty white nylon leads, try washing them with Spray

'N Wash. Place your lead in the palm of one hand and saturate with Spray 'N Wash. Squeeze the lead several times and then rinse in warm water. Your lead will again be sparkling clean. For really dirty leads, let them soak for a few minutes.

I have found that if I slip the show choke collar on my long-haired dog before leaving for the show, the collar is neatly nestled where it belongs by ring time and there is no brushing or combing required to "set" the collar in place.

In an attempt to keep my tack box somewhat organized, I ran across a nifty piece of equipment to have handy: a shower curtain ring (the metal kind). That little "goodie" is perfect for hanging all my dog collars in a single place. Held up in the air, the correct length collar is more easily determined than by picking them up one at a time and comparing the length of each collar. It is easily unfastened when removing the collar of choice and when refastened, it may be put down with all the other collars still neatly joined on the shower ring.

I tried to get my dirty show lead to look really white again and again and even bleach didn't work. Finally, my husband suggested that I put it in a bowl with a tablespoon of Cascade dishwashing soap. I let it soak for about three hours and I had the whitest lead I've ever seen.

The best way I have found to wash nylon dog collars or show leads is to put them in the toe of a stocking or a nylon and simply put it in the washing machine with the rest of your wash.

Tired of losing expensive leads? Make your own leashes using thin parachute cord cut to any length you desire. Buy inexpensive hooks to knot on one end and sew down the loose end of the knot. Make a loop at the other end and sew off the dangling end, also. The resulting leads are cheap, strong and durable. You can send one with each puppy you sell. If you prefer leather leads, substitute boot shoelaces picked up at any shoe store for the nylon cord. A 50-foot package of nylon cord will make about eight leashes.

To get a white show lead once again white was quite a project as I tried using bleach and all sort of other products but with little success. Then I tried washing my show lead by hand with soap and Calgon Bath Oil Beads. I just sprinkle a little in my hands and rubbed them together onto the leash and lo-and-behold the leash became white. I had just used these when washing my dogs and their white collars and roughs were whiter. Wash as usual and rinse well.

White show leads and collars dingy, yellowed or grayed? Mine turn out "white as new" after soaking them in full-strength Dynamo detergent and then rinsing well. This even renewed a white leash I mistakenly tried to bleach (which had resulted in a yellowish color).

Show Training

(See "TRAINING"—"Conformation Training"
and "Performance Training")

Traveling To The Show

(See "TRAVELING and SHIPPING")

Misc.

Here's a great raffle promotion and incentive to get people to clean up after their dogs: for every bag of poop a person drops in a special trash can, they get one free raffle ticket.

I have a large 5-gallon glass container (the type that's used as a water cooler). I've labelled this my "Show Emergency Fund." I put any loose change I've found after doing the laundry, etc., in this container. You don't miss the money if you stash a bit every day or two. I plan on using this for spending money for the shows or some other doggy "splurge" items.

Not needing or wanting several old trophies that were given to me, I decided that the brass Sheltie statues on top of the trophies would make a nice statue. With the careful help of a hacksaw, I now have several beautiful Sheltie statues.

Training

Conformation Training

A 30-foot long line (used for exercising horses in a large circle) made of one-inch nylon webbing makes a great lead to exercise dogs while at shows or places where safety is a concern. They are purchased through wholesale catalogs or tack shops.

For table training my young puppies for future grooming, I use a little one-step stool with a rubber vinyl top. They work great for stacking puppies and for getting puppies used to being on a table. The rubbery top feels like a real table. You may even sit down on the floor or in the yard while stacking the pups. I have even stacked puppies on the stool in order to take their pictures, shoot videos and to measure them.

If you have a dog who is a little apprehensive when a judge comes up to go over him, just take hold of a few hairs along the side of his head and below his ears. Hold him gently, but firmly, with your right hand and take a short hold on the lead with your left hand. You will find this will steady your dog and he will not pull away from the judge.

I have discovered a great way to help those young puppy hopefuls adjust to the noise and echo sounds of indoor shows. I bring the puppy into the house (where he feels secure and comfortable) and play my home videos which I've taken at various shows. It has worked great for me. You can start off with the volume low and slowly increase it as your dog begins to become more and more secure.

I purchased an adult dog who was lead-trained but needed a little more individual attention and socialization. Having given seminars on time management and being short on time myself, I decided to combine the two. I put an Obedience lead on him and tied it to my left-side belt loop. I then proceeded to do some of my daily chores around the house and yard. A very good example which worked well with him was when I cooked or cleaned up after our dinner, he was by my side. The smell of food kept his attention, familiarized him with me and I got the kitchen cleaned—all at the same time. This can also prove to be an excellent time to practice baiting since your dog is ready and the bait is handy.

I thought I would offer this helpful hint for anyone else who might need an alternative training method. Why not just teach your new puppy or dog the obedience hand signal "to stand." Puppies are very eager learners and will catch on in no time. Then, when in the ring, all you have to do is give that hand signal "to stand" as you're gaiting up to the judge. You will also have taught the first part of the Utility hand signal exercise and will be one step closer to obtaining a Utility degree. It's a wonderful way to have a "smart" dog as well as a "pretty" dog.

To prevent my dog from picking up bait from the floor while in the show ring, I place several pieces of liver on the floor (while still outside the ring). Then I gait my dog over and around the liver. If he tries to grab the bait, I use some good obedience corrections. It will take about three minutes of work before going into the ring...just to refresh his memory.

To train your puppies to bait (but not to puncture your fingers), feed them through the crate or fence wires. At a later date, put them with older, stable dogs and train them to bait in a group and to only take the tidbit when called by name. You want the whole group's attention even when someone else gets the treat. Be sure that each dog receives a reward when the correct baiting occurs.

When show-training young dogs, I have found an easy solution to instilling self-confidence. I work the young dog on a brace with an older, seasoned show dog. It helps the youngster to relax and soon he will start to imitate and compete with the older dog and begins to enjoy every minute of it.

When training your puppies to bait, try using Nutri-Cal since dogs love its taste. Nutri-Cal may be purchased through veterinarians and many supply catalogs.

Crate Training
(See "ENCLOSURES"—"Crates")

Ever have a dog who has to be dragged and pushed into a crate? I avoid this by teaching my puppies to happily pile into their crates on command by bribing them. As soon as they are in their individual crates, I reward each puppy by giving him a Milk Bone (or other doggy treat) as soon as he is inside the crate. I also make them get into their crates for their meals. Now it's a race for the crates as soon as I say "Cookies" or "Suppertime." Thank heavens, there is no chasing all over at bedtime or when company arrives. It's great at the shows, too, because they enter their crates willingly.

Feeding each puppy in a crate will create a positive reward associated with going into a crate. Always remember to let the puppy out immediately after he eats so he may go to the bathroom as soon as he has eaten.

If you need to contain your puppy in a crate, remember to put a favorite toy or two in with the puppy.

You can let your young puppies crate train themselves by placing a small crate (#100 Vari Kennel crate) in their play yard. Since they are able to come-and-go as they please, they seem to accept being crated much more readily.

Drink From A Sport's Bottle

Dogs generally think any water they find is drinkable but we know better. Puddles hide toxins and lakes and streams harbor bacteria and parasites. To protect our dogs from these dangers, we often include an extra bottle of water and a bowl for them. You may leave the bowl at home if you teach your dog to drink straight from a squirt-top sports bottle. Start when your dog is thirsty. Squirt a little water into a shallow bowl and let your dog drink. He will still want more, so when he finishes, slowly squirt water into the bowl while allowing your dog to continue drinking. Squirt more slowly than your dog drinks so that he becomes impatient and starts licking the water as it comes out of the sports bottle squirt-top instead of waiting for it to collect in the bowl. A*t that point, turn the bottle sideways so the stream flows across your dog's tongue rather than down his throat.* Now raise the bot-

tle up a little so the dog's muzzle is roughly parallel to the ground. *Don't squeeze the water out too fast.* Your dog needs to learn how to lap and swallow a stream of water. If some water goes down the wrong way your dog will cough to clear his throat. Wait a moment or two before offering more. *Don't hold the bottle too high or your dog will have trouble swallowing water without choking on it because a dog's natural drinking position is with his muzzle pointing down. A dog may learn to drink with his muzzle parallel but if it's much higher than that he will likely gag and cough as water runs down his throat faster than he can swallow.*

Good Manners Training

I keep a towel on a hook right outside my back door. I have taught my dog to sit and wait (when he comes inside) until I wipe all four feet. As dogs are creatures of habit, I must wipe his feet and even on the driest of days, he will wait and "paw the air" (until I wipe him). It really cuts down on the amount of water and mud that he tracks into the house. He stays cleaner between bathings and my carpet stays cleaner between vacuumings.

I start teaching my puppies "to come" at three weeks of age. The day I start feeding them, I push their noses down to the food and make what is best described as a "repeated kissing" sound. I do this every time they are fed. People are always amazed that my six-week-old pups obediently run to me when I call them. Once this is learned, they never forget it.

To get your puppy's attention, put a few pennies in an empty soda can and shake. The noise will make him stop what he is doing. This can be a good training tool.

Grooming Table Training

For table training my young puppies for future grooming, I use a little one-step stool with a rubber vinyl top. They work great for stacking puppies and for getting puppies used to being on a table. The rubbery top feels like a real table. You may even sit down on the floor or in the yard while stacking the pups. I have even stacked puppies on the stool in order to take their pictures, shoot videos and to measure them.

My ironing board (which is up most of the time) makes an ideal and quick substitute for a grooming table (to prepare small puppies for the Conformation ring table). It is higher than most grooming tables for better eye-to-eye contact. It provides great footing, is adjustable as needed and is generally close to the kitchen for that quick treat. *(Never leave your puppy's side while he's on the ironing board.)* I use this all the time and it really works great.

Housebreaking Your Dog

Always put you puppy outside immediately after he eats and/or drinks or is being let out of his crate. Then praise him as soon as he "goes potty."

Housebreak your dog by hanging a bell (at your dog's height) by the back door. When you are taking your puppy outside, ring the bell. As he gets older, he will ring the bell when he needs to go out and will then alert you to come to the door to let him outside.

I always hated "rubbing a pup's nose" in his messes as I feel that is degrading. When your puppy makes a mess, scold him and rush him outside. While he is gone, clean up and liberally dump pepper on that previously-soiled spot. That is all, except for cleaning up the pepper two hours later. Invariably, your pup will return to "the spot" to sniff and I have never had to use that method more than three times before the pup decides that outside is better than inside for that kind of business.

If you are tired of papers covering the entire puppy area, try this: after my puppies get the idea what the papers are for, I take my metal tray from a puppy crate and line it with papers. Placing this in the puppy play area, I remove the rest of the papers and they quickly get the idea that this is their spot. The tray is a nice size, providing your puppies room for walking and still find their favorite spot but is small enough to provide the puppies room to play. Your puppies soon learn where to go, the tray is easily cleaned and the puppies can't slide into messes as they spend the rest of their time playing. The tray is also nice when you have carpeting (since papers leak but metal does not).

I leased a bitch who was used to being kept in the kennel. When she stayed in my home she would pee everywhere. This became very tiring so I went to the store and bought a package of the potty training pull-ups (the largest size they had). I carefully cut an approximate two-inch vertical slit for her tail to go through and it acts like a diaper. She never had an accident again. Amazing what it will hold. *You need to change the diaper as soon as it's soiled so bacteria doesn't build up and for the dog's comfort. Remember to take it off when the dog is crated.*

I partition my kitchen off from the rest of the house when housebreaking a youngster by using indoor shutters and decorative wood trim. The trim pieces are cut, spaced and nailed along the outer edge of the doorway in such a way that one or more shutters may slide into the doorway (depending on the size of the puppy). They are easy for adults to step over but too high for a puppy to jump. The trim pieces and shutters may be stained or painted to match your decor.

I was having some trouble housebreaking an older puppy. I found a most welcome solution. I bought disposable diapers for her. I cut an "X" approximately one third of the way down the diaper for her tail and taped it on. We have not had one accident since. She will hold it until she is outside and the diaper is taken off. *(Be sure you do not leave a dog alone with a diaper on as your dog could try to tear it off and choke on the plastic.).*

Our puppy has a new accomplishment which is both useful to us and also a bit of a nuisance. Her housebreaking has not been 100 percent (partly because she is like our other dogs and just stands by the door to ask to be let outside). If we don't happen to see her right away, she just finds a convenient spot on the floor. So, we got a little bell that was one of our Christmas ornaments and hung it from the doorknob so it is dangling about puppy-head height. It only took her a couple of days to learn that if she bumped that bell and made it ring, someone would come and open the door. Now she rings it when she has to go out.

When a puppy begins spending the night in a crate but isn't old enough to last the night without wetting, I hook two wire crates together. If a puppy is small or the crate's large, I put bedding in one half of the crate and newspaper in the other half. (I put computer paper over the newspaper to keep the puppy from getting newsprint on himself.) When the puppy's old enough to last the night without having to wet, I take away the crate along with the newspaper.

Winter may be severe, especially with wind chills. This makes it both dangerous and difficult to housebreak puppies, not to mention their hairless mother. Instead of buying sweaters which my puppies will outgrow, I cut the arms out of an old loose-knit sweater, tapering the top to reach the tail and the underneath just so it won't get piddled on. I cut holes in the sides for the puppy's front legs. The sweaters were also great for quick trips to the vet, etc., and our puppies thought they were fun. Oh, and Mom got the body of the sweater for a nightgown. The arm holes were for her front legs and a quick stitch and trim down the back made a snug fit so she wouldn't get tangled up. Being loose-knit and not too tight meant that she didn't overheat. For a good fit, the size of the sweater you use will depend on the size of your puppies.

Improving Puppies' Temperaments

(Also see "ELIMINATING BAD BEHAVIORS"—
"Temperament Problems
and Encouraging Good Behaviors")

Leash-Breaking

For our last litter, my daughter braided (substitute macrame for those of you who are talented and want to be fancy) strands of fairly heavy yarn together to make collars for the babies when they were only three weeks old. After several weeks of having these tied on, lead-breaking was easy.

To leash-break young or even the more difficult older puppies, I use an adult who is well-trained and calm. I attach the leash to the collar of the adult dog. Because my hands are free, I do not become the "meany" or even become associated with the leash-breaking process. Try it. It works and beats the struggle.

To make the lead-breaking process go smoothly, carry your puppy away from home and let him walk back with you. This gives him good incentive to walk because puppies almost always want to go home. This is much more fun than trying to drag a screaming puppy away from home. Most puppies trained this way will become "happy workers" who really move out.

Performance Training

A 30-foot long line (used for exercising horses in a large circle) made of one-inch nylon webbing makes a great lead to exercise dogs while at shows or places where safety is a concern. They are purchased through wholesale catalogs or tack shops.

A board across the width of your dog run (around 12" high for a medium-size dog) encourages jumping back and forth for improving your dog's muscle tone and is also good preparation for later advanced Obedience.

An easy way to get puppies to come when you want them is to call them with a "clicker" or a "cricket" (which is a small metal noisemaker available at most toy stores). Just make the clicking noise when you feed them and soon they'll come running whenever they hear that distinctive sound.

I acquired a dog who I hoped to show in Conformation. He had started Obedience training and sat each time we came to a halt. I worked with him for a couple of weeks and I was unable to break this habit. I remembered reading an article which suggested that I use a second lead in front of the hindquarters. I used a simple slip-type lightweight nylon show lead (held in my right hand). I gaited the dog as usual with the lead in my left hand. When the dog showed signs of sitting, I gently pulled up on his hindquarters with my right hand. It took only a couple of short sessions for him to understand that he was not to sit every time we stopped.

I purchased an adult dog who was lead-trained but needed a little more individual attention and socialization. Having given seminars on time management and being short on time myself, I decided to combine the two. I put an Obedience lead on him and tied it to my left-side belt loop. I then proceeded to do some of my daily chores around the house and yard. A very good example which worked well with him was when I cooked or cleaned up after our dinner, he was by my side. The smell of food kept his attention, familiarized him with me and I got the kitchen cleaned—all at the same time. This can also prove to be an excellent time to practice baiting since your dog is ready and the bait is handy.

I start teaching my puppies to "come" at three weeks of age. The day I start feeding them, I push their noses down to the food and make what is best described as a "repeated kissing" sound. I do this every time they are fed. People are always amazed that my six-week-old pups obediently run to me when I call them. Once this is learned, they never forget it.

I thought I would offer this helpful hint for anyone else who might need an alternative training method. Why not just teach your new puppy or dog the obedience hand signal "to stand." Puppies are very eager learners and will catch on in no time. Then, when in the ring, all you have to do is give that hand signal "to stand" as you're gaiting up to the judge. You will also have taught the first part of the Utility hand signal exercise and will be one step closer to obtaining a Utility degree. It's a wonderful way to have a "smart" dog as well as a "pretty" dog.

Train your dogs to accept strange noises and objects which flap in the wind because they may encounter them in the show ring (whether inside or outside). Around your kennel area, hang up some wind chimes, an American flag and some of the pretty wind socks.

When show-training young dogs, I have found an easy solution to instill self-confidence. I work the young dog on a brace with an older, seasoned show dog. It helps the youngster to relax, and soon he starts to imitate and compete with the older dog and begins to enjoy every minute of it.

Training to Improve Movement

I acquired a dog who I hoped to show in Conformation. He had started Obedience training and sat each time we came to a halt. I worked with him for a couple of weeks and I was unable to break this habit. I remembered reading an article which suggested that I use a second lead in front of the hindquarters. I used a simple slip-type lightweight nylon show lead (held in my right hand). I gaited the dog as usual with the lead in my left hand. When the dog showed signs of sitting, I gently pulled up on his hindquarters with my right hand. It took only a couple of short sessions for him to understand that he was not to sit every time we stopped.

Traveling and Shipping

Bedding and Mats For Travel Crates
(See "ENCLOSURES—CRATES, CAGES, PENS and WHELPING BOXES"—"Bedding, Mats, Footing, Etc.")

Car Sickness
(See "HEALTH"—"Car Sickness")

Cleaning While Traveling

After attending a dog show where my dog was violently ill in the hotel room and I had no real clean-up supplies, I now travel prepared. For dog-show trips, I carry a container with cleaning

items such as moist towelettes, car cleaner (like Simple Solution), a roll of paper towels, hand sanitizer, some folded newspapers, spray disinfectant, a can of air freshener and/or Febreeze, a lint roller and some trash sacks. You may use off-brand and small or trial sizes of many of these items (which will take up less room). I use a Rubbermaid-type plastic storage box with a tight lid lock. It's about 12" x 12" x 9" deep and doesn't take too much space in the vehicle. Now I can handle emergency clean-ups and not give motels one more reason to ban dogs from their rooms.

Make it easier on yourself while picking up after your dogs. For pottying your dogs on those dark nights at a motel or on the showgrounds, get yourself a Flexi-leash with a little flashlight attached. It makes finding your dog's poop in the dark much easier. You may find them at Petsmart, Dollar General, etc., and online. I save mine to use at the motels and now there's no more hunting around for after-dark poo (especially in rainy or cold weather).

Make your own Handi Wipes for dog show trips or summer travels by cutting a roll of heavy paper toweling (such as Bounty or Viva) into pieces which will then fit into a Tupperware or Rubbermaid type of covered container. Whip the following liquid ingredients and pour over the paper towels. The liquid ingredients are: 2 capfuls of rubbing alcohol, 2 squirts of baby oil, 2 squirts of baby soap and 1/4 cup of water. Keep in covered container.

We use Baby Wipes for a multitude of reasons (for example: cleaning up a mess in the car, cleaning a "just-used" thermometer, cleaning any area that's been stitched or sutured, a quick ear cleaning before a show, on a messy puppy's face and on babies just learning to eat from a pan). The least expensive ones contain more moisture, and you'll be surprised how many uses you'll find for them.

When traveling, I tape a syringe to the side of any liquid medicines I have in my traveling canine pharmacy. Extracting liquid from the bottle and administering it into the side of the mouth is easier with the syringe *(minus the needle, of course)* with 5 cc = 1 teaspoon.

When traveling to other areas with your dogs, carry along a Real-Lemon. A couple of drops in their drinking water neutralizes strange water and it will not upset them. I have yet to run into the new water malady (from which so many dogs suffer) when I have my trusty Real-Lemon along.

With the threat of so many viruses affecting our dogs and puppies, we are all finding it necessary to take extra precautions. Aside from dog classes and shows from which we potentially track home the unknown, we also have three children and all their friends generate quite a bit of foot traffic throughout our home. I keep a spray bottle of Clorox and old carpet pieces in our garage. The children spray the soles of their shoes or take them off before entering the house. They always wash their hands before playing with our puppies. I also solved the dilemma of visitors coming into our house through the front door. I purchased a rubber-backed doormat (the kind with some type of material in the middle). I spray this heavily with Clorox and ask people to please wipe their shoes on the mat.

With parvovirus threats, we take a special precaution before leaving shows. The dogs are pulled from their crates. The papers are then changed and the inside of each crate is sprayed with Clorox solution. Then each foot is dipped into a jar of solution (a small wide-mouth peanut butter jar is good for this). *Being sure there is no wet Clorox or Clorox fumes left inside the crate, the dog is returned to his clean, dry crate (without making contact with the floor or the ground at the show).* Then, before entering the car, each person gets the bottoms of his shoes sprayed as well.

Feeding While Traveling
(See "Feeding"—"Travel and Feeding")

Identification To Take When Traveling
(See "RECORDS"—"Identification")

In the Vehicle

Although many dogs find that sticking their heads out the window of a car is the best part of the road trip, it's not safe. *Your dog may easily be injured from flying debris. Never travel with a dog in the back of a pickup truck.* Some states have laws restricting such transport and it is always dangerous.

Be sure that your dog is safely restrained in your vehicle. Utilizing a dog safety harness, travel kennel, vehicle dog barrier or dog car seat are the best ways to keep your dog safe during travel. These restraints protect your dog from injury, and they keep your dog from distracting you as you drive. A safety harness functions like a seat belt. While most dogs will not have a problem adjusting to it, you may want to let your dog wear the harness by itself a few times before using it in the vehicle. If your dog prefers a travel crate, be sure it is well ventilated and stabilized. Make sure it's not too large for your dog because if you're in an accident and the crate is too large, your dog may be tossed around while still inside that oversized crate. Many dog owners prefer vehicle barriers (particularly for larger dogs). Vehicle barriers are best suited in SUVs. Smaller dogs are best suited for dog car seats. The car seat is secured in the back seat using a seat belt and your dog is secured in the car seat using a safety harness. In addition to it's safety features, a dog car seat will prop up your smaller dog which allows him to look out the window. No matter what method you choose, back seat travel is always safer for your dog.

Dog harnesses which hook to car seats are available for restraining your dog while he's riding in your vehicle.

Dogs should be confined in carriers while traveling. *Your dog will be unable to leap from open windows, doors or interfere with your driving if they're inside a crate.*

Dog too hot? Just wet two towels in cold water and get some crushed ice. Lay one towel in the bottom of the crate or where your dog likes to rest. Then smooth out the crushed ice on top and lay the other towel on top of the ice.

During travel, being confined in a crate or an animal carrier for long periods of time during the hottest months of the year is potentially dangerous for your dog and may lead to dehydration and heatstroke. In addition, certain breeds such as brachycephalic (snub-nosed) dogs and cats are susceptible to pulmonary distress when temperatures are extreme.

During your stops be sure to provide your dog with some fresh water. Occasionally traveling may upset your dog's stomach so take along ice cubes which are better for your dog than consuming large amounts of water.

If you drive long distances to shows and enjoy listening to books on tape, stop at a Cracker Barrel restaurant. They rent books on tape. Pick up one of their maps showing their restaurant locations. When you are finished listening to that book, turn it in at the nearest Cracker Barrel. They will refund your purchase price minus $3.49 for each week you've had it. This is a very cheap form of entertainment. Most recorded books run at least nine

hours.

If you get low-back pain on those long dog show trips, you might try what works wonders for me. I take a regular-size bed pillow along (mine is Dacron Poly fill) and place it behind my lower back. It may be adjusted up or down a little bit to take the pressure off your back and that will make your trip much more enjoyable. A bonus for me is that I always have my own pillow when I arrive at my destination since I have difficulty sleeping with some pillows (due to an allergy).

It is hoped that everyone knows how *deadly the summer heat is to a dog who is locked inside a car, h*owever there is another danger which is present year-round. A well-known champion sire and his daughter died tragically some years ago. Their owners had left them locked in the car, which they had done many times before. *Sadly, the owners did not realize their brand-new car was airtight until it was too late. Avoid another such tragedy. If you must leave your dog in the car, always leave a window or vent open even during the winter.*

Most travel service areas have designated areas for walking your dog. Be sure to stay in this area (particularly when your dog needs a potty break). Remember to bring along a bag so you may pick up after your dog.

Never leave your dog unattended in a parked vehicle. *On warm days, the temperature in your vehicle may rise to 120 degrees within minutes even with the windows slightly open. On very cold days, the vehicle could possibly become too cold. Also, an animal left alone in a vehicle is an open invitation to dog thieves.*

Pets should be confined in carriers while traveling and your pet will be unable to leap from open windows or doors or interfere with your driving.

Provide your dog with frequent exercise and bathroom breaks, and remember to clean up after your dog.

Sears has a wonderful little item in their camping department. It is a very strong, elastic, rope-like band with a plastic-covered metal hook on each end. They come in different lengths (ours are about two feet long, unstretched). We pile exercise pens, grooming table, chairs, etc., on top of a row of crates when traveling. Everything is strapped down tight and safe in seconds (by stretching these over the top of the pile and attaching to the tops of the crates). Nothing budges or slides...no matter how rough the drive might be. It also makes unloading (at the show) simple. We stack a couple of crates on our dolly with everything else on top. This takes two seconds to secure these elastic bands and we can go anywhere in one trip.

Whatever method you choose to properly restrain your dog in your vehicle, be sure to make his comfort a priority. Just as it's important for your seat to be comfortable during a long road trip, your dog's seat should be comfortable, too. Usually, a favorite blanket or travel bed will do the trick. There are also some safe and very cozy dog car seats available which your dog may find quite comfortable.

When walking your dog outside your vehicle, make sure that your dog is always on a leash and wearing a collar with a permanent ID and a temporary travel identification tag.

Lodging (Motels, Hotels, Etc.)
(Also see "ENCLOSURES"—
"Bedding, Mats, Footing, Etc."
and "FEEDING"—"Travel and Feeding")
After attending a dog show where my dog was violently ill in

the hotel room and I had no real clean-up supplies, I now travel prepared. For dog-show trips, I carry a container with cleaning items such as moist towelettes, car cleaner (like Simple Solution), a roll of paper towels, hand sanitizer, some folded newspapers, spray disinfectant, a can of air freshener and/or Febreeze, a lint roller and some trash sacks. You may use off-brand and small or trial sizes of many of these items (which will take up less room). I use a Rubbermaid-type plastic storage box with a tight lid lock. It's about 12" x 12" x 9" deep and doesn't take too much space in the vehicle. Now I can handle emergency clean-ups and not give motels one more reason to ban dogs from their rooms.

A nerf ball is great to take on the road for your canine ball player. It may be bounced off floors and walls with no noise or damage, and it's a great way to exercise your dog while in a motel room.

A plastic shower curtain may be used to protect a bedspread at motels for those "bed potatoes."

Do you have an early and noisy riser in your kennel? I do. He wakes everyone up. So I put a sheet over his enclosure (just as is done with a bird). Now he stays quiet until I remove the sheet and it's time to get up.

Make it easier on yourself while picking up after your dogs. For pottying your dogs on those dark nights at a motel or on the showgrounds, get yourself a Flexi-leash with a little flashlight attached. It makes finding your dog's poop in the dark much easier. You may find them at Petsmart, Dollar General, etc., and online. I save mine to use at the motels and now there's no more hunting around for after-dark poo (especially in rainy or cold weather).

Preparing To Travel
(Also see "ENCLOSURES," "FEEDING," "GROOMING," "HEALTH," "PUPPIES," "RECORDS," "SHOWS," "TRAINING" and "WARNINGS")

All of my dogs are tattooed and the tattoo is registered with the National Dog Registry. Their travel collars have a tag on them that says: "I am tattooed, please call 1-800-NDR-DOGS." Someone is always at the National Dog Registry, whereas who knows where I may be when I'm traveling. If you plan to travel with your dog, start out with small trips before going on longer trips.

Sedatives from your veterinarian may be given to jittery dogs for unavoidable traveling.

To be prepared for a trip with your dog, pack the following: dog tags (identification with your phone numbers), your dog's photos, leash and an extra collar, a blanket or cushion from your dog's home bedding, prepared containers of your pet's meals, water dish, dog treats (keep to a minimum), dog toys, baby wipes (for cleaning purposes), trash bags and waste pickup bags along with a first ad kit.

When traveling, I tape a syringe to the side of any liquid medicines I have in my traveling canine pharmacy. Extracting liquid from the bottle and administering it into the side of the mouth is easier with the syringe *(minus the needle, of course)* with 5 cc = 1 teaspoon.

Shipping
(Also see "RECORDS")

All of my dogs are tattooed and the tattoo is registered with the National Dog Registry. Their travel collars have a tag on them that says: "I am tattooed, please call 1-800-NDR-DOGS." Someone is always at the National Dog Registry, whereas who knows where

I may be when I'm traveling.

As safe as air shipping is, there was an unfortunate situation where a dog in a Sky Kennel was injured. *The crate was accidentally tipped and the dog's leg was trapped.* Tape down your pegboard floors before shipping.

Be sure to have identification on your dog when traveling. Also include the area code with your telephone number. Two collars are good in case one collar falls off.

Our information packages (when selling or shipping a puppy or dog) include an ID tag that includes the words "REWARD IF FOUND" along with the owner's area code and phone number. It's hoped that the dog will never be lost, but accidents do occur and we feel the knowledge of a reward will enhance the chance of someone returning any lost dog.

Sedatives from your veterinarian may be given to jittery dogs for unavoidable shipping.

Shipping an animal via the airlines? Be aware that if your dog must change carriers when making plane connections, your charges will double. Each airline involved will charge.

Something we do all the time when shipping is to put letters, photos and other papers under the false floor (all securely sealed in Baggies). This is much better than trusting our heavy-handed air personnel not to accidentally scrape our taped envelopes from the outside. Naturally, the health papers do go on the outside of the crate.

The heat-sealing gadgets (such as Seal-A-Meal) are handy for putting a shipping label inside the plastic and then sealing it shut.

The heat-sealing gadgets (like Seal-A-Meal) are great for us doggy folks. These bags are also great for "spillables" that we take with us when traveling (such as cosmetics and any other grooming goo which might ooze out of their container).

Whenever I ship a dog to his new home or ship a bitch to be bred, I put a buckle collar on the dog with a tag which includes my name, address and phone numbers on it. In this way, for a few dollars, I have the peace of mind that if this dog somehow gets away, anyone finding him or her will know how to get in touch with me. Also, the line "REWARD" on the tag will provide even more assurance that I will get my dog back.

When shipping a bitch we enclose all necessary papers (pedigree, test results, etc.) in an empty candy or cookie tin and put this inside the crate. By doing this, papers can't be torn off the outside of the crate and they will remain dry and safe inside the crate. We can also send vitamins, raspberry leaves, etc., for bitches who are to be bred

〰〰 ≫ ≪ 〰〰

Warnings

«» Editor's note: since almost all of the following hints contained a warning, the previously-included italics for those warnings were removed.«»

The 24/7 Animal Poison Control Center's phone number is 800-213-6680. If you're calling from the Caribbean or US Virgin Islands for poisoning assistance, you may call them 24/7 (toll-free) at 877-416-7319. Other Caribbean islands may reach them at (011)-1-952-853-1716.

Bloat

Bloat is a medical emergency. Bloat is a gastric condition

which may be deadly and is an emergency for your dog. Bloat is most commonly caused by too much gas or fluid in the stomach. This gas may extend the stomach causing gastric dilation. Usually, large, deep-chested dogs are the victims but it has occurred in some smaller breeds and puppies who have been allowed to eat too quickly. While the causes of bloat may vary, gulping of food and water is the most common reason (usually during excitable times when yummy treats are given and then exercise follows). This excitability and playfulness may occur during busy times like holidays and family gatherings. Bloat is a deadly condition. Do not permit your dog to overeat (even his own food). Instead of one or two large meals a day, try three or four smaller meals.

Brown Recluse Spider Bites

Since brown recluse spiders are so dangerous, be careful where you put your hands and where your pets are investigating. These dangerous spiders prefer dark spaces and woodpiles. They also like cool areas (in the attic or storage sheds). If you have a need to be in your attic, go up there and turn on a light and then leave it on for about 30 minutes before entering. The brown recluse spider is the most dangerous spider in the USA. Spider bites are dangerous and may have permanent and highly negative consequences. After a bite, the affected skin actually dies. A person or pet may die from its bite.

Cancer In Dogs

The American Veterinary Medical Association has developed the following list of common signs of cancer in small animals: 1) abnormal swellings which persist or continue to grow; 2) sores which do not heal; 3) weight loss; 4) loss of appetite; 5) bleeding or discharge from any body opening; 6) offensive odor; 7) difficulty eating or swallowing; 8) hesitation to exercise or loss of stamina; 9) persistent lameness or stiffness; or 10) difficulty breathing, urinating or defecating.

Choking, Suffocation and Drowning

A wise precaution to take (if you have small puppies exercising in a dog run which has the chain-link cyclone fence fabric) is to put 12" to 24" of 1-inch mesh or hardware wire all around the bottom and on its outside. I had a seven-week-old puppy who put his head through the 2 1/2-inch diameter opening and got stuck. While I held the puppy so he wouldn't struggle, a neighbor (who had heard the commotion) used pliers to unweave the fence (at its base) in order to free this puppy's head. If I had used the wire mesh, this could have been avoided. I was lucky because I hadn't left those pups unsupervised and I saw this dangerous incident as it was actually occurring.

From working in a hospital with premature infants, I have learned when tube-feeding to always let the fluid drain into the stomach by gravity flow (not by force of the plunger). That way, when the flow stops, you'll know that the puppy's tummy is full and you'll prevent the risk of overflow and aspiration.

If you take your dog on a boat or a canoe, a life jacket is just as important for your dog as it is for you. Falling or jumping overboard and drowning is always possible since not all dogs know how to swim. Any dog who spends time near water should have his very own pet life vest.

I was having some trouble housebreaking an older puppy. I found a most welcome solution. I bought disposable diapers for her. I cut an "X" approximately one third of the way down the

diaper for her tail and taped it on. We have not had one accident since. She will hold it until she is outside and the diaper is taken off. (Be sure you do not leave a dog alone with a diaper on as your dog could try to tear it off and choke on the plastic.)

Snack bags, Ziploc bags, shrink-wrap bags and bottles (or any container in which an animal may get his head wedged inside) have caused deaths of many dogs when they pushed their heads into these bags and/or containers and then suffocated. Such containers had originally been made airtight to keep products fresh. Some of these bags are made of a tough, slick material which resists puncturing and tearing. Bags, bottles and all such containers should be kept completely out of the reach of your dogs and children. These containers should be disposed of in such a manner that neither dogs nor children will ever be able to retrieve them from the trash.

This tip is for those who are always worried about their dogs getting into the kitchen trash basket or garbage container and eating chicken bones or any type of dangerous bones. We save spaghetti sauce jars (any type of jar will work) and put all bones inside those jars (with their lids securely closed). Then we throw away the jars. No need to be paranoid anymore about the dogs getting into any type of cooked bones.

Crate Hazards

I want to issue a warning to anyone who uses or recommends using the dividers that come with the wire crates. I sent a pup to his new home and received a call that no breeder ever wants to get. It was from a sobbing, hysterical puppy buyer who got up to let her puppy out to potty only to find the puppy dead (with his head hung between the divider and the crate). She said the divider fit in very tight and was hard to insert. The pup had somehow loosened one of the hooks which secures the divider and got his head caught. Not hearing a sound from him, she assumed that her puppy was unable to make a noise by having his airway cut off. Later, she did call the company that makes the crates and also asked me to warn everyone I knew about this danger. I'm just sick over this and want to warn as many people as possible.

Eating Dangerous Bones
(Also see "PARASITES, PESTS and INVADING VARMINT CONTROL"—"Invading Animals and Varmints")

Cooked turkey, duck, geese and other bird bones are dangerous to your dog because these bones are hollow. They break and splinter easily. Because they are so easily breakable, dogs usually won't chew them thoroughly and those sharp pieces of bone may choke the dog, block or tear his intestines. A dog who has a bone or fragment of bone lodged in his intestines may not even show symptoms for a few days. When those symptoms do occur they may include loss of appetite, depression, vomiting or diarrhea. Sometimes the bone will pass by itself and other times it may need to be surgically removed. So...make sure all leftovers are thrown away properly and totally out of your dog's reach.

Make sure your pet has no access to any food left on the counters or tables.

Take all garbage out and dispose of it in a secure place where no dogs can get into it.

This tip is for those who are always worried about their dogs getting into the kitchen trash basket or garbage container and eating chicken bones or any type of dangerous bones. We save spaghetti sauce jars (any type of jar will work) and put all bones inside those jars (with their lids securely closed). Then we throw away the jars. No need to be paranoid anymore about the dogs getting into any type of cooked bones.

Electrical Shocks, Burns and Death From Electricity

Secure electrical cords to baseboards or make them inaccessible to your dogs. If your dog chews on them, he may suffer electric shocks, burns and could possibly die. To hide those cords (which can't be made inaccessible), you may place empty paper towel rolls or toilet tissue cardboard rolls over the cords. Place construction-type cardboard on the walls to cover over cords which can't be put into cardboard tubes.

Foods Dangerous To Dogs

Do not let your dog eat any of the following (according to peteducation.com and other sources): alcoholic beverages (may cause intoxication, coma and death); avocado (leaves, seeds, fruit and bark contain persin, which may cause vomiting and diarrhea); bones from fish, poultry or other meat sources (may cause obstruction or laceration of the digestive system); cat food (generally too high in protein and fats); chocolate, coffee, tea and other caffeinated drinks and foods (contain caffeine, theobromine or theophylline, which may cause vomiting and diarrhea and be toxic to the heart and nervous systems); citrus oil extracts (may cause vomiting); fat trimmings (may cause pancreatitis); fish—raw, canned or cooked (if fed exclusively or in high amounts may result in a thiamine or a B vitamin deficiency leading to loss of appetite, seizures and, in severe cases, death); grapes, raisins and currants (contain an unknown toxin which may damage the kidneys); hops (unknown compound causes panting, increased heart rate, elevated temperature, seizures and death); human vitamin supplements containing iron (may damage the lining of the digestive system and be toxic to the other organs including the liver and kidneys); macadamia nuts (contain an unknown toxin which may affect the digestive and nervous systems and muscle); marijuana (may depress the nervous system, cause vomiting and changes in the heart rate); milk and other dairy products (some adult dogs and cats may develop diarrhea if given large amounts of dairy products); moldy or spoiled food, garbage (may contain multiple toxins causing vomiting and diarrhea and may also affect other organs); mushrooms (may contain toxins which may affect multiple systems in the body, cause shock and result in death); onions and garlic—raw, cooked or powder (contain sulfoxides and disulfides which may damage red blood cells and cause anemia...cats are more susceptible than dogs); persimmons (seeds may cause intestinal obstruction and enteritis); pits from peaches and plums (may cause obstruction of the digestive tract); raw eggs (contain an enzyme called avidin, which decreases the absorption of biotin—which may lead to skin and hair coat problems...raw eggs may also contain Salmonella); raw meat (may contain bacteria such as Salmonella and E. coli which may cause vomiting and diarrhea); rhubarb leaves (contain oxalates which may affect the digestive, nervous and urinary systems); salt (if eaten in large quantities it may lead to electrolyte imbalances); string (may become trapped in the digestive system; called a "string foreign body"); sugary foods (may lead to obesity, dental problems and possibly diabetes mellitus); table scraps...in large amounts (table scraps are not nutritionally balanced and, therefore, they should never be more than 10 percent of the diet and all fat should be trimmed from meat; bones should not be fed);

tobacco (contains nicotine which affects the digestive and nervous systems which may result in rapid heart beat, collapse, coma and death); yeast dough (may expand and produce gas in the digestive system causing pain and possible rupture of the stomach or intestines); xylitol which is an artificial sweetener (may cause very low blood sugar or hypoglycemia which may result in vomiting, weakness and collapse and, in high doses, may cause liver failure).

Fourth Of July Dangers

Do not take your pet to fireworks displays since fireworks are dangerous to pets. Many pet parents assume that if their pet is not afraid of thunder or other loud noises, he will not be bothered by fireworks. This is not necessarily true. Even pets who are normally not bothered by thunder and other loud noises are often frightened. Then they panic because of the cumulative effects of the fireworks, the excited voices outside and being left alone inside the house. If pets are left outside and unattended, the noise often causes them to run away. In fact, the July 4th holiday is a very busy time for animal shelters across the U.S. as they report taking in a higher number dogs who run away during firework festivities. In addition, many police stations log higher volumes of stray dog calls and barking complaints on July 4th as compared to any other day of the year.

If you know that your pet is seriously upset or distressed by loud noises like thunder, consult with your veterinarian before July 4th for ways to help avoid the fear and anxiety he will experience during fireworks displays.

If your pet seeks comfort in a bath tub, under a bed or other small space...let him go there. Do not try to lure him out. If the space is safe and it makes him feel more secure, let him be alone.

Keep your pets at home (in a comfortable and quiet area with the shades drawn). If your pet is crate-trained, then his crate is a great place for him to stay. Some animals may become destructive when frightened so be sure that you've removed any items that your pet could destroy or that would cause harm if chewed. Leave a television or radio playing at normal volume to keep your pet company while you're attending Fourth of July picnics, parades and other celebrations.

Leave pets at home when you head out to Fourth of July celebrations, and never use fireworks around your pets since exposure to lit fireworks may potentially result in severe burns or trauma to curious pets and even unused fireworks may be hazardous.

Make sure your pets are wearing identification tags so that if they do become lost, they may be returned promptly. Animals found running free should be taken to the nearest animal shelter where they will have the best chance of being reunited with their owners.

Many types of fireworks contain potentially toxic substances (such as potassium nitrate, copper, chlorates, arsenic and other heavy metals) which are dangerous to your dog.

Never leave pets outside unattended (even in a fenced yard or on a chain). In their fear and panic, pets who normally wouldn't leave the yard may escape and become lost or they might become entangled in their chain. Any of these events could be a risk for injury or death.

Glass, Staples and Sharp Objects Being Ingested

If you're fishing, be sure your baited hooks are not accessible to your dog because you wouldn't want him to swallow the hook hidden inside the bait.

What do you do if your puppy (or mischievous older dog) gets into your holiday decorations and eats some of the glass ornaments, another glass object or staples? To be prepared for this type of a potentially lethal happening, go to a pharmacy and buy a box of cotton balls. Be sure that you get the real cotton balls and not the "cosmetic puffs" which are made from man-made fibers. Also, buy a quart of half-and-half cream and keep it in the freezer. Should your dog eat glass or other sharp objects, immediately defrost the half-and-half cream and pour some in a bowl. Dip the cotton balls into the cream and then pull the cotton apart into bite-size pieces. Feed those cream-soaked cotton pieces to your dog. Dogs weighing under 10 pounds should eat two cotton balls (which you have torn into smaller pieces). Dogs who weigh from 10 to 50 pounds should eat three to five cotton balls and larger dogs should consume five to seven cotton balls. You may feed larger dogs an entire cotton ball at once. Dogs seem to really like these unusual "treats" and will eat them without hesitation. As the cotton moves down and through the dog's digestive tract, it will find all the glass pieces and wrap itself around them. Even the smallest shards of glass or other sharp objects will be caught and wrapped within the cotton fiber and, also, the cotton will protect the intestines from damage from these sharp objects. Your dog's stools will appear strange for a few days. Check for fresh blood or a black tarry appearance to the stool and if either of these symptoms appear, you should rush your dog to the vet for a checkup. In most cases, the dog will be just fine.

Halloween Warnings and Hazards

All but the most social dogs should be kept in a separate room during trick-or-treat visiting hours as too many strangers in strange Halloween outfits may be scary for your dog.

Be careful with dogs and cats moving around a lit pumpkin and candles because pets may knock them over and cause a fire. Curious kittens especially run the risk of getting burned.

Be very careful that your dog or cat doesn't dash out the open door during trick-or-treat time.

Do not leave your dog or cat out in the yard on Halloween. There are plenty of stories of vicious pranksters who have teased, injured, stolen and even killed pets on this night and during the time around Halloween.

Don't dress your dog or cat in costume (unless you know he loves it) because it may put a lot of stress on your dog or cat. If you do dress up your pet, make sure the costume doesn't hinder his vision, movement or air intake and that his costume isn't constricting, annoying or unsafe. Be careful never to obstruct your dog's or cat's vision since even the sweetest pet may become snappy when they can't see what's going on around them. If the costume has metallic beads, snaps or other small pieces, be aware that some metals (especially zinc and lead) may result in serious poisoning if ingested.

Doors are made to open and close and both functions may cause trouble for a dog. Opening a door is dangerous because your dog could escape to the outdoors and closing a door is dangerous if a dog gets caught in the door and is then crushed. Trick-or-treaters and party-goers create numerous opportunities for danger if a dog is on the loose. On Halloween or during a party, dogs do best if they're safely tucked away in their habitat or in a safe room (away from all the activity).

During Halloween, cats who have punctured and chewed glow sticks and glow jewelry may be in trouble. While not usually life-threatening, they may cause mouth pain and irritation as well as profuse drooling and foaming.

If you think your dog may have ingested Halloween chocolate, call a vet or the Animal Poison Control (800-213-6680) right away for medical assistance. Untreated, chocolate poisoning in dogs may result in vomiting, diarrhea, lethargy, agitation, increased thirst, an elevated heart rate or seizures.

Instead of giving out candy during Halloween, some people hand out mini-boxes of raisins. Even very small amounts of raisins, grapes and currants are poisonous to dogs and may cause kidney failure.

Keep your dogs and cats inside during the days before and the day of Halloween because many pets are stolen, tortured and killed during these days. Be especially careful if you own a black cat.

Large consumption of sugary, high-fat candy by pets may lead to pancreatitis which is potentially fatal. Signs include: decreased appetite, vomiting, diarrhea, lethargy, abdominal pain and possibly kidney failure or organ damage.

Some Halloween food-related hazards for pets are candy wrappers, raisins and general candy overindulgence.

The use of candles increases dramatically around Halloween. Whether inside pumpkins or adding pumpkin, cinnamon or other holiday scents to the air, candles pop up all over. A curious dog on the loose might get burned by the flame or knock over a lit candle and cause a fire. Placing a candle on a counter or a table doesn't mean that they're safe from a dog. Some dogs are able to climb which makes it possible for them to reach unexpected places.

Thinking of using a fog machine for a spooky effect during Halloween? Keep your pet well away from this machine and its fog. Also, check with your veterinarian to determine whether it's safe for your pet to breathe the fog. If you create fog by using dry ice, be absolutely sure your pet can't touch it or get to it by any means.

Trick-or-treat candies are not for dogs or cats as chocolate is poisonous to a lot of animals. Tin foil and cellophane candy wrappers may be hazardous if swallowed.

Watch out for Halloween decorations and costumes which have feathers or rubber (and even styrofoam may have a lot of decorations) since they may be deadly. Also, the rubber sticky decorations that go on the window or on a glass door may be hazardous.

When pets eat candy, sometimes they also eat the wrappers. Ingestion of foil and cellophane wrappers may cause a life-threatening bowel obstruction which may require surgery. Watch for vomiting, decreased appetite, not defecating, straining to defecate or lethargy.   X-rays may be necessary to diagnose this problem.

While Halloween sound effects (like spooky sounds and loud music) aren't an obvious danger to dogs, they might cause stress to some. If the stress is severe, it might then cause illness.

Holiday Warnings and Hazards

Be careful of holiday decorations and costumes which have feathers or rubber (and even styrofoam may have a lot of decorations) since they may be deadly. Also, the rubber sticky decorations that go on the window or on a glass door may be hazardous.

Be extremely careful that your pet doesn't drink anything containing alcohol. Pets who ingest alcohol may become very sick and may fall into a coma which could lead to an untimely death.

Chocolate eaten by your dog may cause a variety of dangerous symptoms in your dog such as: vomiting, diarrhea, hyper-activity, abnormal heart rate and occasionally seizures. Dark chocolate and baker's chocolate are more dangerous.

Holly and mistletoe may be dangerous for cats and dogs because the ingestion of holly or mistletoe may cause gastrointestinal upset, or in rare cases with mistletoe, cardiovascular problems.

If your dog experiences excessive vomiting or if there is any sign of blood in the vomit, immediately take him to the vet.

It's best to use non-toxic decorations such as wood, fabric or even pine cones.

Keep your pets away from any seemingly-innocuous decorations such as: ribbons, tinsel, glass ornaments, as well as wires, cords and candles. Even Christmas tree water may pose potential danger to pets.

Large consumption of sugary, high-fat candy by pets may lead to pancreatitis which is potentially fatal. Signs include: decreased appetite, vomiting, diarrhea, lethargy, abdominal pain and possibly kidney failure or organ damage.

Make sure your dog doesn't consume sweeteners, such as xylitol, which may cause a sudden drop in blood glucose.

Poinsettias cause only mild to moderate gastrointestinal irritation to pets. Keeping poinsettias out of your pet's reach is still a good idea but there's no need to totally remove a poinsettia.

Some poisons are retained in plants (even after those plants are dead from being sprayed by weed killer). If a puppy or adult chews on the exposed grass or weeds, dogs could become seriously ill. Instead...use salt to kill unwanted grass or weeds. If your dog eats it, the salt will not seriously hurt him but it will kill the weeds.

The use of candles increases dramatically during the holidays. With cinnamon or other holiday scents in the air, candles pop up all over. A curious pet on the loose might get burned by the flame or knock over a lit candle and cause a fire. Don't place a burning candle on a counter or table because pets are able to climb which makes it possible for them to reach unexpected places.

Watch out that neither your dog nor your cat eats turkey as it contains bones which may splinter (causing blockages in your pet's throat and/or digestive tract). Also, eating turkey may cause stomach upset in your pet(from consuming the turkey's grease and fat.

When dogs eat candy, sometimes they also eat the wrappers. Ingestion of foil and cellophane wrappers may cause a life-threatening bowel obstruction which may then require surgery. Watch for vomiting, decreased appetite, not defecating, straining to defecate or lethargy. X-rays may be necessary to diagnose this problem.

Hot Temperatures, Heat Hazards and Summer Warnings

Animals with flat faces (like Pugs and Persian cats) are more susceptible to heat stroke since they cannot pant as effectively as those pets who aren't snub-nosed. These pets, elderly pets, the overweight and those with heart or lung diseases should be kept cool in air-conditioned rooms as much as possible.

Do not leave your pet alone in the car. With only hot air to breathe inside a car, your pet may suffer serious health problems and even death in a few short minutes. Partially opened windows do not provide sufficient air, but they do provide an opportunity for your pet to be stolen.

During travel, being confined in a crate or animal carrier for long periods of time during the hottest months of the year is potentially dangerous for your pet and may lead to dehydration and heatstroke. In addition, certain breeds such as brachycephalic (snub-nosed or flat-faced) dogs and cats are susceptible to pulmonary distress when temperatures are extreme.

Heat stroke at the beach may be prevented by providing lots of fresh, cool water which your dog may drink. A spray bottle with cool water that you may spray on him will also help reducing his temperature. A bonus of having fresh water with you is that you can also clean the sand and salt water from his paws which may cause irritation and dry out those sensitive pads. Also, since you can't guarantee that you will have access to a shady area, bring an umbrella so he can move into the shade. To make sure that hypothermia doesn't occur, bring lots of towels that you may wrap him inside and also to remove the excess cold salt water. Not only may this warm him up quicker, it also helps in removing the sand and salt water from his fur so he won't be in danger of shaking onto someone else.

Heat stroke may be fatal if not treated promptly. Overheating in pets could be seen as: excessive panting or difficulty in breathing, drooling, mild weakness, stupor and even collapse. Pets may also suffer from seizures, bloody diarrhea and vomiting along with an elevated body temperature (over 104 degrees). If you suspect your pet is suffering from heat stroke, get help from your veterinarian immediately.

Heat stroke may be prevented. Pay attention to how your dog is acting and responding during a hot day since there could be the potential of either heat stroke or hypothermia. Some signs of heat stroke in a dog include: rapid panting, bright red tongue, thick, sticky saliva, weakness, vomiting and/or diarrhea, lethargy, weakness, shivering, muscle stiffness, difficulty breathing fixed and/or dilated pupils. If you think that your dog has heat stroke during a hot day, move your pet into the shade and apply cool (not cold) water all over his body to gradually lower his body's temperature. Apply ice packs or cool towels to your pet's head, neck and chest *only*. Allow your dog to drink small amounts of cool water or lick ice cubes. Then...take him to the nearest vet.

If you think that your dog has hypothermia while you're at the beach, take the following actions immediately. Wrap your dog in towels and blankets which have been warmed by the sun. Bring extra fresh water in bottles and leave them out in the sun as this warm water may be applied to your dog to bring his body's temperature back up. If your dog has still not stopped shivering and has continued lethargy, take him to the nearest vet.

It might be best to leave your dog at home when going to large outdoor events, parties and/or gatherings. A large crowd may become overwhelming to your dog, and this type of outing increases the opportunity for injury, dehydration and exhaustion. Most likely, there will probably be a lot of unhealthy or even toxic food and trash on the ground which your dog might try to eat. Also, remember that fireworks and other loud noises may frighten your dog into running away and/or become injured. If you do bring your dog to outdoor events, keep him on a short leash and always be on watch for any potential dangers.

Keep fresh water with you when you go to the beach so you may wash off the sand and salt water which may cause irritation and dry out his sensitive pads.

Never leave an animal alone in a parked vehicle. On a hot

day, a parked car may become a furnace in no time (even with the windows open) because this could lead to fatal heat stroke. Leaving pets unattended in cars in extreme weather is illegal in several states.

Never leave your dog in the car unattended. Despite the many warnings about this, each summer brings numerous accounts of dogs who become sick or even die of heat stroke because they were left inside a car. Even if it does not seem that hot outside, the temperature inside the car may rise to dangerous levels within minutes. If you absolutely must bring your dog with you on errands, make sure you bring another person who can stay in the running, air-conditioned car with your dog. Otherwise, do your dog a favor and leave him home.

Prevent your dog from drinking any water while on an outing with the exception of the safe water which you've brought from home. Salt water may cause dehydration, vomiting and diarrhea. Water in lakes, ponds and rivers may contain parasites and bacteria which may infect your dog. Always provide plenty of fresh, clean water for drinking.

Sensitive paw pads may burn if your dog stays or walks on the hot asphalt and/or on hot sand.

Stay near your dog when playing or swimming in a pool, lake, river or ocean. Contrary to common belief, not all dogs are skilled swimmers. Also, remember that even the most experienced swimmer may become a victim of an undertow, jellyfish or other hazard.

Steer clear of long walks and strenuous exercise on hot, sunny days to avoid prolonged sun exposure. Not only is there a risk of heat stroke, dogs may get sunburned. Consider sunscreen for your dog. If you are planning to spend time outdoors with your dog, find a shady spot and provide plenty of fresh, cool water. Try to take leisurely walks during the cooler times of the day (like during the morning or evening hours). Remember to protect your dog's feet from getting scorched from walking on a hot pavement or hot sand.

Summer heat is very dangerous to a dog locked in a car, however this danger is actually present all year. A well-known champion sire and his daughter died tragically some years ago because the owners of these two dogs had left them locked in their car. Sadly, the owners did not realize that their brand-new car was airtight until it was too late. Avoid another such tragedy. If you must leave your dog in the car, always leave a window or vent open even during the winter. Sometimes leaving a window open isn't even enough to keep your dog from suffering or dying during those hot days. It's much safer to have one person stay inside the car because having someone with your dog will discourage anyone from stealing a dog who has been left alone in a car.

Symptoms of overheating in pets include: excessive panting or difficulty breathing, increased heart and respiratory rate, drooling, mild weakness, stupor or even collapse. They may also include seizures, bloody diarrhea and vomiting along with an elevated body temperature (over 104 degrees).

To avoid dehydration always provide fresh, clean water. Keep your pet in shady areas where pets are cooler. When it's extremely hot, keep your pets indoors.

You may give your pet a light summer haircut to help prevent overheating. Shave the hair to a one-inch length, but never down to the skin (since fur offers protection from the sun). Brushing your pet more often than usual may also help prevent problems caused by excessive heat.

When the temperatures are very high, don't let your dog linger on the hot asphalt. When a dog's body is close to the ground, he may heat up quickly and may then suffer with heat stroke.

When using sunscreen or insect repellent, be sure the product is labeled specifically for use on animals.

Ice, Snow, Extreme Cold Temperatures and Winter Warnings

Antifreeze (which is put into a car during colder weather) may be fatal to a dog and other pets even in small amounts. Any pet who has ingested antifreeze will need immediate emergency care. Symptoms of antifreeze poisoning include: drunk-like behavior, vomiting, excessive urination, drinking and depression. Pets may appear to recover within a few hours, but the antifreeze will continue to poison their systems and is often fatal.

Before letting your dogs out to run in the snow, generously apply Vaseline between the toes on each foot. This will prevent the formation of ice balls (which cause a great deal of discomfort) and will keep the snow from adhering.

Dogs and other pets, like people, are vulnerable to hypothermia and frostbite. Immediately take your pet to a vet if he is shivering, disoriented and lethargic or if his hair is puffed out and standing on end. Frostbite may turn his skin bright red, pale or black. Skin at tips of his ears and on his extremities (including reproductive organs) are particularly at risk.

Dogs kept outdoors should have a dry, draft-free dog house which is large enough for the dog to both sit and lie down in comfort but still small enough to maintain his body heat inside the dog house. The floor should be a few inches off the ground and covered with cedar shavings or straw. The house should face away from wind and the doorway should be covered with waterproof burlap or heavy plastic.

Dogs, outdoor cats and wildlife often will choose to sleep under hoods of cars when it's cold outside. Bang on the hood before starting the car (which will provide any animal the time to escape).

Dogs who are shivering uncontrollably or who exhibit blue tongues could be experiencing hypothermia. Don't bathe this dog since a warm bath may make the dog lose more of his body heat and a hot bath could cause the dog to go into shock. Instead, take as many towels and blankets as you possibly can and wrap them around the dog. Position the dog near a heat vent or a small light bulb. If the dog doesn't return to normal within five minutes after doing this, call the vet or an emergency pet clinic.

Don't ever leave a pet unattended in a car. A vehicle may act like a refrigerator holding in the cold and freezing your pet to death.

If you think that your dog has hypothermia, take the following actions immediately. Wrap your dog in towels and blankets which have been warmed by the sun or by having been put into a warm clothes dryer. Put warm water on your dog's body in order to bring his body temperature back up to normal. If your dog has still not stopped shivering and has continued lethargy, take him to the nearest vet.

Keep your dog leashed when he's outside in the snow and make sure he has an ID tag since dogs may lose scents in snow and then become lost.

During those icy days, the best thing to put on slippery dog runs' surfaces and on all other slippery spots in the kennel yard is Kitty Litter. It is very effective, won't burn the dogs' feet and if they lick their feet, it is harmless to them. It is also the most effective to use if your car is stuck in a slippery spot as the Kitty Litter will provide instant traction.

Use pet-friendly versions of products which melt the ice on steps, driveways and sidewalks. Products such as Safe Paw Ice Melter and Safe-T-Pet Ice Melt avoid chemicals which irritate dogs' paws (and their stomachs, if they lick their paws). These pet-friendly products are usually colored so you can also see where you've sprinkled them.

Use plastic food and water bowls instead of metal bowls because your dog's or cat's tongue may stick and freeze to the metal when it's below freezing and you're feeding your dog or cat outdoors.

Identification and Lost Dogs

(Also see "RECORDS"—"Identification")

All of my dogs are tattooed and the tattoo is registered with the National Dog Registry. Their travel collars have a tag on them that says: "I am tattooed, please call 1-800-NDR-DOGS." Someone is always at the National Dog Registry, whereas who knows where I may be when I'm traveling.

Be sure to have identification on your pet while traveling. Also include the area code with your telephone number. Two collars are better...just in case one collar falls off.

We have a large assortment of different collars our dogs wear and we hated the search required in order to find and change the tags to identify each dog. We solved this problem by purchasing several small clips and small key rings to which we attached each dog's license, tables tag and ID tags. Now when we go out, all we have to do is pick any collar and just snap that particular dog's tags onto his collar.

Jumping Out Of An Enclosure

To discourage dogs from jumping out of an exercise pen, I attach about a 4-inch piece of fine chain to his web collar. At the end of the chain a tennis ball is attached (make sure the chain is no longer than 4" because you don't want your dog to be able to chew the tennis ball). When my dog jumps, the ball bounces against him and he is quickly discouraged from this practice.

Pancreatitis

Do not feed your dog when he's highly excited since the result may cause leakage of enzymes which then damages the pancreas and any surrounding tissue they reach. This breakdown is called pancreatitis. Symptoms of pancreatitis include: loss of appetite, severe and frequent vomiting, diarrhea (which may contain blood), reluctance to walk, weakness, pain, crying, restlessness, irritability or refusing to eat. Many people know their dog is sick but they may be confused (as to whether or not it's serious) because there may be a lack of symptoms or his symptoms are vague and mild.

If you give your dog fatty table scraps (such as potato chips), there is a possibility that an acute pancreatitis attack could occur. Symptoms are: loss of appetite, severe and frequent vomiting, diarrhea (that may contain blood), reluctance to walk, weakness, pain, crying, restlessness, irritability or refusing to eat. If your pet exhibits any of these signs (even if those symptoms are mild at first), get him to your vet immediately!

Pancreatitis may occur only once in a dog's life or it may become chronic (a condition that returns over and over again). It may quickly become fatal or just be a mild attack of pain which is over in a few hours or a day or so. It may cause serious side effects which include: shock, blood clotting disorders, heart arrhythmias and liver or kidney damage. So if your pet exhibits any of these signs (even if they are mild at first), immediately take him to your vet.

Poisonous Snakes and Their Bites

Having your vet give your dog a rattlesnake vaccine works by stimulating an animal's immunity to defend against potentially harmful agents. This vaccine is intended to help create an immunity which will protect your dog from the rattlesnake's venom. The dangers of rattlesnake venom may be greatly decreased by vaccinating your dog against rattlesnakes, however even if vaccinated against rattlesnakes, your dog needs to be seen by a veterinarian if bitten by a rattlesnake.

Snake bites (which commonly occur in spring and summer) could cause death in your pets.

When a rattlesnake strikes an unprotected dog and venom is injected, the toxins in the snake's venom are very painful and may have serious consequences. Even if your dog survives the immediate effects of a rattlesnake's bite, he may be permanently injured by this toxic venom. The snake's venom is made up of a mixture of toxins which spread rapidly through a dog's body. Treatment for a snake bite may include anti-venom injections. Anti-venom is associated with an increased risk of adverse reactions which may complicate your dog's recovery. Other added costs for snakebite treatment include hospitalization, fluids, a number of medications and sometimes even surgery.

Poisons and Poisonings

Acetaminophen (which is found in Tylenol) and other medications, may cause liver damage in dogs. Cats are even more sensitive to Acetaminophen. Ingestion of a single 325 mg. tablet by a 10-pound cat may cause anemia and even be fatal.

Always keep the toilet lid down if you use toilet bowl cleaners. They are often strongly alkaline and tempting for pets to drink.

Antifreeze (which is put into a car during colder weather) may be fatal to a dog and other pets even in small amounts. Any pet who has ingested antifreeze will need immediate emergency care. Symptoms of antifreeze poisoning include: drunk-like behavior, vomiting, excessive urination, drinking and depression. Pets may appear to recover within a few hours, but the antifreeze will continue to poison their systems and is often fatal.

Antifreeze (ethylene glycol) is very poisonous. Even though our dogs are never allowed in the garage, we take special care to clean up any antifreeze which is spilled. We sprinkle baking soda on the antifreeze to reduce its toxicity and then cover both substances with kitty litter to absorb all the liquid. A few minutes later all of this may be swept up and thrown away (in a securely sealed bag and out of the way to stop any animal getting to that disposal bag). If your dog does happen to lick up some antifreeze, induce vomiting and call your vet immediately.

Available for free is the "Antidote and First Aid for Poisoning" chart at most drugstores. Ask your pharmacist for one. Mine is taped inside my kitchen cabinet door with my vet's phone number written on it.

Avoid "dust" snail baits because they are extremely dangerous. This dust may be carried in the wind for many blocks. If the wind carries this poisonous dust to your lawn or to other lawns (such as park lawns) and your dog walks on it and then later licks his feet, that makes for a potentially deadly scenario. Make your dog walk through a pan of clean water. Then rinse his paws and wipe them dry after each walk through public areas or even after walks around the neighborhood...as his life could depend on it.

Avoid snail and slug bait because metaldehyde is one of the main ingredients in most snail and slug baits and it's one of the deadliest. It is extremely hazardous to all mammal life and dogs are exceptionally attracted to it. Metaldehyde poisoning may cause dangerously increased heart rate, severe breathing complications along with profound seizures leading to death. Even if caught early enough to treat, most survivors still eventually die from complications with their liver. Either way, it's an ugly and painful way to die.

Batteries may be toxic to both dogs and cats which may lead to the formation of ulcers in the mouth, esophagus or stomach.

Be certain automotive antifreeze is kept out of reach and any antifreeze drippings are totally removed. Pets are attracted to its scent and antifreeze is highly toxic.

Before feeding your dog eggs, remember to wash the outside of the egg off with hot water. The eggshell may carry the salmonella bacteria. This is also a good idea for the human consumption of eggs.

Be sure to keep mothballs away from dogs as they may be toxic if ingested.

Cats who have punctured and chewed glow sticks and glow jewelry may be in trouble. While not usually life-threatening, chewing these objects may cause mouth pain and irritation as well as profuse drooling and foaming.

Chocolate may cause seizures and death in both dogs and cats. Darker chocolate (such as unsweetened baker's chocolate is more toxic than milk or white chocolate. Even cocoa bean mulch (when eaten in large quantities) may create a problem.

D-Con has changed its mouse and rat poison formulas. If your dog ingests the product, have your veterinarian call D-Con immediately because its treatment is not the same as it used to be! If left untreated, ingesting either product may kill your dog.

Detergents and fabric softener sheets may cause ulcers in the mouth, esophagus and stomach in both dogs and cats.

Don't leave cigarette butts in ashtrays where a puppy may get to them. If eaten, cigarette butts may lead to nicotine poisoning.

Don't let uneaten moist dog food remain in your dog's bowl longer than 5 to 20 minutes. This is due to the fact that bacteria may develop quickly in food which is allowed to stand unrefrigerated.

Don't let your dogs play with tennis balls. A number of newsletters have reported on the futile efforts to save a Scottie in Oregon who suffered fatal liver damage from chewing on and biting into a new tennis ball. Apparently there were some toxic dyes used in the balls as well as chemicals used in ball inflation.

Don't store dog food in plastic "garbage" bags because the plastic will give off toxic fumes (which may then be absorbed by the food). Plastic "food storage" bags are all right to use for storage of dog food as are metal cans, paper bags and plastic containers.

Ethylene glycol is found in antifreeze, windshield de-icing agents and motor oils. Dogs and cats are attracted to its sweet taste but as little as a teaspoon in cats or a tablespoon in dogs may cause kidney failure and then death.

Fertilizers may contain poisonous amounts of nitrogen, phosphorus, potassium, iron, zinc, herbicides and pesticides. Keep cats and dogs away from treated lawns until they are dry. Follow the product's instructions before permitting pets to walk on the lawn.

Flea and tick products, rodenticides (mouse and rat baits) along with lawn and garden insecticides may be harmful to cats and dogs if ingested...so keep them out of reach of your pet. When walking your dog, avoid areas you suspect have been sprayed with insecticides or other chemicals.

Grapes, raisins and currants and even grape juice (even in small amounts) may cause kidney failure in dogs.

Household cleaners (such as bleach, drain cleaners, ammonia and toilet bowl cleaners) may cause gastrointestinal ulcers and other problems in both dogs and cats.

If you have unwanted grass or weeds around your dog's run or exercise area, be careful what you use to kill it. Some poisons are retained in plants (even after those plants are dead from being sprayed by weed killer). If a puppy or adult chews on the exposed grass or weeds, dogs could become seriously ill. Instead...use salt to kill unwanted grass or weeds. If your dog eats it, the salt will not seriously hurt him but it will kill the weeds.

If you think your dog may have ingested any chocolate, call a vet or the Animal Poison Control (800-213-6680) right away for medical assistance. Untreated, chocolate poisoning in dogs may result in vomiting, diarrhea, lethargy, agitation, increased thirst, an elevated heart rate or seizures.

Insecticides in flea and tick products may cause problems if not used exactly according to their labels. Insecticides which are meant for dogs may cause severe toxicity in cats, leading to signs such as: vomiting, seizures and difficulty in breathing. Products intended for treating the yard or house should never be used on pets.

Instead of giving out candy during Halloween, some people hand out mini-boxes of raisins. Even very small amounts of raisins, grapes and currants are poisonous to dogs and may cause kidney failure.

Jimson weed (also known as devil's trumpet) may cause restlessness, drunken walking and respiratory failure in both dogs and cats.

Keep alcoholic beverages away from all pets as these beverages may cause intoxication, depression and comas.

Keep citronella candles, oil products and insect coils out of your dog's reach. The citronella plant (also called the mosquito plant) is actually a member of the geranium family. Grown as a mosquito repellent plant, this plant poses a risk to dogs. The American Society for the Prevention of Cruelty to Animals cautions that all members of the geranium family (Pelargonium) are toxic to dogs...as they contain the active toxins geraniol and linalool.

Keep your pets away from toxic plants. Rhododendron, Japanese yew, lily of the valley, as well as peach and cherry pits, may all cause problems if eaten.

Kerosene, gasoline and tiki torch fluids may cause drooling, drunken walking and difficulty breathing in both dogs and cats. If these products contain antifreeze, they are even more problematic because they are potentially life-threatening.

Large consumption of sugary, high-fat candy by pets may lead to pancreatitis which is potentially fatal. Signs include: decreased appetite, vomiting, diarrhea, lethargy, abdominal pain and possibly kidney failure or organ damage.

Lilies (Easter, day, tiger, Japanese and Asiatic varieties) may cause kidney failure in cats. Lilies of the valley may cause heart rhythm problems and death in both dogs and cats.

Many children with ADHD don't want to take their medications, so they may leave pills on their plates where pets can get to them. These medications may be poisonous to our dogs.

Mothballs (especially if they contain naphthalene) may be toxic to dogs and cats (resulting in vomiting, increased drinking and urination, diarrhea and seizures) and could be potentially life-threatening.

Never give your pet chocolate since chocolate may be very toxic to your pet.

Never use wood chips as bedding for young pups because of the possibility that the chips harbor the bacteria Klebsiella. This organism may cause death in puppies and may make their dam very ill.

Nonprescription medications (such as ibuprofen) may be a problem because many brands have a sweet coating...so it's like candy for dogs yet poisonous to dogs. Ingestion of this medication may lead to severe ulcers and anemia as well as liver and kidney failure in pets.

Onions, garlic, leeks and chives may be toxic to both dogs and cats. When chewed or swallowed, these ingredients may cause anemia and gastrointestinal upset.

Prescription medications (such as antidepressants and ADHD and cardiac drugs) are commonly ingested by pets when pills are dropped on the floor or left on counters. Even a small dose may cause problems.

Putting indoor-outdoor carpeting in the bottom of the whelping box may be deadly to your puppies if their urine or their mother's urine saturates the carpet and the pups then lie in it. The chemicals with which the carpet is treated may combine with the strong urine to produce a chemical similar to sulfuric acid. Well-washed carpeting has probably had all the dangerous chemicals removed. Old throw rugs which have been washed and re-washed are probably the safest and provide the pups secure footing. Be sure to wash these rugs at least once a day to avoid odor and problems with bacteria.

Queensland nuts (also known as macadamia nuts) may cause lethargy, vomiting and difficulty walking in dogs.

Rodenticides (such as mouse and rat poisons) may contain a number of different toxins, which have different effects on dogs and cats. Several common ingredients (like warfarin and coumarin) may cause blood clotting problems and hemorrhaging.

Sago palms are one of a number of toxic plants to both dogs and cats. Ingestion may lead to vomiting, diarrhea and seizures as well as liver failure in dogs.

Snacks enjoyed by your human friends should not be given as a treat to your pet since any change in diet (even for one meal) may give your dog or cat severe digestive ailments. Especially avoid raisins, grapes, onions, chocolate and products with the sweetener xylitol.

Snake bites (which commonly occur in spring and summer) could cause death in your pets.

Stings and bites from insects such as bees, wasps, scorpions and spiders could cause death.

There are more than 1,400 active pesticide ingredients used in an excess of 45,000 pesticide formulas in pesticides. Because of the extremely hazardous nature of some of these pesticides, the EPA has cancelled, suspended or restricted their use. Banned from household use in the USA are: Aldrin, Aresenates, Chlordane, Creosote, Cyanides, DBCP, DDT, Dieldrin, Helptachlor, Kepone, Lindane, Mirex, Pentachlorophenol (PCP), Silvex or Fenoprop, Arsenite, 2, 4, 5-T and Toxaphene. Do not use any of these above-listed products.

Toxic diaper alert! The silica used in the new super-thin diapers is highly toxic to dogs when ingested. Either don't use them or dispose of these super-thin diapers very carefully.

Tulip bulbs may lead to mouth irritation, drooling, vomiting and diarrhea.

Troubled by ants and don't want to use a poison in your dogs' yard or run? Try sprinkling the area with ants with cucumber peelings (instead of using insecticides which may be dangerous to your dogs).

Unbaked bread dough may expand in your dog's stomach. If his stomach twists (cutting off the blood supply), emergency surgery is needed. The yeast in the dough may also produce alcohol which could lead to seizures and respiratory failure.

Use pet-friendly versions of products which melt ice on steps, driveways and sidewalks. Products such as Safe-T-Pet Ice Melt avoid chemicals that irritate cats' paws (and their stomachs, if they lick their paws). These pet-friendly products are usually colored so you can also see where you've sprinkled them.

Veterinary prescriptions (such as arthritis medications) are often meat-flavored which may be enticing to dogs. This may result in stomach ulcers, liver or kidney failure.

When pets eat candy sometimes they also eat the wrappers. Ingestion of foil and cellophane wrappers may cause a life-threatening bowel obstruction which may then require surgery. Watch for vomiting, decreased appetite, not defecating, straining to defecate, or lethargy. X-rays may be required in order to diagnose this problem.

When placing mothballs in the bottom of your trash cans (to discourage flies) be sure to keep mothballs away from the dogs as those mothballs may be toxic if eaten. Keep a tight lid on each garbage can in order to keep the vapor inside the can to make sure dogs can't access their poison.

Windshield wiper fluid may contain methanol or ethylene glycol. Ingestion of methanol may cause low blood sugar and drunken walking in dogs and cats.

Xylitol has been shown to be toxic to dogs (it increases blood insulin levels). Xylitol is a sugar-alcohol product used as a sweetener in some consumer products as well as in baking and food preparation. These products include candy, gum, breath fresheners, sun block and various vitamin supplements. Only one or two pieces of gum swallowed by a 20-pound dog may cause hypoglycemia. Other signs are: depression, vomiting, weakness, seizures and occasionally liver failure. Induce vomiting if a dog has gotten into products such as sugar-free gum.

Xylitol is a sugar-free sweetener commonly found in chewing gum, breath mints and toothpaste. In dogs, it may lead to dangerous drops in blood sugar and liver failure.

Yard products (including snail and slug bait, herbicides and fertilizers) are dangerous for pets.

Zinc toxicity may happen when dogs and cats eat metal or coins. Ingestion of even a single zinc penny may be fatal. Zinc may cause anemia as well as liver, kidney or heart failure.

Protection When Walking

Avoid "dust" snail baits because they are extremely dangerous. This dust may be carried in the wind for many blocks. If the wind carries this poisonous dust to your lawn or to other lawns (such as park lawns) and your dog walks on it and then later licks his feet, that makes for a potentially deadly scenario. Make your dog walk through a pan of clean water. Then rinse his paws and wipe them dry after each walk through public areas or even after walks around the neighborhood...as his life could depend on it.

Avoid snail and slug bait because metaldehyde is one of the main ingredients in most snail and slug baits and it's one of the deadliest. It is extremely hazardous to all mammal life and dogs are exceptionally attracted to it. Metaldehyde poisoning may cause dangerously increased heart rate, severe breathing complications along with profound seizures leading to death. Even if caught early enough to treat, most survivors still eventually die from complications with their liver. Either way, it's an ugly and painful way to die.

Reflector tape on your pet's collar might help cut down on the danger of him being struck by a car at night.

Sensitive paw pads may burn if your dog stays or walks on the hot asphalt and/or on hot sand.

When the temperature is very high, don't let your dog linger on hot asphalt because if you dog's body is close to the ground, your dog may heat up quickly and suffer with heat stroke.

Stings—Bees, Wasps, Hornets, Etc.

Stings and bites from insects such as bees, wasps, scorpions and spiders could cause death.

This method works with people, so it might also work with your pet—carry a penny in your pocket. I was stung by both a bee and a hornet while working in the garden. My arm swelled up so I went to the doctor where I received cream and an antihistamine. The next day the swelling became progressively worse so I went to my regular doctor where I was told that my arm was infected and that I needed an antibiotic. My doctor said to me: "The next time you get stung, put a penny over the bite or sting for 15 minutes." That night, a bee stung my niece. When I looked at her bite, it had already started to swell so I taped a penny to her arm for 15 minutes. The next morning, there was no sign of a sting. We first thought that she simply wasn't allergic to the sting. Not long after that, I was again gardening and I was stung twice by a hornet on my left hand. I promptly got pennies out and taped those pennies to my bites. The pennies took the sting out immediately. We need to keep a penny or pennies on hand...as they definitely work.

Stomach Upsets

Be sure to pack your pet's regular food and water to avoid upsets on a trip. Some animals' stomachs will become upset on food or water they aren't used to consuming.

Trapped and Possible Suffocation

As a breeder of dogs, at one time or another you have probably rushed to the aid of a yelping puppy to find a pup who has managed to get his head wedged between the bars of the exercise pen. In a panic you work to remove the puppy's head from between the bars (while he fights with all his might to resist your help). Newspaper and cardboard modifications to the exercise

pen's bars are fine but these fixes make it impossible to fold up the exercise pen. I found that if you take a roll of weaving strips (used to repair lawn chairs) and weave those strips in and out of the bars of the exercise pen, it then becomes safe, escape proof and easy to fold up and to transport. This weaving material is usually the same height as the exercise pen's bars.

A wise precaution to take (if you have small puppies exercising in a dog run which has the chain-link cyclone fence fabric) is to put 12" to 24" of 1-inch mesh or hardware wire all around the bottom and on its outside. I had a seven-week-old puppy who put his head through the 2 1/2-inch diameter opening and got stuck. While I held the puppy so he wouldn't struggle, a neighbor (who had heard the commotion) used pliers to unweave the fence (at its base) in order to free this puppy's head. If I had used the wire mesh, this could have been avoided. I was lucky because I hadn't left those pups unsupervised and I saw this dangerous incident as it was actually occurring.

Snack bags, Ziploc bags, shrink-wrap bags and bottles (or any container in which an animal may get his head wedged inside) have caused deaths of many dogs when a pet pushed his head into these bags and/or containers and then suffocated. Such containers have been made airtight in order to keep the enclosed products fresh. Some of these bags are made of a tough, slick material (which resists puncturing and tearing). Bags, bottles and all such containers should be kept completely out of the reach of your dogs and children. These containers should be disposed in such a manner that neither dogs nor children will ever be able to retrieve them from the trash.

Traveling With A Pet

Although many dogs find that sticking their heads out the window of a car is the best part of the road trip, it's not safe. Your dog may easily be injured from flying debris. Never travel with a dog in the back of a pickup truck. Some states have laws restricting such transport and it is always dangerous.

A safety harness functions like a seat belt. While most dogs will not have a problem adjusting to it, you may want to let him wear the harness a few times before using it in a vehicle.

Be sure that your dog is safely restrained while traveling in your vehicle. Utilizing a dog safety harness, travel kennel, vehicle dog barrier or dog car seat are the best ways to keep your dog safe. These restraints not only protect your dog from injury, but they help by keeping him from distracting you as you're driving.

Dogs should be confined within a crate or carrier while traveling. Your pet will then be not be able to leap from an open window, door or interfere with your driving.

During your stops be sure to provide your dog with some fresh water. Occasionally traveling may upset your dog's stomach so take along ice cubes which are better for your dog than consuming large amounts of water.

If your dog prefers being inside a travel kennel, be sure his crate is well ventilated and stabilized. Also, make sure it's not too large for your dog because if you're in an accident and the crate is too large, your dog will be tossed around within that oversized crate.

It is recommended that you keep your dog's food to a minimum during travel. Be sure to feed him regular dog food and resist the temptation to give him some of your fast food (such as burger or fries, etc.) as that's not good for a dog.

Many dog owners prefer vehicle barriers, particularly for larger dogs. Vehicle barriers are best suited for SUVs.

Never leave your dog unattended in a parked vehicle. On warm days, the temperature in your vehicle may rise to 120 degrees in minutes (even with the windows slightly open). On very cold days, the vehicle could possibly become too cold. Also, an animal left alone in a vehicle is an open invitation to dog thieves.

No matter what method you choose, back seat travel is always safer for your dog.

Smaller dogs are best suited for dog car seats. The car seat is secured in the back seat. It utilizes a seat belt and your dog is then secured in the car seat by a safety harness. In addition to it's safety features, a dog car seat will prop up your smaller dog which will then permit him to better look out the window.

Whatever method you choose to properly restrain your dog in your vehicle, be sure to make his comfort a priority. Just as it's important for your seat to be comfortable during a long road trip, your dog's seat should be comfortable, too. Usually, a favorite blanket or travel bed will do the trick. There are also some safe and very cozy dog car seats available which your dog may find quite comfortable.

When walking your dog outside your vehicle, make sure that your dog is always on a leash and wearing a collar with a permanent ID and a temporary travel identification tag.

Veterinarians

Keep an emergency number for your vet handy or the emergency vet clinic's number...just in case your regular vet's office is closed.

Water Dangers and Hazards

Do not leave pets unsupervised around a pool or any other water areas as not all dogs are good swimmers.

Rinse your dog off after swimming in order to remove chlorine or salt from his fur. Do your best to keep your dog from drinking pool water (which contains chlorine and other chemicals which could cause stomach upset).

When you and your dog are near water such as lakes, pools, etc., introduce your dog to the water gradually and make sure he wears a flotation device when he is on a boat.

When To Induce Vomiting

> If your dog has swallowed bleach, drain cleaner or a petroleum distillate product, DO NOT allow your dog to vomit because those products will burn his escophagus and mouth during vomiting. Also DO NOT permit vomiting if your dog has already begun to vomit, lost consciousness, has difficulty breathing, is too weak to stand or if the dangerous substance was ingested more than two hours previously.

If you need to make your pet vomit for some reason, put 1/2 teaspoon to 1 teaspoon of salt on the back of his tongue and hold his mouth closed for a few seconds.

You may induce vomiting if your vet has advised you to do so and if you dog has ingested antifreeze (ethylene glycol) no more than two hours ago.

Whelping

Bedding and Linings For Your Whelping Box

A good use for those old mattress pads is to cut them into smaller sizes and use in the whelping box. They provide traction for the puppies and do not wad up like towels. They also work well for drying your dogs off after bathing (as they are really absorbent). I hemmed the outer edges on the sewing machine by folding them over. Blanket binding worked well, also.

Ever wonder what to do with your old sheets and pillowcases? I buy one-inch thick foam rubber and have it cut to fit the size of my crates. Just slip the foam piece into the pillowcase and you have an instant crate pad. The fabric is extremely durable and you may machine wash and dry them. Pillowcases are the perfect size for medium-sized dog crates. When traveling, if you have a dog who drools or who gets carsick, place the piece of foam inside a 13-gallon-size trash can liner to protect it from moisture and then slip this pillow into a pillowcase. For larger crates or whelping boxes, use the sheets. Just stitch up the sides to make a giant envelope.

Hospital supply stores sell washable, moisture-proof pads for use in hospital beds. They are soft, absorbent (they stay dry on top, wicking moisture to the absorbent filling in the center) and provide firm footing for nursing puppies. They are also the perfect size (30" by 34") which means they will fit most medium-sized whelping boxes. Ours have been machine-washed, bleached and dried repeatedly and have held up well through many litters over a number of years.

I do not like the mess of handling newspapers or the laundering of towels during whelping. I just whelped a litter and used Depend's chair pads under the bitch. The whelping box was first prepared with a fitted blanket. Layers of the pads were placed over this fitted blanket. Then as each pad became soiled, I whisked it into a waiting garbage bag. New layers of pads were periodically slipped under the bitch. It was the cleanest whelping I have ever handled. These pads resemble Chux (the blue bed liners) and there are probably other brands and several other sizes also available.

I found that when I was raising puppies who were still nursing, the ruts around the bottom of a very large crate (which I used as a whelping box) could be eliminated by rolling newspapers, taping them together and then putting them inside the crate. *This keeps the puppies from getting sat upon by their mother* (especially when she has seven puppies and she's having a difficult time getting them situated so everyone may nurse).

In using a cardboard box for whelping. I cover the bottom of the box with contact paper before spreading the newspapers. By doing this, I have a disposable whelping box which is easily disinfected and with the contact paper on the bottom, liquids will not soak through. It also adds a decorative touch to the plain box.

I use old bath towels (instead of newsprint) on the bottom of my puppy pen. This gives newborns plenty of traction for finding "mum," is easy to change, simple to wash and my puppies are always clean.

I went to a plastic supply company and bought scraps of high-impact styrene (which were .060" thick). The store cut them for me (at no cost) into 16" by 22" sheets (four each) and I took the remaining pieces home. The 16" by 22" pieces fit into a #200 crate without having to round the edges. They fit on top of the grates. Now there are no slots for toes or tiny paws to slip through and any wetness runs off under the grate. They're washable and bleachable and odor doesn't cling. They may even be used without a grate although the .080" might be a bit better for that use (which is more expensive, of course). I was able to purchase "liners" for four #200 crates, one #500 crate (my whelping box) and enough left over for another #200 crate, if I ever needed it. If people are afraid of puppies chewing the edges, the sheets may be cut a tad larger and then just round the edges for a closer fit.

My young bitch (just having whelped her first litter) had an uncontrollable desire to dig and rip the fresh newspapers that I had so carefully laid down for her. So I tried this and it worked for me. I cut short paper strips and scattered two or three handfuls on top of the newspaper and just a few inside the whelping box. This seemed to satisfy her nesting instinct. After a couple scratches and a few pokes with her nose, we both could settle down.

Need shredded paper to line puppy pens or perhaps to use when shipping dogs? Shredded IBM (computer) paper and un-printed newsprint makes excellent absorbent material and, as an extra bonus, there's no dirty newsprint ink left on your dog.

Since puppies should not be on a smooth surface when they are young, I do not like to use newspapers in my whelping box. Because I work and am gone for long periods of time, I worry about using towels or blankets. The perfect answer, I think, is to use carpet samples. I got the kitchen carpet type (tight loops) from my local carpet store. They may be washed off and work well to provide puppies the traction they need.

Putting indoor-outdoor carpeting in the bottom of the whelp-ing box may be deadly to your puppies if their urine, or their mother's urine, saturates the carpet and the pups then lie in it. The chemicals with which the carpet is treated may combine with the strong urine to produce a chemical similar to sulfuric acid. Well-washed carpeting has probably had all the dangerous chemi-cals removed. Old throw rugs which have been washed and re-washed are probably the safest and provide the pups secure foot-ing. Be sure to wash these rugs at least once a day to avoid odor and problems with bacteria.

Reuse old crib bumpers as liners for dog beds, crates or for whelping areas. They are especially useful for geriatric dogs to lean against.

Sam's Wholesale Club sells (in its automotive department) packages of small hand-size white towels for washing cars. They come in packages of 12 towels, and they are excellent when wash-ing your pet and during whelping of puppies.

Since I do not usually have more than one litter at a time, I only own one wooden whelping box. This year when I needed additional whelping boxes, I found a simple, good substitute. I have a large shipping crate (the fiberglass type). It may be easily divided into its two sections and becomes two makeshift whelping boxes. The only problem is that the bottom is not completely flat but by padding with papers and covering with carpet squares, they worked very nicely. Good idea? When it is not in use for whelping boxes, you have a nice large shipping crate instead of boxes stored and in the way, getting dusty.

To give newborns something for good footing (which will stay in place and is easily cleanable), cut up and edge flat mattress pads. A Sears king-size makes four to exactly fit a Kennel Aire whelping crate.

To line my whelping box, I place a piece of Masonite which is about the size of a crate floor inside the long wire crates. Then I wrap a large piece of terry cloth or beach towel tightly around the Masonite and pin it or Velcro it on the bottom. When I place this inside my whelping box, it takes up the majority of the floor space. It also gives the mom a comfortable bed and the pups firm footing *(with little danger of smothering pups in rumpled towels or blan-kets)*. I have three or four pieces of terrycloth to rotate as I wash the soiled ones.

To prevent the bitch from scratching at the bedding and pos-sibly covering up her puppies, use a 3' by 3' wooden box covered with linoleum on the bottom and all 8" sides. Cut a piece of Ma-sonite board 1" smaller, that is, a piece 2' 11" x 2' 11". Next...use a piece of thin carpet cut 3' by 4'. This gives you 6" to tuck under-neath two sides of the Masonite board. Even though the bitch may still do some scratching, *her weight standing on the carpet-cov-ered board will prevent the puppies from getting covered up by the rug.* I have three pieces of carpet for changing and washing.

Use a 12-panel Extra-Aire by Kennel Aire exercise pen (or ken-nel panels) when keeping newborns or a litter of puppies in the house. Place a large plastic drop cloth *(after it's been aired out)* over the carpet or over whatever kind of flooring you may have. Then spread newspapers down and place shredded newspaper on top of the flat newspapers. If you can get newspaper without print, the print won't get onto the puppies. After the pups are whelped these may be changed easily. Surround the papers with a portable exercise pen which is 24" high. You may step over this and this pen will keep the puppies and their dam confined until the pups are weaned. If we have two or more litters at the same time, we put a partition in the middle. Each of our litters has it's own heating pad. A heating pad is needed, even in the summertime, es-pecially if you're running your air-conditioning (as newborn pup-pies need about 85 degrees temperature for approximately their first seven days). By using this method we have never lost a pup past three days of age.

When puppies are two weeks old, I put a 12" by 16" card-board bed (with a baby receiving blanket and a heating pad) in the whelping box. Then I put disposable diapers over the newspaper laying in the rest of the box. (Use diapers without elastic legs so they'll lie flat.) The diapers are more absorbent than newspaper and provide good footing. The puppies leave their bed and use the diapers. I also put computer paper or unprinted newsprint over the newspaper to keep the puppies cleaner.

When whelping, I buy receiving blankets at yard sales. I cut these blankets in fourths (or quarters) and use them when a pup is being whelped. They are useful in cleaning and drying a newborn. Simply throw the blankets in the washing machine so they're ready to be used for your next litter.

When whelping, I use newspaper during and after delivery of each pup and I always have to scramble to open up new newspa-per after each pup. I work in housecleaning for a medical center and noticed that staff members have these blue pads that they use for babies, etc. These pads have plastic on the bottom and then the absorbent material is on top. What an easy way to keep things dry and clean.

Feeding Newborns

(See "Feeding"—"Newborns")

Feeding The New Mother

(See "Feeding"—"New Mothers")

Heating The Whelping Box

Do you have orphaned pups? With an orphaned litter and depending on the size and age of the litter, I find a plastic dish pan is always handy and convenient. I put a heating pad in the bottom of the dish pan, cover it with a towel and then drape the entire tub with a towel to prevent drafts. It is easily unplugged and portable. To keep everyone warm while at your destination, you'll need only find an electrical outlet for the cord and its plug. Don't forget to take your formula-filled syringes and cotton balls along on any trip.

Each of our litters has it's own heating pad. A heating pad is needed (even in the summertime) especially if you're running your air-conditioning as puppies need about 85 degrees temperature for approximately their first seven days. By using this method we have never lost a pup past three days of age.

For an economical way to heat the whelping box, try a pole lamp. We turn ours upside down and the lamps are just the right height. Adjusting heat is easy since one, two or three bulbs may be used as required.

If you live in a cold climate, a good investment is a Double Mantel Coleman Lantern. Set it on a sturdy chair or something near the whelping box. It will throw out a lot of heat (just in case a power outage occurs) and it also helps to keep those newborn babies warm.

Many people will probably know this, but for those still wondering about heating a whelping box, we use this method: our box is 3' x 3' with 12-inch high sides. We use a Reflector Lamp with a clamp base. The lamp is clamped directly onto the side of the box (pointing straight down). With a 150-watt bulb, the temperature in the box is 85 degrees (plus or minus a degree, in the corners). At around three weeks of age, puppies do not require that high temperature so we change to a 100-watt bulb (which keeps the box at 70 to 75 degrees). The light has never bothered our puppies' eyes and their dam adjusts well to the heat. (The light is also ideal for picture taking.) I do not like a heating pad for fear of a puppy crawling off of it and not being able to find its way back to its available warmth. In addition, I have a bitch who would chew anything (which includes heating pads). In extremely cold weather, we place a space heater in front of the box to keep the chill out of the surrounding air.

We use a heating pad in the whelping pen, but sometimes *mothers like to rearrange it which could result in puppies being unsafely buried underneath the pad.* We secure our pad to the sides of the pen using long strips of duct tape. This pad is then secure and is easily removed when the cover needs to be changed.

When whelping litters, I use the smallest Doskocil crate, (#1911, as an incubator). My heating pad fits into it perfectly and with a towel to cover the crate and the pad on low heat, I place each puppy into the crate to keep him warm and out of the way when the bitch is whelping another puppy. For the first week or so, when the bitch gets her periodic breaks (out of the whelping box), I turn the pad on and place the puppies inside until their mother is ready to get back into the box with her babies. These newborns stay warm and asleep which eliminates any worry of puppies becoming chilled while mother is out of the whelping box.

Mothers Needing Help

If a bitch goes for more than an hour between whelping puppies (and isn't in trouble otherwise), I always give her ice-cold milk (some like it with torn up bread mixed in with the milk). She will gobble it up and labor will usually start again very shortly after drinking the ice-cold milk. Try it as it may work for your bitch, too.

If you have a first-time mama who is less than enthusiastic with diaper duty, try spreading a little peanut butter on the new puppies' tummies and bottoms. Mom should get the idea in one or two applications of the peanut butter.

If your bitch has just had a litter and does not have enough milk for her new arrivals, give her a few swallows of beer. Her milk should begin flowing in abundant quantities. This small amount of alcohol will not affect the puppies.

Instead of bathing or cutting off the skirts of bitches after whelping (in order to remove the blood), wipe the blood off by using straight hydrogen peroxide and then dry with a towel or paper towels. Pour or sponge the hydrogen peroxide through her skirts and then squeeze out with a dry towel. Her skirts will become beautifully clean. *Be sure to completely dry everything before returning mom to her pups.*

To get a C-sectioned bitch to accept her pups, use your fingers and gather the discharge from her vulva and smear it on her pups. One sniff will tell mom that these puppies are hers.

When a brand-new mother lets me know that she doesn't want to eat, I mix one tablespoon of canned cat food well into her food. Few dams will refuse that fishy treat and I figure it's got to be full of extra goodies.

Oxytocin Shots

I made a trip to the vet and asked him for a clean-out shot (oxytocin) for a bitch who was having her litter within a couple of days. The vet reminded me that the shot should be kept cold. Since I wasn't going directly home, I decided I better do some fast thinking about a way to keep it cool. I pulled into a Burger King and (along with my food order) asked for a small cup filled with ice and a lid. I placed the syringe (covered-needle-end first) into the cup through the straw hole. I made sure the barrel part of the syringe was not in the ice. (The cup should be a little more than halfway full of ice.) The cold air between the ice and the lid made a nice refrigerated area and when I reached home, the syringe was just as cool as when it was handed to me.

Puppies' Toenails

(Also see "GROOMING"—"Nail Trimming")

A quick alternative to clipping sharp nails on wiggly nursing pups is to let the pups scramble around briefly on a piece of fine sandpaper. This results in nice smooth nails with no rough edge to scratch mom's tummy. Be sure to use fine sandpaper as this does not seem to hurt the pads.

Records and Record Keeping

(See "RECORDS"—"Medical and Health Records")

Taking A Dog's Temperature

A quick, easy way to take your dog's temperature is to use one of those new digital thermometers. You don't have to "shake it down." Instead, just press the button to turn it on and in it goes (we use one drop of K-Y jelly on the tip). About one minute later, it beeps and you're done. They're made of plastic and are almost unbreakable (a blessing which cuts down time on an unpleasant chore).

Since my bitch is in whelp and whelping day is very close, I have been taking her temperature (rectally) twice a day. The only drawback is when I have to wash the thermometer and disinfect it. Since I wash it by hand, I find it very unsanitary. But one weekend while looking at all the goodies in the drugstore next to the temperature strips, I found a great product called Oral/Rectal Thermometer Covers. These are oral and rectal sheaths for thermometers. Rectal sheaths are pre-lubricated so they'll will be no more hassles with Vaseline. The thermometer is left clean and this process is so simple and sanitary.

The new type of surface thermometer (such as Digitemp which may be found in the medical section of any store) would be a very valuable item for a pet owner to keep handy. The surface thermometers measure the surface temperature and not the internal temperature (as rectal thermometers do). The directions for them state that the surface temperature of humans (measured on the forehead) is five degrees below internal temperature. So when used on humans, normal would be approximately 94 degrees. Since a dog's internal temperature is normally 101 degrees, this thermometer should read about 96 degrees for his surface temperature. I have checked this temperature reading on my own dogs and found it to be accurate (at a normal 96 degrees surface temperature). I measure by holding the strip against the least hairy place on the inner thigh or belly of my dog and the whole procedure takes less than 30 seconds. Used as a quick check on a bitch close to whelping, you should be able to spot the temperature drop which would produce a reading of 94 degrees or below. Although it will not measure fractional changes, it is an easy-to-use tool to check for high or low temperatures when you are watching for a large deviation from normal.

Weak Newborns

(Also see "FEEDING"—"Newborns" and "Tube-Feeding")

A few drops of room temperature liver blood when puppies are first whelped gives them an extra shot of energy for a good start.

A new device (designed by a veterinarian to save lives of baby pigs) may help save puppies, too. Called a Pig Resuscitator, this device pumps air into the lungs of non-breathing newborns. If the animal is not breathing, first clean out his mouth and then tilt his head back in order to open up his air passage. Slip the mask over his nose. Then compress the bellows to force air into his lungs. Next, pull off the mask (to allow fresh air to enter). Repeat until the animal breathes on his own. It's available from Joseph Magrath, D.V.M., Box 148, McCook, NE 69001.

A product called Probiocin (live culture Lactobacillus is excellent for enteritis in newborns and to fight E. Coli. Definitely use this if any antibiotic is given. Also, give it to the bitch. «»Editor's note: based on reading and research in nutritional biochemistry, an effective anti-diarrhea mixture (Bifidobacterium infantis) for puppies is Natren's Life Start (1/8 teaspoon in 1/2 ounce of lukewarm water and 1/2 teaspoon of each in 1 ounce of lukewarm water for adults and especially for the new mother).«»

As the best substitute for bitch's milk, I use the following recipe: 1/2 cup of water, 1/2 cup of Carnation Evaporated Milk (canned), 2 teaspoons white Karo syrup and 1 raw egg yolk. Mix well. It is quite simple to make and I have gotten better results with this than from powdered or prepared varieties. «»Editor's note: based on nutritional biochemistry, if the puppy is orphaned before nursing is completed, bifido bacteria or bifidobacteria (1/8 teaspoon into warm formula) should be supplemented. Based upon further reading and research, goat's milk works well and is less upsetting to a puppy.«»

A tube of Nutri-Cal is a necessary item in my dog supplies. A tiny bit in the mouth of a weak newborn puppy is usually all that is needed to strengthen him. Since dogs love the taste, it is also a handy tool in teaching puppies to bait. Nutri-Cal may be purchased through veterinarians and many supply catalogs.

Do you find in your large litters that you have one weak puppy or that your older bitch's puppies have one weaker one even though it is a smaller litter? We have found that by feeding an additive to all our pregnant bitches from the time they are bred until whelping, we have never lost a small one nor have we had to help a pup. The product is called Stress and is an excellent product. It is made by the makers of Vetzyme products.

Esbilac cocktail may be made by mixing (in a blender): 3 Dixie paper cupfuls (kitchen size) Esbilac to 1 paper cupful of water. Add 1 tablespoon honey, 1 tablespoon lactobacillus acidophilus and 1 tablespoon Pepto-Bismol. Not only does this recipe produce better puppy stools, but it seems to stick to their ribs better as well.

Extra tiny newborn puppies dehydrate very easily especially when subjected to the artificial heat sources (which are sometimes vital to keep them from becoming too chilled and subsequently dying). I have found that keeping a very close watch on them for the first several days is vital and checking several times daily for any signs of dehydration (like pinching up the skin on the back). *If a pup's skin stays up at all, dehydration is beginning.* I keep a bottle of Ringers Solution (purchased from my vet) at home at all times. At the very first sign of dehydration, I give subcutaneous (under the skin) injections of the Ringers using an allergy syringe and needle. You may purchase allergy syringes at many pharmacies (without a prescription) or you can simply get a prescription from your vet or physician. Remove the Ringers from the bottle with one of your regular-size needles, then replace the regular-size needle with the very fine allergy needle (which will be used for the actual injection). I also heat the solution in the syringe by holding it under hot water for a bit or putting it in the microwave oven for a split-second *(without the needle). Test the heat on the inside of your wrist as you would a baby's bottle.* Body-temperature Ringers eliminates the shock to the body that cold solution would cause and it saves puppies.

For weak puppies, we have found that Diamino 4x Vitamins may bring around a weak puppy in 24 hours. We usually use the vitamins for about a week and assist the puppy when he's nursing. These vitamins are available from veterinarians.

From working in a hospital with premature infants, I have learned when tube-feeding to always let the fluid drain into the stomach by gravity flow *(not by force of the plunger). That way, when the flow stops, you'll know that the puppy's tummy is full and you'll prevent the risk of overflow and aspiration.*

Here's a liver-water recipe for fading puppies. Put a large piece (or pieces) of calves' liver in a little bit of water and boil slowly (about five minutes) until the blood comes out. Let it cool, and then drain and save the liquid. Put four drops (no matter what the breed) into an eyedropper and give to a weak puppy. At first, you give four drops to the puppy every two hours for 12 hours, then every four hours. You may do this for however long you feel is necessary and until you feel that the puppy is thriving.

I needed to tube-feed my last litter. My bitch had produced a huge litter of ten puppies and she and I were both exhausted. In my befuddled state, I wasn't sure that I would reset the alarm correctly. How could I get up in time for the next feeding? While sleepily waiting for the milk to become warm, I drank a large glass of water and drinking that water turned out to be the solution to my problem. Later, I urgently woke up without an alarm in time for the next feeding. Because bladder capacity varies, you may need to try drinking between one-half to two glasses of water. Then time your awakening before you have a tube-feeding problem. For me, drinking a glass of water was a simple solution to my dilemma of waking every few hours without an alarm.

One helpful hint I might pass on is an "Orphan Puppy Formula." Here's the recipe: 1 can Carnation milk, 2 cans warm water, 2 tablespoons table cream, 2 tablespoons honey, 2 egg yolks, 1 envelope unflavored gelatin and 1 dropperful Vetamino 4x. I heat up small portions in the microwave at medium power for 35 seconds or less. It seems to be well tolerated, and weight gain is noticed quickly when fed through preemie nipples. «»Editor's note: based on nutritional biochemistry, if the puppy is orphaned before nursing is completed, bifido bacteria or bifidobacteria (1/8 teaspoon into warm formula) should be supplemented. Based upon further reading and research, goat's milk works well and is less upsetting to a puppy.«»

Pedialyte is an oral electrolyte solution (which you may keep on hand) for both newborns and for older dogs. Give a weak newborn puppy a dropperful every hour. Pedialyte is found in the canned milk section of the baby department. It comes in several strengths so *check with you vet for the best strength to use for your pup or older dog.*

The fastest and safest way to warm a puppy (if he is small, weak or cold) is to carry that pup in the front of your blouse or shirt (making very sure that he can't slip out while your carrying him). I had to prove it to myself with two small premature puppies weighing only 3 1/2 ounces. They wouldn't nurse so I carried them around all afternoon in the front of my blouse and, presto ,they are now three weeks old, fine and healthy. «»Editor's note: based upon reading and research, handling puppies in this manner will also help their temperaments when it comes to bonding with humans and wanting to be cuddled.«»

This recipe came from a nurse who works in a hospital. It is useful for weak puppies or finicky eaters: 1 can Carnation, 8 ounces water, 8 ounces plain yogurt, 3 or 4 egg yolks and 3 tablespoons of Karo syrup.

We had a puppy who I had to supplement feed. Although he seemed strong enough, he did not want to even try nursing from his dam again. By putting some honey on a nipple which another puppy had already started, the weaker puppy was able to latch right on and begin nursing.

When new puppies are "on their way," I make sure that I have purchased fresh goat's milk and freeze it in ice-cube trays. I then store those frozen cubes in a Ziploc bag and place the bag in the freezer. If a puppy needs a boost, I can take out one cube of goat's milk and mix it with equal parts of Pedialyte. It seems to work great. If there are leftover cubes, I mix them in with the puppy food during their weaning time.

Whelping Boxes
(See "ENCLOSURES"—"Bedding, Mats, Footing, Etc.,"
"Whelping Boxes" and "Newborns")

Whelping Equipment
I discovered the joys of having a bean bag chair near the whelping box and puppy pen. The styrene pellets inside the bag mold to your shape and provide support for the hours of staying beside the bitch while she is whelping. Later, the bag provides comfort as you recline near the pups to watch them play. These bean bag chairs give great support on a water bed or on the floor. You may provide the pups early bonding with humans while comfortably watching television. My comfort-loving dogs like to recline on the bags but they prefer a bag with less pellets so it molds to their shapes. I've purchased several bags for my dogs at garage sales.

My husband presented me with a mechanic's caddy to ease the hours I spent hovering over my whelping box. It's very handy. It was made by Ex-Cell, has a padded seat, a tray beneath the seat (which could hold towels and scissors) and also has rolling, swivel castors. If only it came with extras such as arm rests, a padded back and a snooze alarm.

Three of my friends have only one or two litters a year. Because we have so few litters among us, we put together a traveling whelping kit (complete with scissors, hemostats, towels, heating pad, dental floss, baby scales, glucose solution, feeding tubes, nursing bottles, Esbilac, silver nitrate sticks, KY Jelly, etc.). If something is used, it is replaced and all items are cleaned and sterilized before the kit travels to whomever's house will need it next. It saves us all time and money, and it's nice to know that the kit is ready (complete and waiting when one of us needs it).

To be sure all necessary items are available (before whelping begins), I buy a plastic lunch pail and gather together the following items: iodine, quick stop, surgical gloves, scissors, forceps, K-Y Jelly and a digital thermometer. These items are kept solely for whelping. I keep both the scissors and forceps wrapped in foil (after being boiled until sterilized).

To make cleaning your bitch easier after whelping (or breeding), wrap her tail from the base to the tip with a non-sticky wrap. Vet Wrap (mine was made by Johnson and Johnson) works well. It works something like an Ace bandage because the elastic sticks together without glue and it's reusable. Vet Wrap may be purchased through your vet. ❐